Playing the State

QUESTIONS FOR FEMINISM

Edited by Michèle Barrett, Annette Kuhn, Anne Phillips and Ann Rosalind Jones, this socialist feminist series aims to address, in a lively way and on an international basis, the wide range of political and theoretical questions facing contemporary feminism.

Playing the State

Australian Feminist Interventions

Edited by
SOPHIE WATSON

VERSO
London · New York

First published by Verso 1990

Verso
UK: 6 Meard Street, London W1V 3HR
USA: 29 West 35th Street, New York, NY 10001-2291

Verso is the imprint of New Left Books

British Library Cataloguing in Publication Data
Playing the state: Australian feminist interventions.—
 (Questions for feminism)
 1. Australia. Politics. Role of Women
 I. Title   II. Series
 323.3'4'0994

 ISBN 0-86091-255-8
 ISBN 0-86091-970-6 (pbk.)

US Library of Congress Cataloging-in-Publication Data
Playing the state: Australian feminist interventions
 (Questions for feminism)
 Includes bibliographical references.
 1. Feminism—Australia.   2. Women in public life—
Australia.   3. Women in politics—Australia. I. Watson,
Sophie.   II. Series.
HQ 1823.P53 1989   305.42'0994   89-24770
ISBN 0-86091-255-8
ISBN 0-86091-970-6 (pbk.)

Typeset by Leaper & Gard Ltd, Bristol
Printed in Finland by Werner Söderström Oy

Contents

Acknowledgements

The idea for this book came from conversations with Anne Phillips in 1984–5. I am very grateful to her for her constant warm support and enthusiasm for the project, particularly through its more rocky moments, and for her comments. I would also like to thank Jenni Neary for her initial input, Annette Kuhn, Jill Matthews and Deena Shiff for helpful discussions, Jim Gillespie for his insights, Paul Patton for comments on the final chapter, and Drusilla Modjeska for listening to my tales. Particular thanks to Kerry Schott for contributing some useful material for chapter 1 and for her suggestions. I am grateful to Chris Ronalds, and the NSW Womens Coordination Unit for providing the illustrations. Typing this manuscript through its various drafts was no mean feat; Kath Bradburn managed to meet tight deadlines with her usual skill and patience.

I am indebted to the contributors, not only for what they have written, but also for their enthusiasm and commitment to the whole enterprise. Putting together a book concerned with aspects of feminism in a country fairly new to me was not always an easy task. Without Rosemary Pringle's unstinting intellectual and practical support and friendship I would not have enjoyed this project as much as I did. I would like to thank her greatly.

Preface

It is now twenty years since feminism emerged once again as a force to be contended with. One aspect of this new wave of feminism has been the interaction of more 'grassroots' feminisms with institutionalized forms and sites of power. The coining of the word 'femocracy' reflects and represents the relatively new entry of numbers of women into the political and bureaucratic arenas. In Britain, with the exception of local or metropolitan government levels, feminist intervention has been limited. In countries where feminists have gained some footholds in government, the possibilities and limitations associated with access to institutional forms of power have posed serious questions to feminists within and outside the institutional structures. What relations can the femocracy have to more grassroots feminisms and how much does its power derive from the feminisms 'outside'? Have feminists had to compromise in the process? Have demands been diluted? And what have the real gains of feminist intervention been? These are some of the questions which are fascinating to explore in the Australian context, since it is here that feminists in the last fifteen years or so have made significant inroads into the arenas that constitute the state. Drawing on contributions from feminist activists, bureaucrats and academics, this book attempts to explore the implications of the Australian experience for feminists in other parts of the world.

This book is divided into three parts. The first section, 'Defining the Rules', sets the context for the rest of the book. Feminist theories of the state are considered, new questions are asked, and new perspectives explored. The specificity of the Australian political framework is made clear. The particular forms of feminism in Australia are argued to be of interest and relevance to feminists the world over, since there the possibilities and contradictions of feminist bureaucratic and political power are both sharply illustrated and contested. In chapter 2 Judith Allen concludes by arguing that feminism does not need a theory of the state, thereby provoking us to question some of the perspectives suggested in the chapters which follow. The next three chapters address the crucial issues of ethnicity and race in the Australian context. Important questions are raised concerning the complexities and contradictions involved in formulating feminist policies and making feminist interventions in a country split by ethnic and racial differences and divisions. Lyndall Ryan concludes this first section by setting out the political context of feminist interventions into the bureaucracy, with a focus here on the federal bureaucracy. The years of the Whitlam administration emerge as a crucial time in the development of feminist public policy-making and reform, which has survived despite the more conservative governments that have followed.

The chapters in the second part of the book, 'On the Field', explore more directly the processes, practices and impacts of feminist interventions into the bureaucratic, political, trade-union and legal arenas in Australia. Have feminist demands been weakened, reformulated or co-opted through the political process or have real gains been made and sustained and struggles won? Where and how have feminists been most successful in their efforts? With whom have alliances been made and where has the support lain? In chapter 7 Hester Eisenstein charts the passage of equal employment opportunity legislation in the New South Wales Department of Education over nearly ten years, providing an illuminating account of the political and bureaucratic complexities and power struggles involved in such a process. The following three chapters explore further important aspects of women's employment, looking at Affirmative Action legislation, women in trade unions, and strategies for promoting women's employment opportunities in the changing environment of industry- and company-level debates, policies and initiatives. The final chapter considers another significant area of reform, law reform, and in particular the area of matrimonial property and legal models of equality.

Part III, 'Debating Strategies', stands back from the bureaucratic and political processes and considers the contradictions and questions raised by feminist interventions into the arenas of the state from a series of vantage points. In Chapter 12, Barbara Sullivan argues that sex equality legislation can only represent one aspect of a broader struggle to improve women's lives. Such strategies, which she refers to as 'degendering proposals', inevitably engage with existing categories and assume a liberal discourse where the argument is simply for extending rights traditionally held by men to women also. The following two chapters are a fascinating account of the experiences of feminist activists in seeking

funding from the state, and the difficulties involved in maintaining a
commitment to feminist principles throughout such engagement.

Cultural production is an area often forgotten in discussions of the
state. As in many countries, feminist cultural interventions have had a
significant impact in challenging traditional images, discourses, knowledges and politics. To counteract the focus on the more frequently
analysed public, employment, and welfare sectors, Chris Westwood,
Manager of the Belvoir Street Theatre, was interviewed, and gave a
colourful illustration of the games women have to play to make themselves heard in the world of theatre, film and television.

The final chapter of the book addresses the problem of the lack of
coherence of the arenas that constitute the state and the discourses
which construct it. The focus here is on the fraternalism that underpins
the modern industrial state, on the erratic nature of the welfare state in
relation to family and gender relations, and on the specificity of
mechanisms of power rather than underlying structures. Although each
chapter can be read separately, they are intended to be read in the order
in which they appear.

PART I
Defining the Rules

1

The State of Play:
An Introduction

Sophie Watson

For some years feminists across the world have confronted the thorny questions posed by engaging with 'the state'. Feminist activists have had to face the dilemmas and compromises imposed by the acceptance of government funding, often necessary so that vital services for women can survive. Feminist academics have attempted to reformulate existing theories of the state to incorporate notions of gender or have constructed new ones. While the new right has gathered force in some parts of the world, in other parts, social democratic governments, left-wing local authorities, and even conservative governments, have become the sites of feminist interventions. In the interstices of the bureaucratic, political and legal arenas, feminists have gained more, or less, of a foothold from which to make their claims.

Australia offers us one of the best opportunities to evaluate what these feminist interventions have meant for feminism and feminist thought. Since the mid 1970s, and the latter years of the reform-oriented and progressive Whitlam government, a small but significant number of feminists have held positions of (relative) power within federal and state governments and bureaucracies, influencing policy and funding for women. The implications of these and other Australian feminist interventions provide the focus for this collection.

The origins of this book lie in my own experience. I came to Australia from England in early 1984, six months after Margaret Thatcher had been elected for a second term. I came from a university where support staff were not being replaced, where brown envelopes had been issued to replace white ones, and where second-class stamps replaced first class. More generally, unemployment was growing, public expenditure was being slashed, and women were fighting to retain the inadequate services they had. I arrived in Canberra to find myself in the midst of a foreign and somewhat dazzling world. The feminists I met exchanged coded gossip about their ministers' plans for the following day, about the policies they were trying to 'get up', about the million-dollar budget they had won for women's research, about the interstate meeting they were flying to tomorrow. I was baffled. What relationship did these women have to the academic or community-based feminisms with which I was familiar? What kind of feminism did they espouse? Why did everyone wear designer frocks and smart Italian shoes to work?

Meanwhile, I found myself being invited as a consultant to the government on family law, on housing and family policies, flown around the country and collected by a Commonwealth government car at the airport. In my research I was given access to information and to discussion with senior bureaucrats under the Freedom of Information Act, when in England I would have been fobbed off by a lower-level clerk. A visit from an English feminist friend and academic, Anne Phillips, who was flown out to a conference and who received similar treatment, and who was similarly impressed and confused by what she saw, inspired this book. I decided to explore some of the questions and contradictions posed by Australian feminist interventions into the state by inviting contributions from a group of diverse feminists with a range of perspectives and experiences of the state. Some women had never written before, some were academics, some bureaucrats and some community activists.

Perspectives on the State

In 1979 British feminists, as part of the London–Edinburgh Weekend Return Group, characterized the state as not just an institution but as a form of social relations. The publication of *In and Against the State* marked a significant moment in British socialist-feminist theory and practice. It addressed both the contradictions and possibilities involved in struggle against the state to create alternative policies and practices from within and outside of its institutions. In the book, we were exhorted to build a culture of opposition. Despite the emphasis on the state as a form of social relations, it still appears to be an entity which limits and determines our lives, which acts in the interests of capital, which defines who we are and what we need, which deflects class conflict, and which obscures class divisions. Similarly capital is posed as having a 'new mode of domination, which seems so confident [but which] is really a desperate gamble'; capital appears as a largely unified, thinking force, while diversity of interests remain unacknowledged.[1]

In Canada in 1983, Varda Burstyn gave a speech to the Winnipeg Marx Centenary Conference where she represented the state as playing a crucial role of mediation and regulation in advancing capitalism's needs 'in such a way as to retain masculine privilege and control – masculine dominance in society as a whole'.[2] In her view, the contradictions between capitalism and masculinism have begun to explode with the economic developments of the last forty years. Women's entry into the paid labour force has not been matched by any notable shift of the domestic divisions of labour, while the breakdown of family units has left increasing numbers of women without even the nominal support of men as fathers. Burstyn argues that these trends have been accompanied by a masculinist ideological onslaught in which the gendered state plays a key role.

In the following year an Australian feminist publication *Refractory Girl*, devoted an entire issue to bureaucratic feminisms, to the 'femocrat phenomenon' and to state initiatives for women. This was an entry into what was by the mid eighties becoming an important debate amongst feminists in Australia. Central to the discussions was the long-running and sometimes hostile debate about co-option and the incompatibility between 'grassroots' feminisms and those of the bureaucracy. In 1987, in Toronto, a conference was held entitled 'Women and the State: A Conference for Feminist "Activisits"'. Lorna Weir described Canadian feminists' familiarity with the 'capacity of the state to "manage" women's popular organizing: the use of grant criteria to restructure feminist groups internally, the creation of salaried "femocrats" to speak officially on behalf of women',[3] as well as the struggles to build a multi-racial women's movement.

In her essay in this collection, written 1988, Judith Allen questions the very concept of 'the state' and argues that it is 'a category of abstraction that is too aggregative, too unitary and too unspecific to be of much use in addressing the disaggregated, diverse and specific (or local) sites that must be of most pressing concern to feminists'. Rosemary Pringle and myself argue for a focus on the specificity of mechanisms of power and on the apparently surface phenomena, rather than a reliance on abstract theory or underlying structures (see chapter 17).

We have come a long way from the simple formulation of the state as acting primarily in the interests of capital, or as an institution which must be either smashed or which will wither away with the inevitable advance of socialism. In several countries, Canada and Australia in particular, feminists have gained increasing footholds within the political and bureaucratic arenas. Legislation has been enacted to end sex discrimination, equal employment opportunity programmes have been initiated, women's units have been established in government departments,

policies have been devised to address inequalities and so on. How are
these shifts to be interpreted? What are the limitations of concepts of sex
equality for feminism? Have feminist demands been diluted or co-opted
through engagement with the institutions and discourses which constitute the state? How has the state mediated and reformulated gender
regulation? Can we make significant gains through playing political,
legal and bureaucratic games? What are the compromises? Is there a
unified set of women's interests which can be articulated? Has feminist
engagement with the state been dominated by white women and been
lacking in multi-racial and multi-cultural perspectives? These are some
of the questions this collection of papers seeks to address.

Feminist Theories

Feminists have theorized 'the state' in a number of ways. For some time
Marxist-feminist analysis was the dominant discourse. Within this
paradigm, a feminist analysis of social reproduction, the family, and
gender was grafted onto an analysis of the capitalist state which was seen
as acting predominantly in the interests of preserving the dominant class
relations and assisting the accumulation of capital. The family was
theorized as the significant site of reproduction of labour power and as
maintaining existing social relations. The reason why, in its efforts to
mediate and regulate capitalism's needs, the state has reinforced
masculine dominance and privilege has been, until recently, less explored
by Marxist feminists, with the notable exception of Burstyn.[4] Reductionist
and functionalist arguments are employed to explain the persistence of
sexual divisions and the patriarchal family form, which end up subsuming gender relations within the all-powerful system of something
called 'the needs of capital'.

   The second dominant approach characterizes the state as patriarchal.
Catherine Mackinnon[5] analyses the legal institutions of the state,
showing how they incorporate a male standpoint and institutionalize
masculine interests. The state is conceptualized not simply as patriarchal
but fraternal,[6] a notion that explores in particular the fraternal nature of
the social contract. The common ground of these theoretical positions is
the notion that the state embodies – or acts in the interests of – dominant groups. Feminist and Marxist-feminist analyses of the ways in which
this happens have become increasingly complex and sophisticated in
recent years. Liberal feminists, in contrast, drawing on the liberal democratic views of the state developed by John Stuart Mill and Jeremy
Bentham,[7] have represented the state as a neutral arbiter or umpire. In
this formulation the state is pluralistic and can be influenced or captured

by different interest groups. Although the institutions of the state are recognized by liberal feminists as being dominated by men, and policies are seen to reflect masculine interests, liberal feminists seek initiatives, legislation and policies that promote equality and address women's concerns. The state is seen as the route to achieve such reforms.

Theories and discourses of the state until the last decade have tended to treat the state itself as a fairly unproblematic category. Thus, even though the state has been recognized as contradictory, as an arena for struggle, as a site of conflict or contestation, or as a framework of apparatuses, there remains a tendency to imply a relative coherence to the state. In the last decade recognition that the state is a category of abstraction which cannot simply be characterized as a unified entity has increasingly informed feminist work on the subject. There are many different varieties of state, spatially and historically. Each of these has its own combination of institutions, apparatuses, and arenas, which have their own histories, contradictions, relations and connections, internally and externally. Judith Allen, in this collection, takes the argument yet further, suggesting that a case still has to be made as to why 'the state' is necessarily a category for feminist analysis.

The extent of cohesion of, and linkages between, the component parts of the state is a focus of concern for state theorists; as is, likewise, how to analyse the increasingly complex international circumstances within which the 'nation state' is situated. Theda Skocpol sees the state as 'a set of administrative, policing, and military organizations headed, and more or less well co ordinated by an executive authority'.[8] Foucault's work has also been of some influence. Foucault's analysis focuses on the relations of power and knowledge and power technologies which are diffused throughout society rather than concentrated in the state. The state is accorded no 'unity, individuality or rigorous functionality'[9] but is nevertheless recognized as an important focus of power.[10]

Recognizing that the state is not a unity implies a series of arenas which constitute the state both discursively and through shifting interlocking connections and practices. At one time there may be stronger links, and a clearer and more coherent set of intentionalities embodied within these apparatuses than at another. Similarly, more or less power can accrue to the state as a set of institutions and players across time and place.

A recognition of the heterogeneity and disunified nature of interests is equally important. Feminist theories of the state, be they liberal, radical or Marxist, tend also to assume a unity of interests between men, between sections of capital, and even between women. The state is thus seen as reinforcing, supporting or acting on behalf of these interests which exist outside it, or can be cajoled, persuaded or forced to do this. Such an analysis fails to conceptualize the state as an arena in which capital's or men's interests are actively constructed rather than given. It also fails to address the notion that the interests of capital or of men may not necessarily be unified. The political objectives or demands of women upon the state presuppose a coherent set of interests outside the political and bureaucratic arenas which can be met, rather than recognizing that these interests are actively constructed in the process of the demands being made and the state's responses. Thus, in the process of responding to some demands and not others, or to some interests and not others, the state is involved in actively constructing these demands. An analysis along these lines may be useful when we are considering how effective feminist interventions into 'the state' have been.

State Workers

The discussion so far has analysed the state as a site of power and social relations, as a more or less coherent network of institutions or apparatuses. Such discussion tends to depersonalize the state and ignore the personnel which constitute it. A central focus of this book is precisely the people embodied in the apparatuses of the state, the impact of gender divisions, and the significance of the entry of feminists and other women into positions of relative power.

That the top levels of the elected bureaucratic and legal systems of the state in most countries are dominated by men is well known. In Australia in 1986 there was one female cabinet minister in Hawke's government; women comprised 9 per cent of federal and state parliaments, and 5 per cent of judges in the federal courts.[11] Currently 38 per cent of the entire federal government workforce are women, a similar proportion to the workforce at large. Among the senior management in Divisions 1 and 2 (the Senior Executive Service) only 6 per cent are women. In January 1986 there were still seven federal government departments with no female senior management at all, and Defence and Taxation (both very large bureaucracies) with only one woman at the senior level. Only one department in the entire bureaucracy had a female head. The lower levels of the bureaucracy are, not surprisingly, dominated by women as clerks, typists, secretaries, and so on, who are more likely to identify themselves as workers than as bureaucrats or as femocrats (who are somewhat of an elite among women).

The dominance of the military apparatus of the state by men (93 per cent of the combined forces in June 1984)[12] has been linked by Genevieve Lloyd to women's exclusion from citizenship: 'the masculinity of citizenship and the masculinity of war have been conceptually connected in Western thought'.[13] The same might be argued of the connections between the judiciary, the bureaucracy, and parliament. Women are marginal in the arenas which confer and define citizenship. The focus of this book is on the bureaucratic and political arenas, not the military. Where women are selected for cabinet posts at state or federal level they tend to be given the portfolios related to family or community concerns, and excluded from the more powerful and prestigious departments of Finance, Treasury and Foreign Affairs. In Hawke's government, Susan Ryan, the only female minister, was appointed to Women's Affairs and Education, and latterly shifted to the less powerful Ministry of State to introduce (unsuccessfully) the unpopular Australia (identity) Card.

This exclusion has been attributed to masculine control in the selection of candidates, and to the routines of Party life, the skills and the forms of behaviour valued. Certainly in Canberra, the women at the top levels of the political and bureaucratic arenas tend to be without dependents and rarely in conventional marital relationships. Social drinking after work and working at weekends is an unspoken prerequisite for high-level positions. Forms of masculine dominance and behaviours are the ascribed norm referred to by Canberra feminists in the bureaucracy as 'playing the boys' games'.

Bureaucracies operate on a closed system of favours, shared perspectives and values, deals, hierarchies of knowledge, and mystification. Marx describes the bureaucracy as a 'particular closed society within the state' which extends its power through secrecy and mystery.[14] Weber attributes bureaucratic power to the possession of expertise, information and access to secrets.[15] There is no one pattern of how feminists have negotiated their positions of political and bureaucratic power. Neither is there a distinctive category of 'femocrat'. Some feminists referred to as the 'tree people' (going to and from the trees with the rise and fall of Labor governments) joined the bureacracy as part of a conscious political strategy to achieve reform. Others have been traditional career public servants, while yet others joined the bureaucracy to escape the poorly paid and insecure community sector; some have also joined the bureaucracy because of the closed doors of academia. Women working in the 'femocrat' areas – in the women's policy units in the prime minister's office and in other government departments – face different problems and contradictions from the women working in the mainstream areas of departments, who are less likely to be referred to as femocrats. Here, uneasy alliances are made and broken; loyalties to ministers or departments frequently conflict with policies formulated elsewhere in the women's units. Bureaucratic languages and abbreviations are quickly learned and spoken, to the fury of feminists 'outside' who feel mystified and excluded from the process.

Feminist intervention into the state in Australia has received mixed responses. In 1984 Lesley Lynch addressed the question of whether femocracy constituted a strategic transference of the struggle to a key arena of influence or an undermining of the women's movement.[16] Using the metaphor of 'bossism and beige suits' she identifies the increasing shift as a careerist and conservative tendency. Three issues are discussed. The notion that femocrats have been co-opted or sold out, which derives in part from their resistance to discuss their work, their claims to be unable to tell the real story, their high salaries, and the pressures on them that undermine their capacity to function as feminists. Lynch sees conformism as another pressure. These include the difficulties of maintaining a high profile as a radical activist, the inability to publicize work issues, and the pressure to 'dress for success'. Femocrats' conformity in fashion is linked with effectiveness at the job, rather than as an ambiguous, contradictory gesture, simultaneously a sword and a shield, as might be suggested by an application of Elizabeth Wilson's ideas.[17] The third issue is that of rejection, the sense that femocrats have of being maligned and misunderstood, often accused or being arrogant or critical of the women's movement's unwillingness to compromise and its naivety.

The extent to which feminists in the bureaucracy have contributed to or effected social change is one of the questions considered in this book. If the state is theorized as a complex set of interrelated but distinct institutions, relations, hierarchies, discourses, interests and players, it follows that there will be a diversity of femocrat discourses and practices. Workers in the institutions of the state inevitably have to negotiate a path of contradictions, conflicts and dilemmas, particularly if they see themselves as feminists. As Suzanne Franzway points out: 'The state is not only a site of contest but is itself implicated in that contest and so, necessarily, are state workers.'[18] Femocrats, particularly those in the women's units, can find themselves marginalized in women's policy areas with little impact on economic and social policy formulated elsewhere, but at the same time deriving their strength and coherence from this separate relation. Feminists working in mainstream areas can find themselves formulating policies which may have a negative impact on some groups of women. Policy-making may involve responding to conflicting demands – from politicians, other bureaucrats, and a whole range of diverse feminist interests outside the bureaucracy – and facing the constraints of government expenditures, directives and legal structures within a prescribed bureaucratic framework. Feminists are thus likely to adopt different strategies at different times and in different situations.

The Limitations of Feminist Intervention

Critiques of feminist intervention as leading to co-option or dilution of feminism embody several obscured assumptions. One, that there exists outside the bureaucratic political arena a coherent unified and defined set of feminist demands or interests which may or may not be met. Second, that rather than being constituted in the interaction with, or arenas of, the state, these interests exist autonomously and prior to feminist intervention. Feminist interventions can be criticized from a rather different standpoint, one which questions masculine individualism and universalism and a liberal equality framework, and draws on notions of sexual difference or autonomy. A recent Australian collection, *Feminist Challenges* develops theory which accepts neither 'gender-neutral' abstract individualism nor social individualism which prescribes women's bodies as subject to men's desires and decisions.[19]

A dominant theme in these texts is that the universal standing in society for which we have been fighting is that of a 'being with masculine characteristics engaging in masculine activities'. As Carole Pateman argues, feminism has tended to adopt liberal and socialist notions of freedom and equality without recognizing that 'their apparently universal categories, such as the individual, the worker, the social or the political, are sexually particular, constructed on the basis of male attributes, capacities and modes of activity'.[20] Sexual difference within feminist struggles, especially those taking place in the state arenas, is either denied or attempts are made to minimize its impact. Since so much of women's exclusion from the public and political spheres has been premised on our physical characteristics, such as our reproductive capacity, assertion of our equal capacity for work has been a necessary path. This has led to arguments for sex equality that sit uncomfortably with arguments for women's liberation, which has 'sought to envalue and develop what have been perceived as women's gender-specific potentials and capacities'.[20]

As Merle Thornton points out, the concept of equality only applies to two things which are said to be equal in some specified respect. Arguments for sex equality rely on an assumption of equal natures which if treated equally will result in equal performance. If the possibility of distinct natures for the sexes is considered, we substitute the argument that men and women should be equally enabled to develop their different capacities so that their different performance will be both complementary and have comparable value. Thornton suggests a path which seeks to remove women's disqualification from public and political life but which moves beyond equality to liberationism. This is a recognition that gender differences (social or biological) imply the need for new

...ays of living which enhance women's potential. The call to re-insert sexual difference into the picture, and to develop theory which recognizes that individuality is not a unitary abstraction and that women have an autonomous place, is an important one. What this means for a pragmatic feminism which seeks to develop policies for women within the political and bureaucratic arenas is of serious concern, since a recognition of women's gender-specific potentials and capacities still underlies most opposition to even formal equality. The dichotomies between private and public, political and social, sex and gender, family, home and work will have to be reconceptualized. Pateman and Grosz's collection provides a useful starting point for such a project.

The Australian State

Part of the explanation for the form of Australian feminist interventions and the femocrat phenomenon lies in the specificity of the institutions which constitute the Australian state. Australia is governed by a federal government (based in Canberra), and six state governments. Australia is a country of only 16 million people, and it is often argued that the country is over-governed, but such arguments overlook the relatively minor importance of local government. The powers of state and federal governments are set out in the 1901 Constitution and there is a continuous tension between the federal and state governments about this power, with frequent legal battles in the High Court to test the jurisdiction of each layer of government. Because there are six states in the federation, Australia is typically governed by a mixture of political parties at any one time; a conservative Liberal/National Party federal government in Canberra, for example, may be accompanied by Labor Party governments in several states, or vice versa.

Economic power is rather firmly in federal government hands. Effectively the federal government has the power to levy income tax while the states' power to tax is more limited. This financial leverage is an important influence on policy and is used quite blatantly at times to achieve the will of the federal government. (The control that Westminster exerts over local authorities in Britain is more complete than the control exercised by the federal government in Australia over the states, but there are some similarities.) The federal government provides about half of the states' revenues, with the rest coming from state taxes on payrolls, gambling, motor car registrations and so on. The federal level of government is about 30 per cent of total Australian GDP while the state level is about 20 per cent of GDP.

The federal government controls defence, foreign affairs and external trade policy, economic policy, unemployment benefits, social security benefits, immigration and (at present) national health insurance. The states have jurisdiction over most education, over hospitals, roads, many community projects, and public housing. But because the states rely on federal funds for about half of their activities, any directional order attached to these federal funds affects state actions, either directly or indirectly. There are also many policies where responsibility is shared more visibly between states and federal government. Policies towards aboriginal Australians, the environment, and transport fall into this category.

The distinctive form of the public service in Australia is crucial to an understanding of how feminists have managed to gain some power within the federal and state bureaucracies. The system is quite different to that of Britain. Although the screening of 'Yes, Minister' on Australian television leaves the Canberra streets empty for the night, this is more from a sense of amusement at the familiar machinations, or incredulity at the British class system than from any identification with it. In Australia, the links between boys' public schools, elite universities and the public service are weaker. This is not to argue that the same forms of fraternity do not exist (see for example chapter 16), but simply that the nexus of patriarchal and class interests is of a distinctive, and probably more shifting kind.

Although with each state and federal government different conditions of service apply, a description of the federal public service illustrates the general picture. Like the British civil service, the career structure is hierarchical, with a nomenclature like that of a football league. At the top of a federal government department sits a Secretary (Division 1); below him (or very rarely her) comes the Second Division of Deputy Secretaries, First Assistant Secretaries, and Assistant Secretaries. This is the Senior Executive Service. Below these Olympian ranks come the far more numerous Third Division. The Fourth Division (mainly word-processor operators and support staff) have recently been incorporated into an expanded Third Division, which will improve the position of the many women who worked in the old Fourth Division, since there is now no bar stopping their entry onto the career ladder of the Third Division.

Although the hierarchy of the federal public service resembles the British civil service, it is, in operation, a more open structure – and one that to an extent reflects the political complexion of the government in power. Political appointments are not made by direct political patronage as in the US. Through Ministerial staffing and liaison arrangements the public service works closely with political appointees, particularly on important projects. Each Minister can appoint up to two senior advisors in addition to their normal Ministerial staffing. These senior advisors in practice work closely with the relevant department, often on a major policy initiative of importance to the government. These political appointments can be made from outside or inside the public service, and such appointments are on a contract of up to three years. The contract automatically dissolves at an election.

In an attempt to open up the top management ranks, all public service jobs that fall vacant in Divisions 1 and 2 (the Senior Executive Service) are advertised both inside and outside the public service to encourage applicants from the private sector, from universities and other government agencies. Freedom of Information law allows any applicant access to their own files to see the reasons given for why they were or were not chosen. In addition Secretaries (that is, heads of department) are frequently rotated; either to another department, or to take up another position, or to remain temporarily unattached. This makes it very difficult for any one person to behave like an omnipotent ruler over some area of government policy for decades on end. All applicants are chosen by a panel of usually three or four people, and the panel will have rules about its composition which are intended to stop discriminatory appointments. It is required that every effort should be made to include at least one woman on the panel, who has to be of at least equal standing to the vacant position; also, a person from outside the department in which the vacancy occurs must be present to offset internal departmental favouritism.

Women in the Federal Public Service

In the federal government the employment of women and their conditions of work have only gradually become less discriminatory. Until 1949 no women were permitted to compete for appointment in the Third Division or higher of the federal government; and it was only in 1966 that married women were allowed to remain in the federal public service. These constraints existed at a time when preference, in the form of affirmative action, was given to the employment of ex-servicemen (until 1960). Until the early 1960s promotion by merit, and with it the possible establishment of a fast-track career structure for the best and brightest, were seen as a British class-based inegalitarian way of doing things. It was argued that only 'silvertails' and 'tall poppies' went to university and that the government was better run by men without graduate qualifications who could work their way up from being the office messenger. There was no point in reflecting the bias in higher education entrance by favouring graduates for public service careers. Even with the establishment of promotion by merit (which discriminates less against women than 'long service' criteria) the distrust of a British-type administrative fast-track stream continues to exist.

The emphasis on efficiency in the public service increased as the size of government expanded, and along with the emphasis on efficiency went the move to promotion by merit. As early as 1960, economic rationalists concerned about efficiency argued that women must be included in the public service career, much to the disgust of heads of department, the Public Service Board (the overseers of public employment), and conservative Prime Minister Menzies. The bar against married women was not removed, however, as it was seen to interfere with the promotion of men.[21] It was only after Menzies retired in 1966 that legislation repealed the marriage bar and recruitment (but not promotion) was required not to discriminate against women at least in a *de jure* sense.

In 1962 (four years before women) handicapped people had won anti-discrimination legislation; and in 1967 diabetics were included. By 1970 over 8,000 people were employed who otherwise would not have been. Married women comprised about 31 per cent of permanent female officers in the Third and Fourth Divisions and 10 per cent of all appointments. More changes were introduced by the Whitlam Labor government which was committed to radical reforms in many areas. In 1973 the Maternity Leave (Australian Government Employees) Bill noted:

> The concept of this bill is to provide for greater equality for women. It removes from the Commonwealth public service a selective and camouflaged discrimination which has no place in the Australian way of life.

This signalled an intention to try and move away from *de facto* discrimination as well as from the obvious *de jure* discrimination. Various studies throughout the 1970s (under both Whitlam and Fraser) revealed the unfavourable career prospects for women. In 1979 there were still only 1.3 per cent of women in senior management positions in the First and Second Divisions, and in 1978 there was no woman on the top rung (Class 11) of the Third Division.

Throughout the early 1980s this became a political issue. The Public Accounts Committee tabled a report that gave details of the lag in women's advancement in the public service and by 1984 the Australian Labor Party platform contained a section supporting promotion by merit and committing the ALP to a series of special programmes to recruit, encourage and train women, migrants, and Aboriginal Australians. The election of the Hawke Labor government in 1983 enabled passage of this policy and in 1984 the Public Sector Reform Act was passed. This made discrimination unlawful on a range of grounds, including sexual preference. It also required that departments set up Equal Employment Opportunity programs and report on their progress to the Parliament each year. Compared to the pre-1949 period, when women could not compete for entry to the Third Division, it is clear that some improvements in female working opportunities have been won. Whether the legal changes will be sufficient to stop *de facto* discrimination is another question.

In 1986 women constituted approximately 6 per cent of the senior executive level (Divisions 1 and 2) of the federal public service. Similar patterns would be found in the states, with some variations according to the local political and social relations. Most states as well as the federal government have women's advisers to the Prime Minister or State Premier. The Whitlam government is the key here as the first government to appoint women's advisers and allocate funds under the International Women's Year to women's units (see chapter 6). This initiative inspired most states to follow suit. The units vary in size and in location depending on the emphasis given to women's issues. Conservative governments not only reduce the size of the women's offices but also tend to shift them from the Premier's Department to Departments of Family Services, Community Welfare or whatever. The recently elected Greiner government of New South Wales has followed this practice. The structure of these units follows the lines of other divisions, branches or sections within the bureaucracy with the head usually appointed at a senior level. There are also women's policy units within other federal and (in some cases) state departments concerned with education, employment and industrial relations, health and so on.

Local Government

In Britain local government and the metropolitan authorities have become one of the key arenas for resistance to the Thatcher government, which in turn has done its utmost to limit the powers of local authorities to raise revenues and pursue innovative policies. Not surprisingly there has been considerable debate in Britain on the nature of the 'local state': the extent to which it represents the 'capitalist state' at local level, or the crucial site of struggle, or the avenue for local democratic participation and so on. The fact that these arguments have been less prevalent in Australia can largely be attributed to the different form of the state in Australia, where government at local level has been primarily concerned with the three Rs – Roads, Rates and Rubbish. The state level of government in Australia actually has more in common with

British local government in terms of its functions, scope and powers. The limited role of local government in Australia has to be understood in a historical context. The failure of local government can be attributed to the British colonial legacy, whereby arrogant, elitist and uninformed politicians and administrators have attempted to impose local government from above.[22] Restrictions on the rights of ex-convicts to hold office or even to vote locally, and a related reluctance by the British to allow local government to emerge at the grassroots level led to an early identification of local governments with reactionary attitudes.

The impact of the Whitlam government on local government was substantial. The emphasis was on regionalism. Whitlam saw the key to achieving greater equality between areas as lying in urban and regional policies which bypassed, in many instances, intransigent state bureaucracies. Under the Department of Urban and Regional Development (DURD) local councils were encouraged to formulate proposals to improve their area through initiatives which genuinely reflected the needs of the community. Finance was to be provided by the federal government on a three-year rolling commitment basis. This provided local authorities with the possibility of taking action to solve urban problems without having to rely on state governments, who were notorious in their lack of interest in assistance at this level. The projects supported included community facilities, recreational facilities, drainage works and even the construction of a hill in a flat and desolate area of Sydney.[23] The commitment to this programme came to an end with the subsequent Fraser government elected in 1975.

A more direct input by feminists into local government came through the avenue of welfare and social planning. The Whitlam period was once again a crucial one. Women played a central role both as the majority of welfare recipients and as the majority of paid and unpaid providers of services. Of significance also was the establishment under the 1972 Labor Government of the Social Welfare Commission. The Australian Assistance Plan represented a key element of the Commission's approach and 'involved the establishment of elected bodies (Regional Councils for Social Development) with functions of social planning, co-ordination and allocation of resources on a regional basis'.[24] Over the last decade feminists have increasingly run as local candidates and have been elected as local councillors, as well as campaigning for and participating in the provision of innovative social and community services by local government. Victoria is the notable example, which reflects a greater level of service provision through local government in that state.

Outside of Victoria there has been a more limited engagement by feminists in local government both at the political level and at the level of service provision. In part this can be explained by the notorious corruption of local politicians in many areas. The other factor is that local government represents the pinnacle of fraternity, the archetypal boys' club. The following extracts from a poem in a local newspaper in a mining region of Queensland illustrate my point:

> I really am excited, the poll has been declared
> I'm Chairman of the Shire, can't wait to get in there.
> My policy is simple, I'll make the staff kowtow.
> No more will petty bureaucrats presume to tell me how....
>
> That wimpy Health Surveyor, I'll fix him up quick smart,
> Do-gooder bands with welfare plans won't even get a start,
> He only wants to build his nest with more and high paid staff,
> Those CDOs with PhDs and boy that's not the half.
> They'll talk in riddled language, they'll bluff the Council sure
> Unless I take a firm hard stand and push them out the door.
>
> The voters just won't cop this stuff, I'm here to do it over
> And crack down on these officers all rolling in the clover.
> We need a new direction, a strong hand at the helm.
> Someone who'll face the music and won't be overwhelmed.
>
> I'll be that man of iron, decisive, strong and tough.... [25]

With the Hawke Government in power at a federal level, there has been a renewed interest in the federal-local connections. This has created some space once again for input and participation at a local level. For example, under the 1984 Commonwealth-State funding agreement on housing policy a new sum of money was set aside for the development of community housing programmes by local government and community groups. This provided the possibility of establishing co-operative housing of various kinds, and has been used by feminists as a way of providing refuges, group homes and other housing forms for women. However, while political power remains concentrated at state and federal levels, any successes at local level will be transitory, if they affect important interests, or relatively insignificant. Unless power is first decentralized, as was attempted under Whitlam, the important levels for most political action in Australia will continue to be the state and federal governments.

Conclusion

Feminist interventions and the growth of the femocracy in Australia, which provide the focus for this book, have to be seen in the context of a particular political period. Most significant was the progressive climate of the Whitlam years, but this impetus was sustained in part during the years of the Fraser government at the federal level, and in those states where Labor governments were in power. With the election of the Hawke Labor government in 1983 there was an expanded commitment at federal level to feminist priorities and to equal opportunity which was matched particularly in New South Wales, Victoria and South Australia.

The book has been completed at a time when the Hawke government is increasingly on the defensive, with its future uncertain as it faces an election in 1989/90. With the revived dominance of the new right in the Conservative parties and with continuing pressures on the economy, progressive feminist reforms could recede from the political agenda. Whatever the future, feminists in the political and bureaucratic spheres suffer from the Labor Party's failure to promote women at high levels and from the resulting absence of women with enough political clout to enter the cabinet. How successful feminists will continue to be at influencing debates and policies at the federal level is an open question. Meanwhile in New South Wales a Liberal government was elected in 1988 under Nick Greiner which has introduced large cuts in public expenditure, withdrawn its support for equal opportunities, consigned its women's co-ordination unit to a more marginal status, and re-introduced regressive abortion law reform on to the political agenda.

What is clear is that the federal system in Australia is crucial in mediating the effects of changes in government. For example, as a state government shifts to the right, a Labor government at the federal level can be crucially important in defending the advances achieved in earlier periods and in initiating reforms. What this points to is the significance of fragmentation of political structures and the need to recognize the Australian 'state' as a complex set of institutions and arenas which cannot be assumed to act as a coherent or uncontradictory beast. The ability of feminists to influence the political agenda and to achieve reforms is inevitably a result of specific political and economic relations, of the composition of bureaucratic and political players, of localized powers and resistances and of the strength of 'feminisms' within and outside the political structures.

Notes

1. London-Edinburgh Weekend Return Group, *In and Against the State*, Pluto Press, London 1979, p. 132.

2. Varda Burstyn, 'Masculine Dominance and the State' in R.E. Miliband and J. Santle (eds), *Socialist Register*, Merlin Press, London 1983.

3. Lorna Weir, 'Women and the State: A Conference for Feminist Activists', *Feminist Review* 26, Summer 1987.

4. Burstyn.

5. Catherine A Mackinnon, 'Feminism, Marxism, Method and the State: An Agenda for Theory', *Signs* 7, 3, 1982, pp. 515–44.

6. Carole Pateman, *The Sexual Contract*, Polity Press, Oxford 1988.

7. John Stuart Mill, *Utilitarianism, Liberty and Representative Government*, Dent, London 1915; Jeremy Bentham, 'Fragment on Government', Basil Blackwell, Oxford 1960.

8. Theda Skocpol, *States and Revolutions. A Comparative Analysis of France, Russia and China*, Cambridge University Press, Cambridge 1979; quoted in David Held et al. (eds), *States and Societies*, Basil Blackwell, Oxford 1983.

9. Barry Smart, *Michel Foucault*, Tavistock, London 1985, p. 130.

10. Michel Foucault, 'The Subject and Power' in H.L. Dreyfus and P. Rabinow, *Michel Foucault: Beyond Structuralism and Hermeneutics*, Harvester Press, Brighton 1982, p. 224.

11. Robert W. Connell, *Gender and Power*, Allen & Unwin, Sydney 1988.

12. Ibid.

13. Genevieve Lloyd, 'Selfhood, War and Masculinity' in C. Pateman and E. Grosz (eds), *Feminist Challenges: Social and Political Theory*, Allen & Unwin, Sydney 1986, p. 64.

14. Karl Marx, *Critique of Hegel's Philosophy of Right* quoted in David Held et al. p. 26.

15. David Held et al., p. 37.

16. Lesley Lynch, 'Bureaucratic Feminisms: Bossism and Beige Suits', *Refractory Girl*, May 1984.

17. Elizabeth Wilson, *Adorned in Dreams: Fashion and Modernity*, Virago, London 1984.

18. Suzanne Franzway, 'With Problems of Their Own: Femocrats and the Welfare State', Australian Feminist Studies 3, Summer 1986.

19. Pateman & Grosz, *Feminist Challenges*.

20. Merle Thornton, 'Sex Equality is Not Enough for Feminism' in Pateman & Grosz.

21. Elaine Thompson, 'Reform in the Public Service: Egalitarianism to the S.E.S. Politics', vol. 21, November 1986.

22. M.A. Jones, *Local Government and the People. Challenges for the Eighties*, Hargreen Publishing Co., Melbourne 1981, pp. 29–30.

23. Clem Lloyd and Patrick Troy, 'Duck Creek Revisited' in J. Halligan and C. Paris, *Australian Urban Politics*, Longman, Melbourne 1984.

24. Jenny Wills, *Local Government and Community Services. Fitzroy: A Study in Social Planning*, Hard Pressed Publications, Clifton Hill, Vic: 1985, p. 7.

25. Gary Kellar, 'The New Broom', *The Gem: The Highland's Independent Newspaper*, July 1988, Gemfields Publishing, Rubyvale, Queensland.

2

Does Feminism Need a Theory of 'The State'?

Judith Allen

The difficulty of adequately conceptualizing the patriarchy/capitalism relationship is the central reason for the difficulty of developing a feminist theory of the state. We don't pretend to have developed one.[1]

Since the late 1970s the category of 'the state' has assumed a certain currency and significance in some feminist theoretical work. The fact that so many feminist objectives appear to hinge on legal and policy reforms in areas including abortion, rape, domestic violence, pornography, sexual harassment, anti-discrimination, affirmative action, and child care, has, for many feminists, warranted a focus on 'the state'. While it would be valid to say that feminist theory has developed analyses of a number of categories – for instance sexual economics, reproduction, sexuality, the female body – and knowledges, distinct from those of other sexual politics positions – such as libertarianism – 'the state' has not been an indigenous category of feminist theory.[2] Rather, it is an import, and, for some commentators and in some instances, an uneasy amalgam: partly the liberal state, partly 'the state' as formulated by contemporary Marxism; but either way a theory of 'the state' with definitions, parameters and analytic tasks forged for political positions *other* than feminism.[3]

Some of the recent history of feminist deployments of the category 'the state' is inseparable from the history of attempts to build the theoretical position of Marxist feminism. This position has been concerned with 'the relations between the organization of sexuality, domestic production, the household and so on, and historical changes in the mode of production and systems of appropriation and exploitation'.[4] Arguably, uses of 'the state' inflected by Marxist-feminist presupposi-

21

tions inherit many of the intractable problems of this position, as an examination of some key textual instances illustrates.

By the early 1980s in Australia and North America, feminist involvement in equal opportunity, affirmative action and sexual harassment cases informed arguments *against* feminist appropriations of Marxist versions of 'the state' and arguments *for* a feminist theory of 'the state'. 'Failure' to provide a theory of 'the state' was represented as a major gap in feminist theory. The solution offered by some critics was the formulation 'the patriarchal state' or 'the state is male' or, in more specific variants, 'the patriarchal welfare state'. Such formulations offered clear advances on previous meanings of 'the state' in feminist theory.[5]

On a number of grounds, however, it is timely to review the history and current position of 'the state' within western feminist theory in a thoroughgoing manner. This chapter constitutes only some preliminary questions towards such an enterprise. Attempts to adapt the category 'the state' for feminist purposes by the addition of adjectives – 'patriarchal', 'male' – do not address the fundamentally problematic character of the term 'the state' as a formulation to be put to the service of *feminist* analyses and objectives. Feminism has not been guilty of oversight or failure in *not* developing a distinct theory of 'the state'. Instead, feminist theorists' choices of theoretical agendas with priorities other than 'the state' have a sound rationale that deserves to be taken seriously. 'The state' is a category of abstraction that is too aggregative, too unitary and too unspecific to be of much use in addressing the disaggregated, diverse and specific (or local) sites that must be of most pressing concern to feminists. 'The state' is too blunt an instrument to be of much assistance (beyond generalizations) in explanations, analyses or the design of workable strategies.

We should not be surprised that 'the state' holds less than a privileged, richly nuanced place within feminist theory. Historically, feminism has had one central claim distinguishing it from all other prevailing political positions: that the oppression of women, *as a sex* is in the interests of men *as a sex*; and the one central objective of feminism has been to end women's oppression *as a sex*.[6] Feminism refuses to be, because it cannot be, modified by the conflicting claims and objectives of other political positions such as liberalism and Marxism – and still be recognizable as feminism.[7] Within feminist theory and empirical research, categories other than 'the state' emerge as more urgent and significant. These include 'policing', 'law' and 'legal culture', 'medical culture', 'bureaucratic culture', 'organized crime', 'fraternalism', 'paternalism', 'misogyny', 'subjectivity', 'the body', 'sexuality', 'men', 'masculinity', 'violence', 'culture', 'power' and 'pleasure'.[8]

An examination of some case studies of the Australian history of areas of crime and criminal law reform of concern to feminists discloses the limited analytic purchase of 'the state' (at least as conceived thus far) for feminist history and theory. While some findings from this history could be designated as examples of the contradictory nature of 'the state', 'its' potential to be a site of conflicting interests, there are serious questions as to the extent of contradictions which can be accommodated by theories of 'the state' before such theories lost coherence or effect as theories.[9] Attachment to inappropriate theoretical categories can obstruct feminist recognition of urgent tasks for feminist analysis and explanation. More minimally such categories become irrelevant, possibly burdensome theoretical baggage.

The State and the Oppression of Women

Feminist texts of the early 1970s rarely discussed 'the state' as a separate or privileged category of analysis. Instead, the terms 'government', 'political system', 'state', even 'the establishment' were used coterminously, while feminist critics of the welfare system and its administrative bureaucracy used the conventional formulation 'the welfare state'.[10] These texts indicate that these terms were understood as designating spheres or forms of male dominance over women, of patriarchy without identifying a separate category 'the state'. The force of this work tended to dispel any notion that women's oppression originated from, or was orchestrated by, any single authority. Many forms and levels of men's dominance and women's oppression were identified and explored. Current feminist theory remains heavily indebted to the pathbreaking work of the early 1970s.[11]

The debut of the distinct category of 'the state' in feminist theoretical work accompanied the advent of the first sustained Marxist-feminist articulations. Attempts to make a workable marriage between the terms and concerns of Marxism and those of feminism involved loose adaptations of then current Marxist theories of 'the state' in relation to women. Further, Marxist-feminist interest in the question of 'the state' was stimulated in Australia by feminists' relation to the Whitlam Labor Government 1972–1975, to its successor Conservative government 1975–1983 and to the present Hawke Labor government since 1983.[12] Similarly, feminism became a contender, lobbyist and commentator on shifts in government policy in North America and in Britain.[13]

A series of Marxist (or socialist)-feminist anthologies and texts from the late 1970s attempted to articulate a more rigorous case for the place of 'the state' in feminist theory.[14] Amongst this work, Mary McIntosh's

influential 1978 article 'The State and the Oppression of Women' stands
out as a particularly clear example of the nature of engagement between
Marxism and feminism advocated at this time. It is worth noting some
key aspects of her arguments, especially her characterization of 'the
state' and 'its' rationales and interests.

In the first place, McIntosh claims that the core of women's oppression transpires within two systems, the family household and wage
labour. The question to ask about 'the state' for McIntosh is the part it
plays in establishing and sustaining these two systems and women's
dependent position within them. Secondly she argues that

> The state, like society cannot be analysed simply in terms of patriarchy.
> Capitalist society is one in which men as men dominate women; yet it is not
> this, but class domination that is fundamental to the society. It is a society in
> which the dominant class is composed mainly of men; yet it is not as men but
> as capitalists that they are dominant ... [t]he state must be seen as a capitalist
> one or at least one that is to be understood primarily in relation to the capita-
> list mode of production.[15]

Without offering any justification other than evident faith in Marxist
analysis, McIntosh rejects the notion that sex domination is fundamental
to 'the society', and thereby gives 'the state' a Marxist rather than a
feminist characterization. A third feature of her argument is that, apart
from 'its' support for a dependent position for women in both the family
and the workforce, 'the state's' relationship to women is more a benevolent non-intervention than repressive intervention. Women's relation
to 'the state' is 'indirect', for women belong to a private sphere.
Evidence for this claim is drawn from crime and criminal justice, where
men are overwhelmingly the majority of those arrested and imprisoned.
McIntosh concedes however, that 'state' non-intervention into the
private sphere occupied by women is less than benevolent when women
are denied protection from rape and domestic violence.[16] Many of the
issues of most central concern to feminism centre on relatively unpoliced
abuses of women's bodies which take place in or are related to the so-
called 'private realms of sexuality and the family. Yet the way in which
McIntosh has drawn 'the state' precludes an interrogation of the significance of such 'non-intervention'. She writes:

> while study of such specific injustices is important for *immediate* [my empha-
> sis] political campaigns ... it can tell us little about the part played by the state
> in the oppression of women.[17]

Were the case to be made for 'the state' as a category for feminist analysis (a case which remains to be made) then non-intervention into and

non-deterrence of men's widespread criminal practices against women, far from telling us little, might tell us much about the part played by this 'the state' in the oppression of women.

McIntosh's argument relocates women's oppression as a *descriptive* aspect of the family household and wage labour system of western capitalism, because 'this oppression as such is neither their defining characteristic nor their *raison d'être*', nor is it the objective of 'the state' in relation to these two systems.[18] In this spirit, McIntosh denies that 'the state' serves 'male' interests, because she takes this to imply that such interests and the kind of sexual power relations predicted are being theorized independently of, rather than being determined by, the mode of production.[19] If, following McIntosh, women's oppression is not to be identified as a fundamental, defining characteristic of family, work, society, 'state', McIntosh's lack of an alternative analysis of this resilient, common feature of pre-capitalist, non-capitalist, capitalist and socialist social formations leaves the feminist reader uncertain as to what exactly is being claimed for the category 'the state' in analysis of the oppression of women. The tenor of argument about women's oppression begins to resemble some accounts of how nineteenth-century Britain unintentionally got itself an empire: it was no system or sector's objective or *raison d'être*, it just happened to accompany other developments. The account leaves women's oppression and 'the state' unexplained.

By the 1980s, the Marxist-feminist position was showing the wear and tear of unsuccessful union. In part it became caught in the broader 'crisis in Marxism' and was criticized for its theoretical inadequacies as an account of women's oppression by men.[20] Marxist feminists attacked other feminists' uses of independent formulations of women's oppression, such as 'patriarchy' and 'phallocentrism', and denounced as misguided (and even reactionary) feminist explorations of separatism, political lesbianism, 'difference', 'autonomy' and related concepts popularized by French feminists. Approaches distinct from Marxist feminism were labelled 'cultural feminism' and separated from political (read 'real'?) feminism.[21]

Despite such criticisms, feminists not committed to Marxism (among others) disclosed the profound phallocentrism of Marxism (along with all other systems of thought). The most striking features of Marxism's phallocentrism identified included: its commitment to traditional philosophical concepts of knowledge, truth, reason, the universal rational intellect, dichotomous or binary thought especially the subject/object dichotomy; a unified reality, scientificity, and the levelling of difference to a (male) norm. Politically it was criticized for leading to vanguardism, the attempt to homogenize disparate, specific movements into a unitary revolutionary movement that refused to acknowledge irreconcilable differences of experience and analysis, and thus incommensurate political objectives.[22] The case for a hyphenated relationship between feminism and Marxism had never been satisfactorily made in theoretical terms, but even the practical, political terms of the case that had been made were disintegrating under such circumstances.[23]

'The State' in Post-Marxist Feminism

In this context, what became of the relation between 'the state and the oppression of women'? Three approaches can be identified in feminist work refusing or revising the claims of 1970s Marxist feminism. The first of these was the argument that feminism needed a post-Marxist theory of the state. Advocates of this view tried to devise terms in which this might be done. The work of feminist political philosopher Carole Pateman – particularly her work on 'the fraternal social contract' and on the meaninglessness of political/legal categories such as 'consent' when applied to women – inspired feminists engaged in the project of theorizing a notion of 'the state' *for* feminism. In Australia, Pateman's work was used in the formulation of 'the patriarchal state'.[24] In North America, within a radical feminist analysis of consent and rape, MacKinnon argued forcefully:

> The question for feminism for the first time on its own terms is: what is this state, from women's point of view? . . . [T]he state, in part through law, institutionalizes male power. If male power is systemic, it is the regime.[25]

The substance of MacKinnon's argument involves drawing connections between the sexually positioned, objectivist, male point of view entailed in phallocentric western knowledge and culture on the one hand, and forms of law, politics and governmentality on the other. As such, she has an unmistakable quarrel with McIntosh's claims that men's dominance and women's oppression are not fundamental to the organization of culture and politics. Far from a descriptive fact, a side effect, of arrangements for other purposes – namely capitalist ones – the objectification of women is the *raison d'être* of all aspects of culture and politics.[26] 'The state' seems for MacKinnon to be coterminous with 'the law' and it 'treats women the way men see and treat women'.[27] The state constitutes the social order in the interest of men ensuring male control over women's sexuality and framing all policies according to male experience.[28]

The force of MacKinnon's argument is adjectival. She takes 'the state' as given, and, like McIntosh, at no point does she define any distinctly *feminist* understanding of its parameters. Her efforts are devoted to ways a given 'the state' can be characterized for feminism. In the genre, her case is of unique profundity, and is an enduring, generative contribution to feminist theory. And yet the argument provides no compelling reason that feminism needs a distinct theory of an entity like 'the state' at all. For, in MacKinnon's schema, the 'maleness' of what liberals and Marxists call 'the state' is a function of the 'maleness' of everything else in patriarchal society. She does not establish a feminist definition of 'the state' distinct from the liberal or Marxist state. Instead, in her highly plausible argument, popular culture is male, knowledges are male, sexuality is male; as are economics, religion, language and football. The resemblance between this quality of 'the state' and every other aspect of patriarchal culture undermines the case for this specificity of the 'male state' at the very moment she urges it. So, the case remains to be made as to why the range of areas lumped together in liberal and Marxist theory as the larger abstraction of 'the state' – subsuming, in various versions the government, the executive bureaucracy, police, prisons, the judiciary, and agencies regulating social policy, health, education, defence, and various statutory authorities, public culture and heritage, labour and industry and so forth – should be adopted by feminist theory as the same conglomerate of the same name, thus indistinguishable from the liberal or Marxist entity 'the state' – notwithstanding the adjective 'male'.

Alongside such attempts to retain a concept of 'the state' but defining it as having a 'patriarchal' or 'male' character, a second post-Marxist tendency emerged within feminism. Recognizing the extent to which feminism had been prone to modification and incompatible alliance with non-feminist discourses, work began to appear analysing an indigenous theoretical core for feminism. The category 'the state' has not been central in this work. One of the most significant texts exemplifying this tendency is Marilyn Frye's 1983 text *The Politics of Reality: Essays in Feminist Theory.* In a series of short and original essays she addresses key concepts for feminism; including: 'oppression', 'sexism', 'phallism', 'sex exploitation and enslavement', 'anger', 'separatism', 'power', 'race supremacy' and 'lesbianism'.

Frye contends that the greatest obstacle faced by feminism is the epistemological difficulty men and women have with seeing women as oppressed, as members of 'a group of category of people that is systemically reduced, molded, immobilized'.[29] Unlike other oppressed groups, women are not physically confined or segregated together, but are geographically and demographically dispersed, inhibiting the group perception that is possible for classes and races. Frye contends that women *can* be seen as indigenous in a number of ways. Whatever the differences between women based on class and race (and these can be immense) 'women of all races and classes are together in a ghetto of sorts'.[30] It is defined, not by geographical boundaries, but by the function of service to the men of their own class and race. The nature of such service is non-reciprocal – men do not serve women as women serve men. Surveying the systemic material, sexual and psychical disadvantages experienced by women, Frye insists on a sex asymmetry:

> For any woman of any race or economic class, being a woman is significantly attached to whatever disadvantages and deprivations she suffers be they great or small.... If a man has little or no material or political power, and achieves little of what he wants to achieve, his being male is no part of the explanation. Being male is something he has going *for* him even if race or class or age or disability is going against him. Women are oppressed, *as women.* Members of certain racial and/or economic groups and classes both the males and the females, are oppressed *as* members of those races and/or classes. But men are not oppressed *as men* ... and isn't it strange that any of us should have been confused and mystified by such a simple thing?[31]

For this kind of feminist analysis, it remains unclear what status 'the state' could be given that would significantly contribute more than the terms already in play. The spheres of activity aggregated together in liberal and Marxist concepts of the state have no special, determinate or privileged status in Frye's *feminist* account. This in part is consistent with MacKinnon's argument about 'the state' being an expressive regime of men's interests – but it would seem that for Frye, the areas taken in some accounts to comprise 'the state' are part of the broader zones of phallocratic culture, which require no distinct theoretical formulations. For a feminist theorist whose work is so marked by conceptual clarity and simplicity, it is telling that 'the state' is not embraced as offering indispensable clarity or simplifying any complexity that feminist theory needs to address.

A third tendency apparent in feminist writing since the early 1980s is a formulation of 'the state' as something like the neutral arbiter or at least *potentially* principled agency of liberal theory (that could be deployed to improve women's situation). Feminists involved in the bureaucracy, particularly in anti-discrimination, equal employment opportunity and affirmative action have been prominent in this (initially) more optimistic formulation of 'the state'. As such they have been critical of Marxist notions of the state which would brand work on such legislation and programmes as mere reformism.[32] Similarly, feminist formulations of the state as 'male' or 'patriarchal' are criticized by feminists working with 'the state' because such formulations imply that such work is futile co-option. Thus, to MacKinnon and Pringle and Game, Hester Eisenstein replied in 1985:

I think it is inaccurate to say that 'the state is male' but it is accurate to say that up to now the state has been male if by that we mean that until recently public power has been wielded largely by men and in the interest of men.... The possibility of altering that fact may now lie within our grasp.[33]

The possibility of altering 'that fact' to which Eisenstein refers is the record of substantial feminist interaction with government and bureaucracy in Australia, especially in the 1980s, and the prominent role feminists have played in the drafting of radical, even subversive, legislation at both national and state levels. In particular, the years of the Wran Labor government in New South Wales 1978–1986 were marked by unprecedented law and policy reform activity, much of it in feminist terms or at least inflected by certain feminist perspectives. Domestic violence, rape, incest, prostitution, and juvenile girls' status offences were addressed in law and in the revision of police procedure and public welfare provision.[34] Meanwhile the reform of school curriculum, the promotion of women teachers, affirmative action management plans in industry and higher education, and the implementation of sexual harassment and other grievance procedures were among the many areas of feminist achievement within government, bureaucracy and trade unions during this period.[35] It is entirely understandable that amidst such achievements, feminist bureaucrats, lawyers, policy consultants and academics would react with scorn or hostility to any formulation implying that 'the state is inherently male', or that they work with 'a patriarchal state' through which men's interests in the dominance and oppression of women will always win, feminist tinkerings with this law or that policy notwithstanding.

Eisenstein's response to the formulation of the 'male' (or 'patriarchal') state is to criticize this as a 'very compressed and dense set of assertions' that needed 'unpacking'.[36] She takes it as proof that feminism needs to 'deglobalize' its concepts.[37] However, it becomes clear that her problem is with the adjective 'male', not the hugely abstract noun 'the state'! It is the characterization 'male' that is taken as the extreme, globalizing claim. So, at the end of all this feminist discussion, the imported category 'the state' remains intact, unviolated by anything more than the odd adjective 'male', sometimes adorned, sometimes 'unpacked' – or rather, is it packed away to protect the familiar liberal/ Marxist parameters of the unquestioned state? A history of some of the crimes that have been of such concern to feminists recently working with government and bureaucracy in Australia may suggest that it is the formulation 'the state' that needs to be deglobalized if feminists are to have anything useful to say about these practices, and the uneven and changing responses they have elicited.

Historial Disaggregations

The study of the histories of crimes involving women, so often the subject of the kind of non-intervention noted by McIntosh, can suggest not so much that what is conglomerated as 'the state' is absent or irrelevant, but rather that eliding together government, police, judiciary, coroners, courts and relevant bureaucracies in terms of 'the state' may obscure vital historical specificities of each of these categories. Feminism has remained ignorant of these at the cost of political effectiveness. This does not have to be true in the future.

The example of abortion serves as a graphic instance of the problem of the aggregative character of the formulation 'the state'. Rosalind Petchesky (whose book on abortion mentions 'the state' in the title) attempts to explain the 'relegalization' of abortion in some American states in the 1970s in the following general terms:

> State intervention in fertility control occurs for three different purposes called forth by a combination of social conditions and conscious political activity. These purposes are population control, the regulation of sexual behaviour, and the state's need to maintain social order and the legitimacy of its rules and rule making system. When legitimacy breaks down and the state is no longer able to enforce its policies.... then concessions have to be made that will restore legitimacy without seeming to compromise the dominant ideology informing a given policy and thus the authority of the state.[38]

The Australian history of abortion calls this kind of general pronouncement about 'the state' and 'its' actions into serious question. The reduction of average family sizes from eight or more offspring in 1870 to between two and three by the 1930s elicited pro-natalist denunciations from many sources of cultural and political authority. In New South Wales, a Royal Commission into the Decline in the Birthrate was called in 1903, involving industrialists, business leaders, representatives of all political parties, medical, legal and religious authorities. After sittings during a full year, entailing the interrogation of dozens of salient witnesses and the tabling of considerable research and submissions, much of the final evidence produced concerned abortion and infanticide. Despite what authorities called Australia's dangerous shortage of population, the commission concluded that women were responsible for deliberately causing the decline in the birthrate, chiefly by means of criminal abortion and contraception. Between a quarter and a third of conceptions were terminated. The law was being flouted and many witnesses called it unenforceable. As abortionists were permitted to advertise in the daily paper, with services offered at very affordable prices, it would seem that the criminal law which forbade abortion at any stage in pregnancy (and threatened severe penalties) had little force and legitimacy.[39]

This situation did not result in 'the state' granting concessions to the perpetrators of abortion in order to restore 'its' own legitimacy. Conversely, the policing of abortion was rare before the 1903 Royal Commission and remained rare after.[40] Moreover, extant case papers and transcripts suggest that abortionists were only identified as a result of their patients' death or critical illness, generally when the woman had been between four and seven months into the pregnancy. Put differently, action was taken only against some of those performing dangerous procedures on late term cases; and while both doctors performing curettages and midwives inducing miscarriages competed on the market, increasingly it was midwives who were most liable to arrest. Finally, of the small handful arrested, fewer than a quarter received jury conviction in the period 1900–1949.[41] With the advent of civilian use of penicillin, abortion related deaths dramatically declined, while infections could readily be treated privately or concealed from official scrutiny.

From the 1950s, abortion services had become substantially medicalized, and rates of abortion prosecutions declined from an already low level. Many feminists who were teenagers and students in the 1950s remember abortion then as an area of secrecy, risk and enormous expense. Their cultural access to the service had deteriorated compared with women of earlier generations. The activities of abortion law reformer Dr Bertram Wainer revealed that at least in Australia's two most populous states, New South Wales and Victoria, by the 1950s the police substantially organized abortion and extorted profits from its providers. In 1967 some doctors were being charged $600 a week to stay in business without arrest; others, especially non-medical abortionists, were forced to pay police 10 per cent of each fee. Wainer estimated abortion had become a twelve million dollar industry. Phone taps and police-appointed receptionists kept police extortionists informed as to the volume of trade. When arrests took place they were no longer the result of death or critical illness. They were carefully orchestrated raids on unprotected operators in which women would wake up on the operating table with the theatre full of noisy men to find their photograph being taken.[42]

By the end of the 1960s with the high overheads involved, the price for a medical abortion reached $200, too much for working class women, especially migrants and Aborigines. A backyard market emerged undercutting the protected operators' fees. Mortality and critical complications increased. Wainer attempted to persuade medical abortionists to take strike action – to cease paying police corruption and to bring their prices down to remove the market of the backyarders. In

1970, after intimidation and several attempts on Wainer's life, Victoria police arrested unprecedented numbers of doctors, charging them with abortion-related offences, in an attempt to prove there was no police corruption.

The result was an exodus of women needing abortions to Sydney, where they had curettages performed under appalling conditions.[43] After Wainer's exposé of police graft in Sydney abortion services on national television, a crackdown took place, with 163 doctors arrested and charged in 1971. Ultimately none were convicted. In the case later called the Levine ruling, Mr Justice Levine secured the acquittal of Dr Louis Wald and five others by instructing the jury that the crux of the criminal law of abortion hinged on the word 'unlawfully' in the 'whosoever shall unlawfully procure miscarriage. . . . ' Levine ruled that a doctor who performed abortions outside of hospitals, and considered the procedure appropriate after considering physical, mental and socio-economic aspects of the woman's situation without securing a second opinion, need not be thought to have acted unlawfully.[44]

The basis for police corruption thereby was undermined and the advent of a Federal Labor government committed to full publicly funded health care made the establishment of free-standing abortion clinics viable. Medical abortions became relatively cheap, in 1974 costing the woman $8 of $80, the scheduled fee for curettage – a far cry from the $200 or more dollars paid by women a decade before.[45] Now, in 1988, the medical fee is $240, but women are compelled to pay 40 per cent of this, due to a range of pressures that might be called a foetocentric backlash, readily capitalized upon by right-wing Labor treasurers. Nonetheless average fertility continues downward to the current rate of one to two children per woman.

Obviously this is only part of the story of the place of abortion within Australian culture over the past century. Much more remains to be said about its connections with particular kinds of heterosexuality, the vexed questions of power and disempowerment for women, and the history of the bodily and psychical dimensions of this prevalent experience of women, especially in the pre-pill context before the 1960s.[46]

But in the present framework, are any of these complicated changes usefully addressed through the classification of 'the state'? Are any of Petchesky's three different reasons for state intervention – population control, sexual regulation and legitimacy maintenance – evident in the Australian history of criminal abortion? Was it 'the state' which intervened? Were the allegedly predictable interests of 'the state' served anywhere in the story?

No doubt a version of available theories of 'the state' could be patched together to make all of these historical pieces appear to fit into a seamless, coherent whole. 'The state' could be represented as a site of conflict, a contradictory – not to say, a *very* contradictory unity, beset by the law of uneven development – some parts saturated in pro-natalism and foetocentrism; others addicted to the bureaucratic rationality of the newly professionalized men of medicine; others functioning pragmatically as profitable enterprises; still others committed to the liberal virtues of the modern, small, consumption-oriented child-centred family. The question really is how useful is an aggregated explanation/analysis of this history in terms of 'the state'.

It is apposite now to return to Petchesky's claims regarding the reasons for state intervention in fertility control. Whatever population control was taking place – and this occurred on a momentous scale – it was hardly 'the state' which intervened to secure this outcome. In the main, it was women. As for sexual regulation, it is not entirely clear which, if any, points in the Australian twentieth-century history of abortion fit this proposed state objective – unless it is the inference that the overall situation of the criminalization of abortion has been designed to curb excessive, or illicit sexual liaisons or else to ensure a link between coitus and reproduction. But then, it is difficult to explain why 'the state' allowed and even funded family planning clinics that are open to all. It is not convincing that any of the developments described comprise attempted sexual regulation.

This only leaves legitimacy maintenance, of Petchesky's triad of rationales for 'state' intervention. Possibly the Levine ruling fits the bill of concession in the face of mass lawlessness and confident defiance of the law. This kind of theory would suggest that 'the state' is actually the hostage of popular agency, that it can afford to criminalize only that which is policeable; and that only unpopular illegalities are policeable. Surely feminism has generated new questions and produced new findings that would have problems with this as a general theory of 'state' intervention. Arguably, men's resort en masse to domestic violence against women (currently estimated to occur in the course of one in three conjugal cohabitations), to the rape and sexual abuse of daughters (the experience of one in four daughters), and to inestimable sexual offences against women outside the family (from rape to indecent exposure) all provide counter instances.[47] These offences have been of extremely low Australian policing priority during the century since 1880, and offenders have enjoyed immensely good odds against arrest; even when prosecutions have occurred convictions have been exceptional rather than routine.[48] Why does not this situation create a crisis of legitimacy for this 'the state'? Why have not these popular masculine practices, so often declared by police to be unenforceable and thus unpunishable, become formal areas of concession to men via decriminalization?

Perhaps a cynical feminist answer would be, there may as well be no law if, with existing legal procedures surrounding the prosecution of these offences, decriminalization is the effect, if not legality. This may be so; but the point is that we do not arrive at a clear understanding of the stakes entailed and the forces in play by means of theories of 'the state'. If the answer 'male power' is offered by MacKinnon to her question 'What is this state, from women's point of view?' it seems likely that her 'state' is not the same beast as the state of liberalism and Marxism. It is arguable that retention of the term obscures the very marked distinction her argument makes between the regime of male power and the liberal or the Marxist state.

Conclusion

So, does feminism need a theory of what liberalism and Marxism call 'the state'? I would contend that feminism requires and provides theories of other more significant categories and processes. Feminism has much more urgent need of nuanced, historically and sexually specified theoretical categories such as 'police' and 'policing', 'misogyny', 'legal culture', 'medical culture', 'bureaucratic culture', 'paternalism', 'organized crime' and 'public corruption', 'men', 'male subjectivity', 'male sexuality' and 'masculinity'. While calling some (or all) of these concepts part of 'the state' is the prerogative, even the imperative of current forms of Marxism and liberalism, feminism may gain from resisting this call. It is not an indigenous feminist need. Arguably, feminism has been a tolerant fellow traveller, along routes dictated by the theoretical needs of others, for quite long enough. As Rosemary Pringle writes:

> Feminists have their own utopias, their own theoretical and practical priorities. . . . Feminists need to detach from socialism in order to pursue their own long term aims. This does not mean that they are automatically unfriendly or contemptuous, merely that they have their own priorities and providing a socialist agenda in the current political situation is not one of them . . . I would question whether socialist feminism or any of the other labels have much meaning in the late 1980s . . . The distinction between liberals, radicals and socialists no longer adequately describes the debates that are taking place within feminism. Perhaps a majority of feminists decline any of these labels and would question why anyone would continue to apply them.[49]

Feminism would not need a theory of the state unless or until it becomes clear how the oppression of women is a function of some larger entity that warrants feminist theorization. MacKinnon contrasts feminism with Marxism and liberalism because feminism neither claims universality, nor failing that, reduces to relativity. It does not seek a generality that subsumes its particulars or an abstract theory or a science of sexism.[50]

On the evidence available to date, feminism does not need a theory of the state.[51] There are more useful tasks to be done.

Notes

1. R. Pringle and A. Game, 'From Here to Fraternity: Women and the Hawke Government', *Scarlet Woman* 17, Spring 1983, pp. 5–6.
2. See for instance, L. Leghorn and K. Parker, *Women's Worth: Sexual Economics and the World of Women*, Routledge & Kegan Paul, Boston 1981; M. O'Brien, *The Politics of Reproduction*, Routledge & Kegan Paul, Boston 1981; S. Jeffreys, (ed.), *The Sexuality Debates*, Pandora, London 1987; E. Grosz, 'Notes Toward a Corporeal Feminism', *Australian Feminist Studies* 5, Summer 1987, pp. 1–16; L. Irigaray, 'Is the Subject of Science Sexed?' *Critical Inquiry* 1, 1985, pp. 73–88; B. Caine, et.al. (eds.), *Crossing Boundaries: Feminisms and the Critique of Knowledges*, Allen and Unwin, Sydney 1988.
3. C.A. MacKinnon, 'Feminism, Marxism, Method and the State: Toward a Feminist Jurisprudence', *Signs* vol. 8, no. 3, 1983, p. 682.
4. M. Barrett, *Women's Oppression Today: Problems in Marxist-Feminist Analysis*, Verso, London 1980, p. 9.
5. See for instance, R. Pringle and A. Game, 'From Here to Fraternity', p. 6; C.A. MacKinnon, 'Feminism, Marxism, Method and the State', pp. 643–4; and C. Pateman, 'The Patriarchal Welfare State' in A. Gutmann (ed.), *Democracy and the Welfare State*, Princeton University Press, Princeton, New Jersey 1988, pp. 231–60.
6. M. Frye, *The Politics of Reality: Essays in Feminist Theory*, The Crossing Press, Trumansburg, New York 1983, p. 1.
7. C.A. MacKinnon, 'Feminism, Marxism, Method and the State', p. 639.
8. See for instance, my 'Policing Since 1880: Some Questions of Sex' in M. Finnane (ed.), *Policing in Australia: Historical Perspectives*, University of New South Wales Press, Kensington, New South Wales 1987, pp. 188–222; C. Pateman, *The Sexual Contract*, Polity Press, Cambridge 1988; R. Pringle, *Secretaries Talk*, Allen and Unwin, Sydney and Verso, London 1989; A. Kuhn, *The Power of the Image*, Routledge & Kegan Paul, London 1985; S. Kappeler, *The Pornography of Representation*, Polity Press, Cambridge 1986; and R. Rowland, *Woman Herself*, Oxford University Press 1988.
9. This point is well argued in A. Phillips, 'Marxism and Feminism', in Feminist Anthology Collective (ed.), *No Turning Back: Writings from the Women's Liberation Movement 1975–80*, The Women's Press, London 1981, p. 90–91. See also, R. Pringle, 'Socialist Feminism in the Eighties', *Australian Feminist Studies* 6, Autumn 1988, pp. 26–7.
10. See for instance, K. Millett, *Sexual Politics*, 1970, reprinted by Avon Books, New York 1971; G. Greer, *The Female Eunuch*, Paladin, London 1970; S. Firestone, *The Dialectic of Sex*, Abacus, London 1970; J. Mitchell, *Woman's Estate*, 1971, reprinted by Vintage Books, New York 1973; and S. Rowbotham, *Woman's Consciousness, Man's World*, Penguin, Harmondsworth 1973.
11. See for instance, A. Oakley, *Sex, Gender and Society*, Temple Smith, London 1972; and P. Chesler, *Women and Madness*. Doubleday, Garden City, NY 1972. For commentary on this work see D. Spender, *For the Record: the Making and Meaning of Feminist Knowledge*, The Women's Press, London 1985.
12. See for instance, A. Game and R. Pringle, 'Women and Class in Australia: Feminism and the Labor Government' in G. Duncan (ed.), *Critical Essays in Australian*

Politics, Edward Arnold, Melbourne 1978, pp. 114–34.

13. See for instance, E. Wilson, *Only Halfway to Paradise*, Tavistock, London 1979; B. Campbell and A. Coote, *Sweet Freedom*, Picador, London 1982; Z. Eisenstein, *The Radical Future of Liberal Feminism*, Longman, New York 1981; R.P. Petchesky, 'Antiabortion, Antifeminism, and the Rise of the New Right', *Feminist Studies* vol. 7, no. 2, Summer 1981, pp. 206–46.

14. See for instance, M. McIntosh, 'The State and the Oppression of Women' in A. Kuhn and A.M. Wolpe (eds.), *Feminism and Materialism: Women and Modes of Production*, Routledge & Kegan Paul, London 1978; E. Wilson, *Women and the Welfare State*, Tavistock, London 1977; R. Hamilton, *The Liberation of Women*, Allen and Unwin, London 1978; Z. Eisenstein (ed.), *Capitalist Patriarchy and the Case for Socialist Feminism*, Monthly Review Press, New York 1979; H. Land and R. Parker 'Family Policies in Britain' in J. Hahn and S. Kammerman (eds.), *Family Policy*, Columbia University Press, New York 1978.

15. M. McIntosh, 'The State and the Oppression of Women', p. 259.

16. Ibid., pp. 258–9.

17. Ibid., p. 259.

18. Ibid., p. 259.

19. Ibid., p. 266.

20. For Discussions of these issues, see P. Patton, 'Marxism in Crisis: No Difference' and my 'Marxism and the Man Question: Some Implications of the Patriarchy Debate' in J. Allen and P. Patton (eds.), *Beyond Marxism? Interventions After Marx*, Intervention Publications, Sydney 1983, pp. 47–72 and pp. 91–112.

21. See for instance, H. Eisenstein, *Contemporary Feminist Thought*, Counterpoint, Boston & Unwin, Sydney 1984, pp. xx, 115, 125–45; A. Echols, 'The New Feminism of Ying and Yang' in A. Snitow, et al. (eds.), *Desire: The Politics of Sexuality*, Virago, London 1984, pp. 62–81; A. Curthoys, 'Politics and Sisterhood', *Arena* 62, 1983; E. Willis, *Beginning to See the Light: Pieces of a Decade*, Wideview Books, New York 1981; and L. Segal, *Is the Future Female? Troubled Thoughts on Contemporary Feminism*, Virago, London 1987.

22. M. Campioni and E. Gross, 'Love's Labors Lost: Marxism and Feminism' in J. Allen and P. Patton (eds.), *Beyond Marxism*; pp. 121–134 and S. Rowbotham, et al. *Beyond the Fragments*, Merlin Press, London 1979.

23. J. Allen, 'Marxism and the Man Question', pp. 98–99. See also, C.A. MacKinnon, 'Feminism, Marxism, Method and the State: An Agenda for Theory', *Signs* vol. 7, no. 3, Spring 1982, pp. 515–44.

24. R. Pringle and A. Game, 'From Here to Fraternity', p. 6.

25. C.A. MacKinnon, '.... Towards a Feminist Jurisprudence', pp. 644–5.

26. Ibid., pp. 635–8.

27. Ibid., p. 644.

28. Ibid., pp. 644–6.

29. M. Frye, *The Politics of Reality*, p. 8.

30. Ibid., p. 9.

31. Ibid., p. 16.

32. H. Eisenstein, *Contemporary Feminist Thought*, pp. 139–40.

33. H. Eisenstein, 'The Gender of Bureaucracy' in J. Goodnow and C. Pateman (eds.), *Women, Social Science and Public Policy*, Allen and Unwin, Sydney 1985, p. 115.

34. For further discussion of these see my forthcoming book, *Sex and Secrets: Crimes Involving Australian Women Since 1880*, Oxford University Press, Melbourne, Chapters 8 and 9.

35. See for instance, essays on these subjects in M. Sawer (ed.), *Program for Change*, Allen and Unwin, Sydney 1985.

36. H. Eisenstein, 'The Gender of Bureaucracy', p. 114.

37. Ibid., p. 114.

38. R. Petchesky, *Abortion and Women's Choice: The State, Sexuality and Reproductive Freedom*, Verso, London 1985, p. 116–17.

39. See R. Pringle, 'Octavius Beale and the Ideology of the Birthrate' *Refractory Girl*

3, Winter 1973; and my 'Octavius Beale Reconsidered: Infanticide, Babyfarming and Abortion in New South Wales, 1880–1939' in Sydney Labour History Group (ed.), *What Rough Beast? The State and Social Order in Australian History*, Allen and Unwin, Sydney 1982.

40. See my *Sex and Secrets*, Chapter 4.

41. Ibid.

42. B. Wainer, *It Isn't Nice*, Alpha Books, Sydney 1972, pp. 71–4; *Sydney Morning Herald*, 11 November, 1970.

43. Ibid, p. 104.

44. *New South Wales Parliamentary Debates*, 3rd Series, vol. 99, 1972–3, p. 200.

45. E. Snyder, *Abortion in Sydney*, Pre-Term Foundation, Surry Hills 1976, pp. 6, 15, 34.

46. For discussion of some of these issues, see my 'Abortion, (Hetero) Sexuality and Women's Bodies', *Australian Feminist Studies* 5, Summer 1987, pp. 85–94.

47. See for instance, J. Scutt, *Even in the Best of Homes*, Penguin, Ringwood 1983; E. Ward, *Father-Daughter Rape*, The Women's Press, London 1983; J. Hamner and M. Maynard (eds.), *Women, Violence and Social Control*, Macmillan, London 1987.

48. See my 'Policing Since 1880', pp. 200–212.

49. R. Pringle, 'Socialist Feminism in the Eighties', pp. 29–30.

50. C.A. MacKinnon, ' ... Toward a Feminist Jurisprudence, p. 640.

51. A recent article – D. Dahlerup, 'Confusing Concepts – Confusing reality: A Theoretical Discussion of the Patriarchal State', like all the other articles in its anthology, (A. Showstack-Sassoon (ed.), Women and the State: Shifting the Boundaries of Public and Private, Hutchinson, London 1987, pp. 93–127) – takes 'the state' once again as given. Her entire, fragmented discussion is devoted to where women fit into broader left analyses of state power, and the extent to which feminism has and has not succeeded in establishing a case for 'the state' to be conceptualized as serving patriarchal interests.

3

Ethnicity Meets Gender Meets Class in Australia

Mary Kalantzis

Feminism in Australia is a political movement and a published discourse. Its activities range from Equal Employment Opportunity (EEO) practices in the public service to 'cultural' production in such forms as academic literature and documentary film-making. For most immigrant women of non-English-speaking background, the cultural arena of feminism is foreign, in many more ways that one. Feminism represents, to speak perhaps too stereotypically, a middle-class 'Anglo' culture, far removed from everyday experience. And this despite well-meaning concern on the part of many feminists for those groups suffering the compound oppressions of class and ethnicity, as well as gender. Symbolically, an almost cult concern is shown for the plight of the migrant woman outworker, and with considerable real justification. Yet this concern is from a singular cultural perspective: middle-class libertarian liberalism, quite alien to the immediate needs and aspirations of its subjects.

Indeed, many migrant women with a non-English-speaking background have gone through revolutionary transitions much greater, and frequently demanding much more personal courage and determination, than the careers and life-projects of the leaders of the EEO industry or the feminist film-makers on their government grants. Whilst not speaking feminism, the language of criticism and re-assertion of power, the practical struggles of many immigrant women are akin in critical spirit and outcome to feminism itself. These struggles often involve a dramatic self-transformation, assuming some elements of the radically new culture of industrialism, whilst retaining what is powerful and positively human in traditional women's culture. And, as often as not, they also involve failure, isolation and oppression, as racism meets sexism and class with a peculiar vengeance.

39

In recent years, the cultural gap between the Australian feminist movement and immigrant women with a non-English-speaking background has closed somewhat but their encounters are still problematic. To cite one instance, Franca Arena, a Labor member of the New South Wales Legislative Council (or Upper House) and Australia's first woman parliamentarian of a non-English-speaking immigrant background, has set up an 'Ethnic Women's Network' which meets regularly in Sydney's Parliament House and which has developed significant political clout. Franca's stated goal for the network is to provide an arena for women of non-English-speaking backgrounds to meet with the members – and the procedures – of government on its own turf, in order to demystify that institution. It has proved to be a very successful exercise in constructing a constituency, in giving women of non-English-speaking backgrounds direct access to government ministers and heads of governmental authorities, and in giving them entry into the magical mystery tour of the state. Yet the exercise is fraught with contradictions and tensions, primarily because, for many of these women, participating in such an experience is more significant as one that brings them into the mainstream than as one that expresses their 'ethnic' difference. The 'privileged' nature of this encounter is reinforced at every meeting when the grey-suited men, guarding Parliament from the likes of ordinary people, especially 'accented' women, delay the participants unnecessarily with the etiquette of protecting the institution.

The positions held by the women in these gatherings and the shifts they are undergoing in their lives, are neither clear-cut nor parallel. They are emblematic, however, of the, as yet unspoken, divide between immigrant women of a non-English-speaking background and mainstream 'Anglo' feminists. For example, one of the first meetings of the group was addressed by a key feminist activist now working within state structures in the service of her sisters. At great length, and in passionate terms, she described how important it was for her to defy patriarchal bonds, to break out of the straitjacket of catholicism into which she had been socialized through an education at the hands of nuns, to leave behind traditional Irish values of family and womanhood and to choose to be a single independent person. And this to an audience of non-English-speaking women which included Muslim women in purdah who had come along to this meeting to ask for support to change their work practices in order to allow them their traditional prayer sessions; and mothers who wanted their children to be taught their mother tongue and cultural traditions within the state school system.

On the other hand, there have been sessions where middle-class women activists from South American background have bemoaned the fact that Australian women's organizations are politically backward and that Australian political life is generally suffocated by macho 'Anglo' ockerism, epitomized by the array of government ministers invited to address the meetings. The 'Anglo' femocrats who turn up accompanying their ministers sit quietly at the back and groan at the sight of these men who will never learn. They know they have no voice to speak – to preach to the women of non-English-speaking background in such a setting – but they are secure in their power back in the offices, as minders of ministers and minions of the state.

This chapter attempts to address those most difficult social questions, those that arise when class, gender and ethnicity meet. Of course, class, gender and ethnicity are always meeting, but they only appear as a 'problem' for groups where the process of intersection portends inequality and marginalization. This is precisely what makes this topic so difficult. It is really about huge historical and social questions which mainstream social analysis conveniently ignores. For example, the points at which middle-class culture meets male culture meets 'Anglo' culture are implicitly considered by social science to be 'normal' or 'natural' or an irrelevant backdrop. Furthermore, if we are really concerned with social relations and not cultural pathology, any discussion of immigrant women throws into question the enormous complexity of the relationships of a whole finely stratified or segmented society. The woman question is simultaneously the man question. The 'ethnicity' question is simultaneously the dominant culture question. And the question of each permutation of class simultaneously implicates the unholy synergy of class relations.

So we have, on the one hand, a feminism which is culturally distant from those of its subjects whose lives are so difficult, and on the other, a series of fundamental social questions which are enormous in their scope and complexity. It is hardly surprising, then, that the literature in this area is fragmentary and as yet poorly developed. The following is one early contribution, a high-speed chase through some of the issues. The first section discusses the social background; post-war migration to Australia and the place of women immigrants in Australian society. The second discusses the concepts of ethnicity, class and gender, and the process of the decentering or fragmentation of everyday life and identity which accompanies the migration process with a peculiar intensity. Finally, taking up the question of political ways forward, the role of the state is analysed, both in the context of women's rights issues and the development of multi-culturalism, which are certainly not always complementary.

Women and Post-War Immigration

Australia's post-war immigration, in world-historical terms, has been quite extraordinary. Only Israel has experienced more immigration over the same period relative to the size of the existing population, but in quite an unusual set of historical circumstances. In sheer statistical terms, the post-war Australian experience even exceeds the great tide of immigration to the USA in the early years of the twentieth century. More than three million immigrants have arrived in Australia since the migration programme began in earnest in 1947. The population has increased from under eight million to over sixteen million. One person in three is an immigrant or the child of an immigrant. During the post-war boom, Australia had the highest rates of population and workforce growth of any OECD country, with immigrants filling 61.2 per cent of the additional jobs between 1947 and 1972.

Labour market position is one starting point for situating immigrant women in a sociological context. In 1947 only 12 per cent of the Australian workforce had been born overseas, 70 per cent of whom were of British origin. Of the workforce, 22 per cent were women. By 1976, 26 per cent of the workforce were born overseas, representing an immigrant population only 40 per cent of whom were British-born. Women now form 36 per cent of the workforce. In other words, there has been a significant shift in the labour force, with substantial relative increases in the participation of women, immigrants and non-English speakers. Perhaps the most dramatic change is the increased number of married women in the workforce, from 15 per cent of the female work-force in 1947 to 61 per cent in 1979.[1]

Over the decades, the composition of this immigrant population has become increasingly diversified. When the mass immigration programme began, there was a strong emphasis on British immigration. Arthur Calwell, the Labor politician who was Australia's first Minister of Immigration, gave the assurance that for every foreign migrant there would be ten people from the United Kingdom; or that, at least, those foreigners who were allowed in would be 'assimilable types' such as the Dutch. However, the racist direction of immigration policy and the project of assimilating those who were 'different' was to prove unworkable in the long term. In fact, even in the short term, the immigration quota of one per cent population increase per annum could only be met by bringing in refugees from Central and Eastern Europe. Recruitment was soon to extend to Southern Europe, and by the time of the European economic 'miracle' of the late sixties and early seventies, when European sources of immigration were running dry, to Turkey and the Middle East. By the 1980s, the net had spread even further afield with substantial immigration from South East Asia and Central and South America.

By the 1980s, 25.8 per cent of Australian women aged 20–64 had been born overseas. Splitting this figure by origins, 11.4 per cent of Australian women were born in non-English-speaking countries other than Australia: 2.3 per cent in North-west Europe, 1.5 per cent in Eastern Europe, 7.7 per cent in the Mediterranean region, and 3.0 per cent in Third World countries, particularly South-East Asia and Central and South America.[2]

How do those various groups, as defined by immigrant, or non-immigrant background and gender, fare in Australian society? Employment is a central marker of social class and social status. Several key writers have thus taken the labour market as a base point from which to measure the experience of different groups. Collins divides the Australian labour market into four major segments. The first consists of Australian-born and Anglophone male migrants who earn the highest pay and who are employed in the tertiary sector or in skilled jobs in the manufacturing sector. They have clearly defined career structures and are disproportionately represented in power structures, such as the trade unions and politics. The second segment, of non-Anglophone migrant males, is located mainly in semi-skilled and unskilled jobs in manufacturing and construction. This is the 'factory fodder' of industry, frequently poorly paid, in exhausting and dirty jobs and with very low participation in power structures and little hope of career advancement. The third segment is Australian-born or Anglophone immigrant women, who are paid less than first or second segment men and tend to work in traditional areas of women's employment in the tertiary sector. In a fourth segment, women immigrants from non-Anglophone countries are concentrated in the parts of the manufacturing sector hardest hit by economic restructuring. They pay is lowest and working conditions poorest, frequently being involved in piecework or outwork.[3] To this categorization De Lepervanche adds fifth and sixth segments of Aboriginal men and women respectively, many of whom are marginalized to permanently unemployed, fringe-dweller status.[4]

These generalizations are only the beginning of an analysis of the place of immigrant women. Indeed, whilst containing a basic element of truth, they are crude over-simplifications. Within Collins's third segment, there is considerable differentiation according to background. Mediterranean women hold poorly-paid jobs of much lower status than do North-West Europeans, East Europeans and South-East Asian Women.[5] This is very much linked to class background in the country of origin and level of education. Mediterranean women work in the worst jobs in the industrial workforce, and are those most vulnerable in the current economic restructuring. They suffer severe occupational health and safety problems such as repetitive strain injuries, low levels of English language proficiency, and lack of support from male and 'Anglo'-dominated unions.[6]

Even this subdivision of a labour market segment is confounded by complexity, however, as each cultural subgroup of immigrant women is by no means homogeneous in class terms. Reworking 1981 census statistics, Evans concludes that between 9 and 14 per cent of employed Australian women of all backgrounds own their own businesses, with women of Third World and Mediterranean origin being more likely to be entrepreneurs than other groups.[7] This reflects significant class differentiation within even a seriously disadvantaged subgroup such as Mediterranean women, and some genuine and impressive stories of upward social mobility. It also reflects official statistics in which outworkers are categorized as self-employed. Self-employment, furthermore, includes family-run shops and milk bars in which working conditions and rates of return are sometimes as bad as the worst of industrial jobs. And, as Collins points out, the proportion self-employed in immigrant groups has dropped dramatically in the structural economic re-adjustments of the post-war decades, as supermarkets, for example, eclipse the corner store.[8] There is evidence, however, of growth in some forms of 'self-employment' such as outwork in the clothing industry. This leaves us with complex and contradictory subdifferentiation which does not deny the general thrust of overall descriptions of labour market segmentation, but which serves as a warning against simplistic arguments about any necessary outcomes in the overlay of gender, class and ethnicity.

The matter is complicated still further by generational differences. Contrary to conventional wisdoms about the relation of labour migration to the self-perpetuating phenomenon of social class, there is evidence of significant intergenerational mobility. The above discussion was about first generation workers. What happens to second generation children?

Neo-conservative critics of multi-culturalism have recently began to argue that specialist education and welfare servicing is unnecessary because people of non-English-speaking background are doing well. The first generation, it is admitted, pays a price and is relatively immobile, but this is supposedly compensated by significant second generation upward mobility, primarily the result of education. Williams argues that a strong family and cultural 'preference' for education produces high levels of participation in education on the part of non-English-speaking background children.[9] Birrell speaks of family support and ethnic valuing of education which produces upward mobility. 'They have been competing with Australians who have generally lacked the same intensity of parented support or protection from distracting influences, notably peer youth culture.'[10] In the same vein, Bullivant writes of the 'migrant drive' and the 'ethnic work ethic'. The 'Anglo' working class are, by comparison, 'the new self-deprived'.[11] And indeed, those groups which in a first generation fare so badly on the labour market, seem to be catching up through the education system in the second. Southern European background students, for example, achieve greater representation in higher education than the Australian norm.

But this inter-generational differentiation must itself be finely differentiated. Relative educational advantage or disadvantage is distributed unevenly between ethnic groups, with some more recently arrived groups faring particularly badly. Generalization about the educational performance of ethnic groups also ignores the fact that they are themselves deeply divided socio-economically and by school performance: even if one small stratum appears to be succeeding, the majority is not. Moreover, by comparison with aspirations that accompany the personal or family ambition and 'self-selection' in the migration process, the results are poor. And these mobility problems are in all probability temporary, as the post-war boom becomes a distant memory and the welfare state is rolled back.[12]

Situating non-English-speaking background girls into this already contradictory and multi-faceted situation, there is considerable evidence that their odds of success through education are longer than their male counterparts. Whilst retention rates are higher in the secondary school than those of their English-speaking background peers, their aspirations and performance are lower than both their male non-English-speaking background counterparts and their female peers in general. In some cases, schooling for a girl is valued highly, but only because it enhances her prestige and manageability, rather than because it lays a foundation for career choices and alternative futures. Girls are also placed in a particularly difficult context of culture clash in which wildly contradictory pressures all collide: their parents' high educational expectations; their exposure to the liberal culture of romance and self-determination; the traditional role model of a 'good' mother and wife; and mainstream sexism and racism which make the traditional role seem a comfortable and familiar retreat.[13]

When Ethnicity Meets Gender and Class

Class, gender and ethnicity overlay each other in social reality in an
extraordinary complex profusion of ways. Having described some of
these in the Australian context, we will now take one step back to
discuss the key terms of theory and analysis. In recent decades, the
litany of concepts of class, gender and ethnicity has emerged as a way of
accounting for lines of social inequality. It is just no longer fashionable
to say that class is, in the last analysis, all. Nor does it seem that society
can be reduced, in essence, to two fundamental classes. Yet, despite the
unquestionable good sense behind the litany, it is too glib. It is just a
reassurance of good faith, in deference to new types of politics. The real
and nagging demands for recognition of these new politics have translated themselves into a new and often poorly thought-through conventional wisdom: that class, gender and ethnicity (or race) are the key lines
of social inequality, the big three, and each oppression compounds the
other, formula-like. I want to argue, instead, that the three categories do
not sit together as descriptions of social realities which are comparable
or even of the same order.

'Culture' or 'ethnicity' is perhaps the most difficult and problematic
of the three, partly because it is such a vague term. 'Culture', for
example, varies in meaning from cultural anthropology's holism (a
whole way of life, including material artefacts, kinship structures and the
social arrangements of subsistence) to the much narrower connotations
of 'high' or 'folk' culture.[14] The culture of 'multi-culturalism', loosely
synonymous with ethnicity in social policy and social analysis in
Australia, is firmly within the narrower connotation of folk culture. In
this respect it is frequently a politically and ideologically skewed term
and, in many important respects, of limited use. Certainly ethnicity is a
powerful social reality, and racism, misreading surface appearances as
social causes, even more powerful. Yet the concept of ethnicity – culture
as delimited in the multi-culturalism of state policy – is still deeply
problematic.

The salespeople of the multi-cultural industry often use fruit salad,
not even with a quiver of self-mockery or a sense of fatuousness, as a
metaphor for Australian society. Australia is a cultural-linguistic fruit
salad bowl, with the bowl as the pluralist, open, liberal democratic state,
and folk cultures with their 'community' languages float freely about in
it like little slices of fruit, happy to be ingredients in the great cuisine of
modernity, yet maintaining their distinctive flavours in tolerant
harmony.

The metaphor is not just fatuous, it is ironically symbolic of the fact
that food is one of the main elements of the construction 'ethnicity'. In

schools and the media, for example, the iconography of the multi-cultural is exotic food, clothing and dance. Difference is the message but only those colourful manifestations of difference that we can celebrate and appreciate for their colour. But, however much their middle-class clients might enjoy eating out at ethnic restaurants in the cosmopolitan city, 'ethnic' restaurants frequently involve working conditions for family members which are far from attractive. Despite the appearance of difference, the structural reality of food in industrial society is as a commodity in a money economy. Behind the food there is another world.

To stay with food for a moment: a woman of rural Lebanese immigrant background walks into a shop and buys Lebanese bread, just one in the colourful array of breads. The multi-cultural city is in action. But the woman works in a factory for a wage (abstract labour and not direct subsistence). She has separate realms of work and domesticity, the week and the weekend (rather than the work and the familiar being integrated in traditional rural forms of farming). She is housed in suburbia for which she has to pay rent or a mortgage (and not subsist on land). She has to be a consumer, and negotiate the welfare and education systems – all forms of culture (in the other broad anthropological sense) essential to social reproduction but totally new and alien to her. Even if she were to work in a family restaurant, maintaining some remnants of traditional work forms, the change in the world of full-blown commodity exchange is dramatic. There is nothing much multi-cultural about this. The culture of multi-culturalism is not even all that relevant.

The fetish for difference not only often leads to a superficial and apolitical reading of culture, it is also unreflectively conservative. Preserving communities or folk cultures for posterity as museum-pieces is not simply positive – as if we have to maintain a sort of cultural national estate. In fact one of the great ironies for the liberalism that champions ethnic preservation and cultural pluralism, is the illiberal, indeed frequently racist and sexist identifications which as much as anything else gives cultures an air of folk primordiality. Communities certainly resist assimilation and articulate their grievances through ethnic identifications and this is frequently progressive. But minority identifications are a two-edged sword, particularly for women. In any event, the battle to preserve ethnicity, very much an interest for certain generations of immigrants and particularly for male 'community leaders', may well be a losing one. Communities and cultures are mixed, contradictory and conflict-ridden things. They are certainly not clearly defined and socially self-isolating. Apart from the question of whether preservation is a good thing or not, it may not even always be possible.

Behind the trivialized and conservative view of culture is a dual hidden agenda of assimilation/marginalization. If we talk less about survival strategies and more about the colourful manifestations of pluralism, we can conveniently neglect some of the elementary issues of social welfare. So, for example, a smattering of 'community' languages is presented in schools in a poorly funded and fragmentary way as a token of our multi-culturalism, without taking effective pedagogy as measured in social outcomes very seriously. Behind the colourful differences and despite the ideological façade of multi-culturalism, immigrants are assimilated, ruthlessly but inevitably, into the system. But it is often a marginalized assimilation with relative lack of power and economic autonomy for the immigrant.

The domain of multi-culturalism is not only the traditional and the exotic. It is also, in commonsense parlance, the domain of non-English-speaking immigrants, or the 'ethnics' in current pejorative usage. Surely Elton John, Kentucky Fried Chicken and *Eyewitness News* are not culture for the purposes of multi-culturalism. The multi-cultural-pluralist reading of Australian society reconstructs the dominant group as 'Anglo-celtic', an extraordinary cultural hybrid. At this point, however, relations of dominance are conceived to be matters of inter-cultural misunderstanding rather than structural relations, with the dominant culture distinguishing itself through Yorkshire pudding and Irish ditties, or perhaps meat pies and beer advertising jingles.

None of this discussion is intended to give the impression that ethnicity is not important. Ethnicity is one of the great social issues of our time. The discussion is only to unravel some aspects of its politics and usages. In short, multi-culturalism is used to construct a happy ideology of pluralism to the neglect of wider structural relations. The powerful reality of ethnicity, however, is that in spite of the modernist theories and social policies of the melting pot or assimilation, there has been a visible and enduring effect of mass migration. Differences have survived the move, more or less and for better or for worse. But industrialism limits the space inhabited by these differences, to the weekend more than the week, to leisure more than work, to the domestic more than the public arena. Theories of social structure tend to ignore this, presumably irrelevant, space. Theories of ethnicity tend to neglect the way in which social structure defines and delimits this space. And then there is racism, which links structure and culture/ethnicity, reconstructing the appearances of difference, both cultural and phenotypical, as a root cause of structural inequality.

Capitalism as social structure is constructed around wage labour and commodity production. The history of modern times has been one of the relentless generalization of the commodity form across the globe and into everyday life. This massive internationalizing and universalizing trend has produced imperialism in its first and blindly brutal phases when it conquered indigenous peoples and appropriated the resources of the so-called 'New World'; later there was colonization and labour migration from diverse sources to consolidate its progress; and then the internationalization of labour, capital and commodities. These are not just matters of structure, but profoundly matters of culture, which have tended to make everyday life experience and expectations fundamentally uniform: around the structure and culture of the commodity form.

But concomitant with this structural/cultural universalization, the integration of a growing proportion of the human population into the material life, relations of class and desires of capitalism, has been the dramatic juxtaposition of differences. Not only have workers of diverse background been thrown together and an immense profusion of culturally different commodities been put on the market in metropolitan industrial societies, but states have had to consider servicing the plurality and re-thinking some of the fundamental tenets of assimilating nationalism. 'Multi-culturalism' is the response on the part of the liberal democratic state to manage and service a diverse population. The use of ethnicity as a political bargaining tool is also new. In essence, the goal is still structural incorporation, but in a more sophisticated form so that difference comfortably and respectably inhabits the private, and the social relations of the commodity are enhanced rather than confounded by the necessary logistics of labour immigration.

The liberalism of multi-culturalism is very contradictory. It is born, not of traditionalisms which are characteristically illiberal in the definition of their boundaries, but of the cosmopolitanism and individualism uniquely characteristic of late industrial societies. Difference is fine. All that matters is the smooth reproduction of the commodity form. Ethnic politics is even more complex: a rallying point against racism and the structural marginalization of minority groups; reconstructed by the liberalism of the state as its own rhetorical mission; then against both the initial radical impulse and the state's liberal management, it becomes a means of conserving supposedly primordial cultures, including their racism and sexism.

The late industrial state and the culture of the commodity are equally liberal when it comes to issues of gender. Certainly, the nuclear family and the 'family wage' are structures of unequal gender differentiation new to capitalism. But in the spread of the commodity even these are destroyed. More traditional domestic functions are commodified; the family wage is cut; and women increasingly enter the workforce. In the high culture of this liberalism are the Equal Employment Opportunity mafia and the professional 'Anglo'-feminists. Yet when this liberalism meets ethnicity and multi-culturalism, it finds itself in cultural conflict with traditions which pay little respect to individual autonomy, economic independence and gender equality. The same culture of liberalism, on the other hand, is the basis of competitive individualism, the fragmentation of community and alienation in everyday life. The liberal state in late industrial society, in other words, might in some cases and in a totally contradictory and hypocritical way, be on the way to becoming non-sexist as an integral part of the process of extending the culture of the commodity.

Behind the double tendency of late industrialism towards increasing diversity alongside structural homogenization, is the development of a relativist philosophical framework around notions of the individual and difference. In everyday terms, this philosophy translates into the following terms:

> *We are all unique individuals. We are all different. Our differences are our own business and they are of equal value. You do your thing and I'll do mine. Anything is possible in a world of differences. You can choose what you want to be. You can have your own culture. You, the individual, should control your own destiny. You know what is right for you. Explore, experiment, discover for yourself what you can be. Negotiate your rights. Look after yourself.*

This is one of the most powerful messages of the contemporary world. We are all formally equal in our differences. Radical doubt and the self are all we are left with. A sense of decentred existence comes from the rapidity of change, the juxtaposition of differences, the maelstrom of modernity.

The 're-evaluation of all received values', to use Nietzche's words, is a fundamental cultural phenomenon of our time. Ours is a world of contradiction, in which there are both structures that bind and radically open options. In pre-industrial societies, disintegrating remnants of which many of Australia's immigrants left, one was born into fairly well-defined and durable social relations, of work, womanhood or manhood. Now all this appears open. How does one choose? What is the centre for judgment and decision-making? This is the phenomenon of decentering.

Decentering is doubly difficult for immigrants from traditional rural backgrounds. Despite the happy multi-cultural ideology of diversity, tolerance, and cultural maintenance, dramatically new structures of everyday life put pressure on traditional ways of seeing the world and behaving in it. For men, there is often a loss of self-esteem as their families become more independent and they are reduced to a childlike status in menial factory work. There is also a loss of authority because they are unfamiliar with the new ways of their adopted homeland. The psychological effect can be devastating, with profound implications for their wives, who often have to cope with this as well as their own adjustment, and care for their children at the same time.

For women, there is the double burden of paid work and domestic work, in conditions that do not fulfil former ideals of motherhood. Financial independence is both liberating and perplexing, opening options which destroy identifications that once seemed natural and inevitable. Yet these same options of freedom involve breaking with deep senses of community, and in the case of women, family relations of care and responsibility.

For second generation immigrants, the problem is even more serious. The parents can retreat into the absolute moral maxims of their past. They can explain their pain in relation to some 'knowable' loss. The past serves as an explanatory centre, from which perspective they can lament their children's waywardness. For the next generation this retreat is not so easy. With the rhetoric of gender-role equality that is preached at school but hardly realized in reality, contesting gender roles at home can appear futile to girls, given the likely cost of being cut adrift and alienated from their families. They become caught in the intersection of a double racism – between being stereotyped as ethnic and morally backward by the dominant group, and being warned by their parents of 'Anglo-Australian' cultural and moral 'looseness'. Will they become victims of assimilation or acquiescent dupes of traditionalism? The conservative option is often taken as an attempt to ground their lives in a decentered world. This is simultaneously an affirmation of what is positive in traditional female roles, including a deep sense of care and community, and a recognition of what is personally fragmenting and alienating in the world of choice and liberal individualism. In many ways, too, the dominant culture of liberal modernity, including much career feminism, is characteristically male and unattractive: an indifference to feelings and care, a competitive hardness, an exhausting self-centredness and a blind aggressiveness.

So, the class-gender-ethnicity equation is not a simple one of compound oppressions with a clear solution in the form of liberation. Affirmation of ethnicity is a two-edged sword: a resistance to racism and domination yet itself potentially conservative and racist. The ethic of liberal feminism is also a two-edged sword, liberatory yet belonging to the fragmented, individualistic, self-serving culture of industrialism. The structures of social class and the world-historical process of the generalization of the commodity, on the other hand, delimit the politics of gender and ethnicity and at the same time remain indifferent to their outcomes so long as these do not threaten the system of wage labour and commodity consumption.

Women, Ethnicity and the State

Two critical and reforming sets of politics have had a significant impact on the state in the past few decades: the politics of gender and the politics of ethnicity. Yet the two are by no means always compatible as argued so far in this chapter. Indeed, the two have mostly been distant and reserved about each other's objectives. The impact of the women's movement on the state, however far it still has to go, has been significant. Women here have achieved equal rights in matters of divorce. They have gained equal pay, formally if not in practice. There is anti-discrimination and equal employment opportunity legislation. There is paid maternity leave. Institutionalized pre-school child care is increasingly available. But the cultural aspirations to economic and personal independence behind these developments are characteristically more those of middle-class, English-speaking career women than non-English-speaking immigrant women. Or, at least, these women are not so strongly in a position, either within the home or in the broader context of their relative social marginalization, to avail themselves of the benefits of these changes.

We need to keep in mind that in the new country the cultural and social distance created by the lack of English skills, unfamiliarity with Australian traditions and institutions, and the dislocation from homeland culture as a result of migration, can come together to produce a situation of cultural segmentation for some groups of non-English-speaking background women, leaving them outside of any dynamic cultural movement around feminist issues. The state for many non-English-speaking background women is a forerunner of feminist concerns in that it provides them with rights and access to support for which their cultural background experience does not prepare them. These seem to be there by magic and not linked into the consciousness of the men and women of that group who have to negotiate receipt of these rights or live in the world where others take them for granted. The multi-cultural movement, on the other hand, developed in such a way that the fundamental welfare needs of non-English-speaking background women were neglected and a mostly male and conservative ethnic community leadership was systematically incorporated. This needs to be explained in historical terms.

The ideology of assimilation lasted in official rhetoric until the late 1960s, even if the terminology had shifted cosmetically towards 'integration' through the decade. By the early 1970s, however, assimilation was clearly not working. Many immigrants were obviously remaining culturally distinct. Specialist welfare and education needs were emerging as the settlement and welfare 'problem' became statistically bigger. There was a growing feeling that a more sophisticated approach would be needed to stem the tide of return migration, principally to the 'economic miracle' in Europe. Finally, there was the emergence of 'ethnic' organizations and, possibly a 'migrant vote'.

Al Grassby, Labor Minister for Immigration from 1972 to 1974, is frequently credited, and with considerable justification, as being one of the founding fathers of this multi-culturalism. But there is also important discontinuity which this historical conventional wisdom ignores. Grassby's concern was not with difference, pluralism and cultural diversity; it was for a unified 'family of the nation', rid of forms of social injustice such as those suffered by many immigrants. In fact, Grassby very rarely used the term 'multi-cultural' as Minister for Immigration. The fundamental welfare reformist orientation of Labor was to the concept of 'disadvantage' and to lines of socio-economic division. Indeed, 'migrants' (a word to lose favour in the era of Fraser/Galbally multi-culturalism) were to be understood as a subset of the general class of those disadvantaged socio-economically and discriminated against. Symptomatic of this policy stance was the break-up of the Department of Immigration into the various 'mainstream' departments of labour, welfare, education, and so on. The problems of migrants were considered, at root, to be general matters of social welfare and social justice.

Losing the elections of 1972 and 1974, certain members of the Liberal Party began to consider that a decisive 'migrant vote' could be possibly mobilized. Fraser, Mackellar and MacPhee were particularly important in re-orienting Liberal policy. Their efforts eventually came to fruition in the Conservative government of the late 1970s. The landmark in this process was the Galbally report of 1978 which became the basis of multi-cultural policy until the mid-1980s. Galbally multi-culturalism in sharp contrast to Grassby's 'family of the nation', was a clear, determined and extremely cost-effective element in the neo-Conservative pruning and reconstruction of the welfare state. It was based on real cutbacks in government funding. In fact, it produced a reduction in overall government expenditure as its recommendation (which was accepted) that tax rebates for overseas dependants be abolished, more than paid for the programmes it set in motion. Galbally multi-culturalism involved shifting migrant services from the general rhetoric of social welfare to marginal 'ethnic specific' services. This in part involved constructing 'ethnic' communities as self-help welfare agencies and giving them minimal financial support. It gave power to frequently conservative and male dominated 'community' leaderships. 'Ethnic Schools' and 'Grants-in-Aid' were typical of this approach.

Thus the shift in the language for reading cultural difference and formulating settlement and welfare policy was from a unified 'family of the nation' to multi-culturalism; from disadvantage to difference; from concern with general socio-economic issues in which migrants were included (a Laborist view of reform) to the paradigm of cultural difference in which cultural dissonance is the main problem; from a social theory of class as the primary social division to a social theory of multiple social divisions, none of which have priority. Ethnic groups in the new multi-culturalism were implicitly viewed, not as class-divided, but as homogeneous. 'Leaders' of ethnic groups could thus be viewed as 'representative', and, at the same time, potentially vocal pressure groups could be incorporated into the spirit of the state and given some responsibility for their own 'community's' welfare provision.

This is not to say that there has not been significant progress, with the setting up of English language learning programmes for children and adults, 'ethnic' radio and television, a telephone interpreter service, specialist welfare services and a policy-oriented office of Multi-cultural Affairs in the Prime Minister's Department. This is the history that in Australia has produced a dilemma for feminists and progressives in general. Surely respect for the other, the underdog, the minority is in itself a progressive thing. Surely multi-culturalism and its apparent call for ethnic maintenance must be progressive. After all, it is concerned with self-determination, tolerance and celebration instead of denial of difference. So onto the bandwagon the state has created they all hop. At the very least their welfare brief is enlarged. But then it gets complicated. When you let 'them' speak, they say things that make you uncomfortable.

Two sites in which this is most clear at the moment are Equal Employment Opportunity and education. The question of participation in employment is a vexing one for the state given that women are half the voting constituency and even in its own institutions they are grossly under-represented at all the different levels. It has tried to respond to the demands of the organized women's movement through its EEO structure. Mainstream western industrialism, as it incorporates ethnic minorities or women into its structures, for example, has to accommodate and service a level of difference. Movement to a 'merit' principle of employment and promotion partly enshrines this accommodation. Common-sense working conceptions of merit of the past have not sat purely upon the needs of industrialism, but have also included prejudices about skin colour or gender. The dominant form of white, male merit is buffeted by questions and struggles which prove the irrelevance, injustice and unnecessariness of sexist and racist prejudices to the essential structures of industrialism. Critically, these struggles gain cogency (but also remain limited) because the merit criterion is itself culturally specific and structurally enduring. In other words, one can be

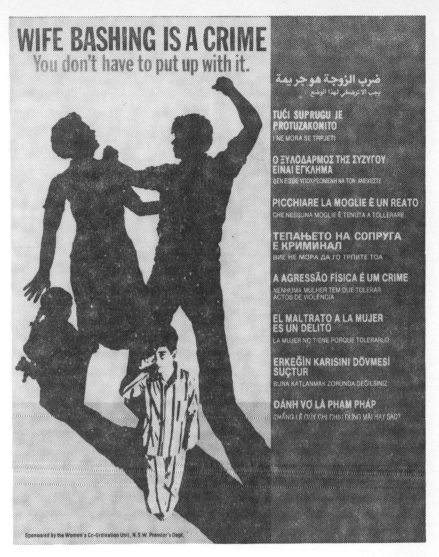

Poster put out by the NSW Women's Coordination Unit and displayed widely on billboards throughout the state

black or a woman or both and just as meritorious in terms of systems needs and social effectiveness. The common-sense alliance of white, male and merit comes under fire without fundamental criticism of the deeper cultural specificity of merit to industrialism. So, the working conception of merit changes as unnecessary prejudices are removed, but merit itself remains the constant, fundamental, structural requirement of industrialism: those aptitudes and capacities that its sycophantic or critical operatives require to be effective. This has involved limited transformation of the concept of merit. Merit now should not prejudice differences. It is about essential systems requirements and not visible cultural or physical differences which are in fact, irrelevant to employment. Skin colour and gender should not now prejudice one's merit for employment.

But in every moment of respect for difference, even in moments of celebration of difference and plurality, there is also a moment of cultural incorporation. The cultures of peasant agrarian villagers or of domestic womanhood, for example, have no merit in terms of significant job promotion or intervention into mainstream power structures. Merit becomes an ideal, perhaps even a form of liberation or a basis for cultural self-transformation, often not in any articulate or explicit way, but through developing expectations and struggling to learn the logistics of social effectiveness. Becoming meritorious is part of a process of cultural incorporation.

Intervention through education is another critical area where ethnicity meets the politics of gender. Here we have mandatory state policies on multi-culturalism and non-sexism. But they do not sit easily together for all the reasons outlined above. The non-sexist policy to date has concerned itself mostly with addressing girls about their options and taking affirmative action to enlarge the choices made available to girls. But, and this is of particular significance to girls of non-English-speaking background whose families still value traditional gender roles and aspirations, without addressing the boys directly and focusing on their behaviour and choices, the lives of the girls can simply be made much more difficult.

The question of focus is also a problem for multi-culturalism. The main response has been that if students' backgrounds are brought within the discourse of the school, and if each group is immersed in the details of each other's difference, then tolerance and understanding will emerge. The teachers are trained for this exercise via suspect methods, as the following illustrates.

A simulation game about Greek marriage, devised and led by an 'Anglo'-Australian man was held at a training conference on multi-cultural education for teachers and departmental consultants. Variations of this approach can be found in the films, background papers and kit teaching material that have been created to represent 'the migrants'. The game went like this: It was announced by the group leader that Greeks have arranged marriages, that this was one feature of their culture and that the participants would play a game that would simulate that experience. The players were asked to choose their roles, whether to be male or female, young or old, their status and so on. They were then supplied with rules with which to arrange the dowries and the marriage. The intention of the game was to absorb tolerance by an immersion in Greekness: to understand by feeling what it is like to be Greek.

Everyone played the game with much gusto and hilarity. But for all concerned it was a misleading experience. First, the statement that Greeks have arranged marriages is *de facto* racist. Arranged marriages have nothing to do with 'Greekness' *per se*. People of Maltese, Italian, Vietnamese and even English background (if one remembers the marriage machinations of royalty with their feudal lags) are, or have been, involved in them. Second, the players were allowed to choose their gender, status and age. Whatever miracles can be achieved in our contemporary world, choosing to be male or female in a traditional Greek society is not one of them. That very element of choice distorted the experience and allowed for the fun. Third, arranged marriages cannot be understood at the phenomenal level of their detail. In traditional peasant societies that were subsistent and based on kin working units, bringing any new person into the fold, with whom the means of subsistence would now be shared, was the whole group's concern. Arranged marriages were thus structurally necessary for the reproduction and survival of that system. With it, of course, developed all sorts of customs and mores, in particular the necessity of virginity and its relationship to the exchange contract. Now, in the process of migration out of the structures that supported these practices, symbols and mores, to a society that is based on independent income earning units and the culture of choice and self-satisfaction through romance, it is difficult for the original cultural practice to continue. The children can choose because they can support themselves. Indeed they have to be formally independent and mobile.

Simulating the cultural practice in an ossified way without locating it in historical context leads seemingly to two pedagogical options. The first is to try to teach the children their parents' traditional values and practices and encourage them to reproduce them as valuable cultural forms. Or, in contrast, you can assert that in the land of the free and brave, the child can choose to do anything. They can choose to be free like everyone else in Australia and make their own decisions. One approach is ethnic maintenance. The other is assimilation. Of course,

neither is an unproblematic 'solution'. It is not just a question of determination or determining. The two processes are constantly in relation.
But multi-culturalism has not seen its way out of this dilemma yet. And
such is the confusion still that one fears the project might be abandoned
before anyone has had a chance to reflect and modify their approach.

There is another way. It involves, not immersion in difference and
familiarity with phenomena, but the necessity to know the processes
involved in one's becoming when their origins are so diverse. It is a
peculiarly contemporary issue because of the way that pluralism is
generalized in all our experiences. It is not enough to know the phenomena, nor is it enough to have an understanding of some driving structural
imperative. They are not dislocated in the lives of many people. The
issues of gender and ethnicity emerged out of modernist struggles
against patriarchy and imperialisms of all kinds. But in some cases it
appears that the difference that was spawned and defended denies the
modernist emancipatory direction that gave it birth. So the state, which
now imposes the modernist social democratic victories, has also had to
cater for difference. It condones separatist Muslim schools that steer
their girls in a very traditional direction and Greek cultural associations
whose main aim is to ensure marriage between Greeks. We are left with
a paradox, a paradox that cannot be approached by mainstream
feminists simply asking women of non-English-speaking background to
join in their game, nor by viewing the state only within the logic of the
dominant social arrangements.

This chapter has attempted to portray the complex relationship of
feminism to the politics of ethnic self-assertion. Rather than simply
assume that counter-hegemonic politics are necessarily complementary,
it has shown some important ways in which they profoundly contradict
each other's intentions. These contradictions manifest themselves in real
tensions and divisions, cracks which are often papered over by the nice-
sounding litany of class-gender-ethnicity. On the one hand, mainstream
institutional feminism is rooted fundamentally in that liberal, libertarian
culture of individual freedom unique to late industrial societies. On the
other hand, whilst the politics of ethnicity involves many fatally regressive and quiescent elements, non-English-speaking background women
also frequently live in a uniquely women's culture which is itself
countercultural to the dominant ethos of conventional success in late
industrial society. Dialogue between the mainstream feminist movement
and non-English-speaking background women would fruitfully open
much feminism to critical scrutiny for its own cultural and historical role
and at the same time open the lives of many non-English-speaking background women to the positive elements of the culture of liberal industrialism, without losing the profound sense of the social that they

have brought from cultural settings not so far down the track of industrialism. The solution to the complexity and contradiction is not *vive la différence*. It is critical dialogue and the forging of a new culture, beyond nostalgic traditionalisms and beyond the liberal modernity of the culture of the commodity.

Notes

1. Jock Collins, 'Immigration and Class: The Australian Experience', in G. Bottomley and M. de Lepervanche, *Ethnicity, Class and Gender in Australia*, George Allen and Unwin, Sydney, 1984, pp. 10–11.

2. M.D.R. Evans, 'Immigrant Women in Australia: Resources, Family and Work', *Mimeo*, Department of Sociology, Australian National University, n.d., p. 14.

3. Collins, pp. 12–13.

4. Marie de Lepervanche, 'Women and the State in Australia', *Mimeo*, Department of Anthropology, University of Sydney 1985, p. 18.

5. Evans, pp. 16–17.

6. Gil Bottomley, 'Mediterranean Women in Australia: An Overview', *Mimeo*, Macquarie University 1984, pp. 3–6.

7. Evans, pp. 38–40.

8. Collins, p. 15.

9. Trevor Williams, *Participation in Education*, Research Monograph 30, Australian Council for Educational Research, Hawthorn, Victoria, 1987, pp. 70–71.

10. Robert Birrell, 'The Educational Achievement of Non-English-Speaking Background Students and the Politics of the Community Languages Movement', *Mimeo*, ANU Centre for Economic Policy Research Conference 1987, pp. 20–21.

11. Brian Bullivant, 'Are Anglo-Australian Students Becoming the New Self-Deprived in Comparison with Ethnics? New Evidence Challenges Conventional Wisdom', *Mimeo*, Australian Association for Research in Education Annual Conference, Melbourne 1986, pp. 11–13.

12. See Mary Kalantzis and Bill Cope, 'Why We Need Multicultural Education: A Review of the "Ethnic Disadvantage" Debate', Centre for Multicultural Studies, University of Wollongong, Occasional Paper 3, October 1987.

13. Mary Kalantzis, 'Aspirations, Participation and Outcomes: From Research to a Curriculum Project for Reform', *Including Girls: Curriculum Perspectives on the Education of Girls*, Curriculum Development Centre, Canberra, 1987.

14. Raymond Williams, *Keywords*, Fontana, 1976, pp. 76–82.

15. de Lepervanche, p. 23.

16. See also Bill Cope and Mary Kalantzis, 'Speaking of Cultural Difference: The Rise and Uncertain Future of the Language of Multiculturalism', *Migration Action*, Mary Kalantzis and Bill Cope, 'Multiculturalism and Education Policy, in Gil Bottomley and Marie de Lepervanche, *Ethnicity Class and Gender in Australia*, George Allen and Unwin, Sydney 1984, pp. 82–97; Stephen Castles, Bill Cope, Mary Kalantzis and Michael Morrissey, *Mistaken Identity: Multiculturalism and the Demise of Nationalism in Australia*, Pluto Press, Sydney 1988.

4

Colonization and Decolonization: An Aboriginal Experience

Barbara Flick

The British colonization of this country had a dramatic effect on the Aboriginal nation. I want to discuss just a little chapter of this invasion and the effect it had on me, a Ualaroi woman from northwestern New South Wales.

Within the first eighty years of white settlement in New South Wales the Aboriginal population dropped from around forty thousand to less than six thousand people. This dramatic drop in our population had a great impact on our families and communities. It is now an undisputed fact that the invaders slaughtered thousands of my people. Throughout this country of ours are many places where the remains of my people lay exposed to the elements. They lay where they fell. Men, women and children. The reason for this slaughter – the land was being cleared of Murris (us) for the growing of sheep and wheat.

Many of my people died from foreign diseases, diseases they had no immunity from. They still die today in large numbers from curable diseases. The devastation was so great that the government of the day decided that we as a race of people were going to die out. And so began the era that became known as 'easing the dying pillow'. We were rounded up and moved hundreds of miles from our own 'country' and placed in large concentration camps controlled by government agents, the mission managers. My mother was born on the Angledool Mission near Brewarrina. She once took me to the tree that she was born under.

The dark clouds hung heavy over the people. Many people defied the government's orders and went back to their own country. They walked. Desperately the families tried to hold themselves together. The old laws for living and relating to each other socially were being destroyed by the interference of government people. My father Joe Flick, in an interview with my sister Karen Flick in January 1988 described this devastation:

> Well, that is my culture. See, it is all laid out in one big puzzle and it's all put
> together; it's all there. The way I look at my culture, it is all there. It would be
> always there, stayed there, until 200 years ago, a big whirlwind come along
> and blew our puzzle to pieces, and now here we are trying to pick up all those
> little pieces and trying to put it all back together again, and in my life, we'll
> never get it all together.

Further fragmentation of our families occurred during the Protection
Board era in New South Wales. This was the organized removal of a
whole generation of our children who were taken, trained and used as
slave labour in the homes of whites. The police were used to help take
the children. Children from around the age of ten years were expected
to work from before sunrise to well after dark. Cooking, cleaning,
washing, ironing, rearing the children of the whites, even though they
were children themselves. The boys were forced to do heavy manual
work and other jobs around the pastoral properties that many of them
found themselves on. Beatings occurred regularly and people today still
carry those scars. The deeper scars are in their minds. They have shared
them with us. Many tried to find their way back home to their families.
Just as many were tracked down and dragged back by the police. They
ran away again.

We have never accepted the colonization of our country. Murri
women have struggled to protect, with the strongest mothers' instincts,
our families. We have striven to build a future out of all of this destruction and devastation.

My father's people came south from Queensland. His parents
had taken him, his brothers and sisters go bush in order to dodge
the tentacles of the welfare authorities, eventually settling around
Collarenebri.

I have vivid memories of the women who growed me up. My great-
grandmother, Ada Woods; my maternal grandmother, Sylvia Walford;
my paternal grandmother, Celia Flick; my aunts, Isobel Flick, Clare
Mason, Rose Flick, Rose Fernando, Noelene Walford and of course my
ever-patient mother Isabel Flick.

Ada Woods told me about the Willy Wag Tail and how he was the
one to bring bad news of a death in the family. If this bird hung around
you had to throw stones at him to make him go away. The bearer of bad
tidings. She told about how you could communicate with other members
of the family a long way away if you concentrated and meditated the
right way. She told me, don't let anyone take a lock of your hair. If they
wished you harm, they could burn your hair and make you sick. This

wonderful old woman died when I was about thirteen years old. She sewed us rag dolls and pillows. She herself had raised twelve children. She had been blind from the age of thirty years when she contracted German Measles.

Nanny. Sylvia Walford. My special protector. She would wake me late at night to feed the possums Sao Biscuits and water. She taught me to fish. She took me to the circus. She kept my school work. She wrapped me in a cocoon and talked to me about the magic of the river. Her death taught me about mortality.

My mother was, and remains a constant force in my life. She has given love to all her five children. She has taught us compassion and caring. She has had a great influence on our political lives. Her strength in her own political convictions has been a source of inspiration to me.

Aunty Is. (Isobel Flick.) When teamed up with Mum she became a force to be reckoned with in the small conservative town of Collarenebri. She still lives in Collarenebri and remains the most influential person in that town.

My father was a shearer and spent most of his time on the track working or looking for work. So it was Aunty Is and Mum.

In the late 1960s these two women took on the establishment and desegregated the picture theatre at Collarenebri. The picture theatre was divided into two sections. One for the whites and one for the blacks. I didn't understand why. It was a strange feeling to see all the white kids from school walking past us with their noses in the air. They knew what segregation meant. It meant they were better than us. Didn't it?

So there we were, divided by ropes. The theatre owner and his assistant would walk around and if they found us (they sometimes did) sitting low in the whitefellas seats, they would belt us on the head with their torchlights.

Then *Ben Hur* starring Charlton Heston came to town. The whole town was turning out to see it. Mum and Aunty Is decided it was time for political action. They stood at the small ticket window and demanded the theatre be desegregated. Trouble-making blacks? Wasn't that what he called them? Well they told him that they would block his patrons and prevent them from purchasing their tickets until the ropes were taken down. There they stood. Defiant. Two black women in that crowd of whites. Talking calmly. Can't you see how proud they were. Their heads held so high.

This may seem like a small thing to you but in Collarenebri in the 60s it was a big event. This was the way that Murri women took responsibility to try and make a more equitable society for their children to live in. This story makes my heart big and full. Tell us again Mum, Aunty Is, tell us again. And the lights in their eyes show the pleasure.

My mother worked from a very young age and so did all my aunts. They have many stories to tell about that time. Some of those stories are the sort that we call 'If you didn't laugh, you'd cry' type. My aunt Isobel Flick from Collarenebri tells this story:

> It wasn't easy comin' into the white society. What about the time the wugin (white woman) told me to put the shirt on the horse. She's ironin' her husband's nice white shirt. This was my first job and I was tryin' to do everything right. She said, 'Here Isobel dear would you mind puttin' this shirt on the horse.' See I never heard of a clothes horse. She pointed out to the verandah so I went out and I was thinkin' 'she did say put the shirt on the horse?' So I thought – Oh well. When I gets out there, there was this old draught horse, a real big old draught horse. And he was just grazin' around close to the verandah. And I was just about to . . . I was thinkin', oh well, I was thinkin' how silly it was. And I was just about to kick the door open to go out and have a go at this job when she came out and she said, 'I'll take that dear, now would you go in and check the milk on the stove. I think it might be nearly boiling over. Quickly dear.' So she took the shirt off me then. And I was thinking, 'I don't care what happens to the milk. I'm gonna watch you put this shirt on this horse.' And she walked over and put it over this thing on the verandah. And that's how I learned about that.

So, although there was a lot of tragedy during those times, there are also times that are remembered by the women, that were amusing, and these they remember vividly; and if you are ever fortunate to be in the company of people like my mother and my aunt and their friends you will be entertained at great length about funny things that happened to them.

I say again. We have never accepted colonization. We have learned to survive.

Historical circumstances both welcome and unwelcome caused the birth of many children of mixed parentage to be born. People who identify themselves as Aboriginal come in many shades of colour. We have a right to our cultural heritage and we maintain that the colour of our skin is not a measuring stick whereby we should be told of how much of our heritage we are entitled to. Our cultural heritage cannot be diluted simply because our skin may be lighter than our people in other parts of this country who have had more recent contact with non-Aborigines.

Marcia Langton, an Aboriginal anthropologist explains:

> . . . the land for Aboriginal people is a vibrant spiritual landscape, it is people in the spirit formed by the ancestors who originated in the dreaming; the creative period from time immemorial. The ancestors travelled the country

engaging in adventures which created the people and the natural features of the land, and established the code of life which we today call the Dreaming or the Law. The Law has been passed on through countless generations of people, through the remembrance and the celebration of the sites which were the scenes of the ancestral exploits. Song, dance body, rock and sand painting, special languages and the oral explanations of the myths encoded in these essentially religious art forms have been the media of the Law to the present day.

Despite conscious government attempts to destroy us, despite the dispossession of the land and access to these sites that our ancestors tell us about, we have survived. Our culture has survived. What Langton has expressed in words are the feelings of generations upon generations of Murris.

It has only been recently that the Murri women's contribution to the maintenance of our culture and existence in the face of the destruction of our communities has been recorded. In the earlier days the only anthropologists around were male and they talked to the men. Murri women were ignored and the role that they played in our society was judged by European males with their prejudiced views of where women fit in. Our history as Murri women lives and thrives in our own oral history tradition.

It is very difficult to live in a society where you are forced to straddle two lifestyles. It is difficult to deal with a male-dominated non-Aboriginal bureaucracy but this offers many challenges. The strength that comes out of being a Murri woman, low in the pecking order, generally speaking is good enough and strong enough to make that lifestyle feasible, interesting and amusing when it's not sending you into stress overdrive.

I say that our struggle for independence is one that could be described as a marathon rather than a sprint. There are compromises along the way. There are times when compromise cannot be entertained. There are times when we are forced to take the scraps from the table in order to bargain. We recognize these scraps for what they are.

We hunger for the loss of our lands and we continue to struggle for repossession. We continue our demands for our birthrights. We struggle for the rights of our children to their own culture. They have the right to learn about our religion and our struggle and they need to be instructed by us in the ways in which this world makes sense to us. We'll tell them the stories about our ancestor spirits, their travels and their adventures. And about morality and the attitudes that we have towards all living things in our world. We can make them strong.

In 1988 in Australia we have a situation where the infant mortality rate is 2.7 times higher for Aboriginal than for non-Aboriginal children. The life expectancy for Murri adults is twenty years less than for the rest of the country. There is an urgency in our struggle. Our people are dying at a much faster rate than ever before. The older people are dying now and information is dying with them.

The role of Murri women has changed in many ways. Ceremonial responsibilities have changed in many parts of the country but in other parts of the country it hasn't changed much at all. Women are involved in organized campaigns in educating our children to reject alcohol and other drug-based activities. One campaign that has and continues to be very successful in Central Australia is the 'Rock Without Grog' campaign, where Murri rock-and-roll bands perform in a drug-free environment controlled by Murris.

Women are organizing into political units known as Aboriginal Women's Councils. The Western Aboriginal Women's Council in western New South Wales in the summer of 1984 strongly campaigned against the government's proposal to set up an army training base near Cobar. The women were concerned about two things. First was the damage to the environment that would occur as a result of the army traffic through the area and the activities that they suggested they wished to be involved in. The second reason was that this place is rich in old rock paintings. It is one of the places that women have taken children back to and told them the stories. The government decided not to go ahead with this proposal.

Today, a growing number of Murri women have identified their struggle against colonization as a regional struggle. We have strengthened contact with indigenous people in the Pacific and Asian regions and have joined with them for a nuclear-free region. We have supported them in their independence struggles. They have joined us in our demands for land justice.

I strongly believe that the struggle of indigenous people to control their lands and to protect the environment will, if we are successful, make this region of the world a safe place in which to live. We have spoken very strongly against the presence of United States bases in our country. We don't want these bases to involve us in global destabilization.

Yes, we have made many sacrifices. We have compromised. We have been forced to compromise in order to survive. But we will continue to sustain the struggle. Our children will continue this struggle for justice. We believe that this is honourable.

5

The Aboriginal Struggle in the Face of Terrorism

Rose Wanganeen

I want to discuss the Aboriginal struggle in the face of terrorism. I will trace this struggle from the first day of invasion to the present and show how one form of terrorism terrorized my life and I'll tell you the forms of terrorism that my people have been expected to accept for the last 199 years. Terrorism to the Aboriginal people covers five areas:

- Individual terrorism
- Sexual terrorism
- Family terrorism
- Community terrorism
- Terrorism as a nation of people

So with that in mind, we blacks have been behind the eight ball for 199 years, through no fault of our own, but believe me when I say, I feel a sense of closeness and togetherness. In a spiritual way, are our ancestors rising up and saying 'Enough'. With their spiritual guidance are they leading us deeper into this resistance? I truly believe, as a nation of people, we are spiritually one nation.

I also would like to point out that our struggle has always been a national liberation struggle. We, like our brothers and sisters in Kanaky, Fiji, Aotearoa (New Zealand) and South Africa have all experienced terrorism and resisted it. We have never given up our sovereignty. We, like other indigenous people of the world, do not, and will not, just co-

NOTE: This speech was delivered to the first plenary session of the Socialist Feminist Conference held in Sydney in October 1987.

exist as a minority in our own homelands. We are going to be the rulers of our own destiny.

Terrorism in the Australian context is defined as a denial that we exist as human beings. That right was taken away on the day of the invasion in 1788, when they claimed that Australia was an unoccupied and empty land. They called it Terra Nullis. To this day they still deny that we are a sovereign people who have our own land, language, religion and our own laws.

Let's look at the history of terrorism in Australia. There have been various forms of terrorism that were used against my people. They were conducted by the government in co-operation with the police and bureaucracy. Terrorist acts have also been carried out by individuals and groups. The first form of terrorism was outright war and attempted genocide. When the act of genocide was practiced, the mentality was 'Let's start with the babies and children.' These precious, innocent victims were buried up to their heads and then the soldiers proceeded to gallop over them with their horses, killing them.

Another form of terrorism used was germ warfare. Diseases like smallpox were deliberately let loose on our communities. This tactic killed thousands of men, women and children, so that a round of ammunition was saved to kill the next black, who stole food to feed his family, just to survive. They then walked over the corpses to steal and lay claim to the land. Syphilis, pneumonia and other diseases were unleashed – we had no resistance to these foreign diseases.

Economic warfare was another device the governments and their followers used to settle our country. To survive off it, cattle and sheep were introduced. Waterholes were poisoned, killing thousands more men, women and children. Today some of the waterholes are gone, but that does not stop them. As recently as five to six years ago flagons of wine were poisoned in the Territory.

These three tactics of terror could not wipe us out – our resistance forced them to use less obvious methods. OK, so they no longer used methods of economic, germ and outright war but moved us into a transitional stage, where the government and their followers began a psychological, cultural and social war. They terrorized our minds, culture and our social structure. We were 'rounded up' like cattle and herded on to missions and reserves that were like concentration camps and were left to die out slowly, with the white man's diseases raging through my people. The terminology used was 'to smooth the dying pillow'.

During this period, for us to acknowledge our aboriginality was an invitation for terrorist acts, for psychological as well as physical abuse. At the same time the government and their followers adopted policies and practices relating to our welfare, our health, our education and our housing. The authorities removed any aspect of self-determination and attempted to make Aboriginal people totally dependent on government facilities, resources and handouts. The use of our traditional language, ceremonial and religious rites were prohibited. Restrictions were placed on our movements, both outside and inside the boundaries of the missions and reserves. Payment for labour with alcohol was introduced. Rape and the enslavement or prostituting of Aboriginal women were carried out. Pregnancies were a result of this degradation, hence the categorizing of us: 'Oh! are you a full blood; half caste; no maybe only one quarter caste. Oh! well you're not a real Aboriginal'.

These tactics of terror were meant to kill us off slowly. They were meant to kill our culture, our family links, spiritual beliefs and our links with the land and to destroy our language. To make us ashamed, afraid, terrified to be who we are. The same way the first tactics claimed hundreds of thousands of lives, these tactics also have stolen the language of thousands more. But once again these tactics have failed to defeat the Aboriginal Nation.

However, terrorism is still used in the present day; our sovereignty, our nationhood and our language is still not recognized or accepted by the majority of white people and your governments. Our land continues to be colonized, stolen and raped for its wealth. Racist attacks and the deaths of Aboriginal people at the hands of racist cops, prison wardens and individuals is a continuation of genocide and of the violence to terrorize and oppress us. The policies and practices of the government today attempt to create and maintain a level of fear and immobilization which takes away the ability of our people to control our lives. The government continues to use a structure which denies control over our rights to make decisions for ourselves.

We have been demanding our rights for 199 years, yet still today we are denied our sovereignty, our land; our people die on average twenty years younger than white Australians; we are the most imprisoned race in the world; and we are still dying at the hands of racist authorities. The sounds of boots and batons on black flesh today join the echoes of the screams of our ancestors. These sounds of murder remain the same – the acts of genocide and terrorism continue. Our resistance can only get stronger. We will stop the terror and we will have justice.

If I could just go back to the transitional stage. I am a product of that stage and my mother before me. My mother missed out on the in-doctrination that I received from my Granny. Nanna had been at the receiving end of the alcoholism, that is the physical abuse, and my mother had been through the same abuse with my father, with the psychological damage he was causing. So, unbeknown to me, Nanna was indoctrinating me with statements like 'Don't marry a black fulla, they're no-good bums, they're nothing but drunks'. Nanna couldn't see the damage she was doing. She was terrified for her grandchild. Through no fault of our men they were the victims of that transitional stage. Victims that are persecuted. So, I was conditioned never to marry a black fella. I married two white men – I also divorced them. I was under the under-standing that they were going to give me all I needed. Nanna was wrong, they couldn't give me my language. That indoctrination has stopped at me. I am stronger now, as a woman. I will pass on my strength to my daughter. I am getting closer to fulfilling my language. Nobody will terrorize my language again. Thank you.

6

Feminism and the Federal Bureaucracy 1972–1983

Lyndall Ryan

The entry of feminists into the Australian federal bureaucracy from 1973 was dependent upon a number of factors; the resurgence of the women's movement in 1970 in response to the massive changes for women in the 1960s; the emergence of a liberal feminist political organization, Women's Electoral Lobby (WEL), which developed goals and strategies in relation to the state; and a political climate which fostered the view of a neutral state, whose services should be extended to the disadvantaged.

This chapter considers the origins of Women's Electoral Lobby and its success in placing feminist issues on the public political agenda during the 1972 federal election campaign. It then examines the entry of feminists into the federal bureaucracy and their experiences in policymaking during the Whitlam years. The focus then shifts to the survival of feminist bureaucrats and to their opportunities for policymaking during the period of Conservative government that followed. It concludes with some points about the experiences of feminists in public policymaking.

Women's Electoral Lobby and the Federal Election Campaign of 1972

Women's Electoral Lobby emerged in Melbourne in February 1972 when eleven women, impressed by the feminist form guide published by *Ms* magazine in preparation for the US Presidential campaign, gathered to discuss a similar campaign for the Australian federal election also due later that year. Their concern was to place the six basic demands of Women's Liberation – free, safe abortion on demand, 24-hour child

71

care, equal employment opportunity, equal access to education, free contraceptives and equal pay – on to the political agenda of the federal campaign.

WEL's strategy for raising these issues was to send a questionnaire to every candidate in the 1972 election; to publish through the women's movement and the local press the results of this questionnaire; to rank the candidates like a form-guide for every electorate in the country; and to campaign for the candidate who was not only the most sympathetic to women's issues, but also the most likely to effect the social reforms desperately needed by women.[1] In some electorates, WEL held public meetings to which all the candidates were invited and their views on these six issues were canvassed. Some candidates (the overwhelming majority were male) refused to fill out the questionnaire. The results showed that few candidates of either major party had a sensitivity towards women's issues, so it proved a consciousness-raising exercise for all, including the media.

WEL was without doubt the political bombshell of 1972. It dramatically changed the nature of public debate by and about women. It quickly replaced other groups like the Union of Australian Women, the Country Women's Association and the National Council of Women as the major women's organization in Australia. It was young, dynamic and politically astute. Its questionnaires were constructed by female sociologists, its public meetings conducted by female media-wise professionals, its press releases written by women journalists, its speeches written by female political scientists, its economic analysis prepared by female economists, its campaign far more sophisticated than any of the political parties. WEL argued that the talent of women was being disregarded to the detriment of the nation. Women suffered discrimination on the grounds of sex, not ability. Few were in positions of influence or power, because institutions of power discriminated against them. The Lobby's arguments were compelling.

WEL saw itself as the pragmatic wing of Women's Liberation. It differed in at least one dramatic way from its sister organization. Instead of eschewing the state and promoting revolutionary change, WEL demanded the right to participate in the decision-making processes of the state, and its share of the national cake. By the end of the campaign WEL had established important contacts with the major political parties, yet remained detached, arguing that no political party in Australia had either a predominantly female membership or a preponderance of women in key positions.

Any woman could join WEL and immediately become part of a wide network and informal structure. WEL met in small groups weekly with convenors and spokeswomen responsible for particular areas. State convenors were elected by consensus of all State members. There was no constitution or hierarchical structure, so that women had no compulsion about joining and suffered no pressures once they were there. Most members joined to gain political experience in lobbying, writing submissions and press releases, speaking in the media and generating interest in the WEL objectives. By the end of 1972 WEL had a membership of about 1700.[2]

One of the important branches of WEL was in the Australian Capital Territory (ACT), based in Canberra. Many of its members had lived in the US where they had joined the National Organization of Women (NOW). Now they were underemployed or even unemployed without any opportunities to test their skills and experience. There was also considerable overlap in membership between WEL and Women's Liberation which enabled a strong dialogue to develop between theoretical and pragmatic issues. It was WEL ACT which lobbied for the appointment of a women's adviser, for anti-discrimination legislation and for equal opportunity programmes. Between 1973 and 1975, WEL ACT maintained strong pressure upon the Whitlam government to pursue an integrated child care policy, to introduce the supporting mothers' benefit and abortion legislation. In Melbourne, WEL successfully appeared before the Commonwealth Arbitration Commission to present the case for the introduction of the adult minimum wage in 1974.

WEL's national network enabled successful lobbying for the appointment of women's advisers in other States. As a liberal feminist organization concerned with equal opportunity, its goals suited the Whitlam government's radical liberal concerns, and fitted the national mood. At a time when Aboriginals were demanding land rights and the White Australia Policy was being laid to rest, Women's Liberation as the stormtroopers and Women's Electoral Lobby as the pragmatic face of feminism found a space in the political agenda that had previously not existed.

Feminists Enter the Commonwealth Bureaucracy 1973–1977

Upon its election in December 1972 the Whitlam government lost no time in taking up some initiatives presented by WEL. In a few quick gestures to indicate its support for women's issues, the government intervened in favour of the equal pay case before the Arbitration Commission and removed the sales tax on contraceptives. Simultaneously a number of feminists were appointed to the staff of several ministers, presaging that feminists had come to the outskirts of the bureaucracy. In

early 1973, the government advertised for an adviser in women's affairs
to the Prime Minister. This was to be a political rather than a bureaucratic appointment, held at the whim of the Prime Minister. Over 400
women applied and eighteen were shortlisted. The appointee, Elizabeth
Reid, a tutor in Philosophy at the Australian National University, was a
member of Women's Liberation. The appointment and the process
caused uproar in Women's Liberation and forced it to confront the
relationship of socialist feminists to the state. Elizabeth Reid's appointment made her accountable to the Prime Minister, but not to Women's
Liberation. Her high salary was also seen as a sell-out to the interests of
the women's movement generally and to socialist feminism in particular.
Her successors would face similar accusations and become the object of
intense scrutiny in terms of personal actions, appearance and clothes
from a suspicious women's movement. Summers argues that the
divisions caused by this suspicion enabled politicians to ignore women's
issues in times of crisis.[3]

Reid's appointment, however, heralded a serious commitment on the
part of the Labor government to introduce feminist ideas into government decision-making processes and to begin planning for more
permanent feminist representation in the bureaucracy. Many of the
other women shortlisted soon joined the bureaucracy and became the
first 'femocrats' – a term of abuse in the women's movement. Once
feminists entered the bureaucracy they were immediately struck by the
possibilities for change in terms of policymaking, bureaucratic structure,
and the delivery of services. The years 1973–75 produced an aura of
revolutionary government, prepared, even anxious and eager to try new
approaches, new ideas and new structures. Socialist feminists who had
joined the bureaucracy needed all their theoretical training to prepare
for such tasks.

In some respects similar to the British Labour Government of 1945 in
its first term of office, the Whitlam government was also responding, in a
period of affluence, to a range of new issues. It attempted to open up the
public service and to create bureaucratic structures that would reflect
 changing community needs. It established a large number of new
commissions and committees of enquiry in virtually every field of
government activity, which brought in as policy advisers many new
people with expertise that was not available in the bureaucracy and with
views broadly sympathetic to the government. However, the overriding
political and administrative fact was that at no stage did Labor attain
complete parliamentary power. The lack of majority in the Senate
permeated every aspect of the government's political and administrative
life.[4]

While the committees of enquiry and think tanks like the Priorities

Review Staff were important additions to the machinery of government, there was little change to the central bureaucracy itself. Except in new areas like the Department of Urban and Regional Development and the Community Health Program, there was adherence to the view of a public service equally able to serve both political sides. Feminists could get into policy making but they had greater difficulty getting into the operations level and the delivery of services to women.

Nevertheless, the feminists who joined the bureaucracy believed they had an important role to raise bureaucratic consciousness about women, to question bureaucratic procedures, to provide policy advice to ministers and to foster programmes for women. By 1974, feminists outside the bureaucracy were establishing their own services for women, women's refuges and rape crisis centres, which had no government funding. The feminist bureaucrats argued that these initiatives would not survive without adequate government funding. This led to conflict between those feminists in the bureaucracy and those who stayed outside in their community groups. Sara Dowse has argued that all these feminist voluntary community groups would have expired from exhaustion, as many did, without sustained government funding. If feminists were to provide services for women, they had to develop a relationship with the state that enabled feminist ideas about women's programmes to be put into practice. This debate has continued.[5]

In the first year of Reid's appointment, her concerns focused upon changing the direction of the pre-school and child care programme, arranging the monitoring of Cabinet submissions and their impact upon women and answering the huge volume of correspondence that her appointment had generated. By 1974 the Department of Prime Minister and Cabinet agreed to establish a Women's Affairs Section within its Welfare Division and in July 1974 Sara Dowse, a member of Women's Liberation and a journalist in the Australian Information Service, was appointed as head. At first Dowse was the only feminist, for the Department was suspicious of any candidates with feminist leanings. By mid 1975 there were two feminists in the Section and by 1977 the Section members were predominantly feminist. The Section's brief was to attend to Elizabeth Reid's correspondence, some of which formed the basis for policy initiatives, to prepare briefings and speech notes for her and for the Prime Minister on women's issues, and to monitor Cabinet submissions as they affected women. For example, the Women's Affairs Section had considerable input in the funding of women's refuges by the Community Health Programme; it monitored the child care programme, and it developed links with other areas of the bureaucracy in relation to women's affairs.

The year 1974 proved the zenith of Reid's influence and vision. She succeeded in committing the Whitlam government to a major change in direction in the provision of pre-school and child care services and salvaged a considerable budget with which to fund it. She succeeded in committing the government to major political and financial support for International Women's Year in the hope that it would raise the consciousness of women throughout the country to feminist issues and produce a spin-off effect for the Whitlam government. She created the first effective feminist bureaucratic enclave and successfully argued that women and women's issues were an integral part of the bureaucratic structure. The year 1975 was thus expected to be the one in which feminists would start achieving major results within the bureaucracy.

Child Care

The Interim Committee for the Children's Commission established in September, 1974, was to be the major deliverer of a feminist programme, the funding of community-based projects for an integrated pre-school and child care programme costing $75m. The Interim Committee developed out of two major reports: *Project Care*, from the Social Welfare Commission and *Children's Services* from the Priorities Review Staff. The former was the blueprint for an integrated programme, the latter the strategy for achieving its goals by the creation of a statutory body with responsibility to a neutral minister, the Special Minister of State, who was not responsible for programmes like health, welfare, education, employment or community development. The feminists involved were convinced that they could retain access to a neutral minister to monitor the programme.

While this was admirable in principle, it failed in practice. The Child Care Act of 1972, passed in the dying days of the previous Liberal government, had established a small Secretariat to service it. The creation of a new programme in a new statutory body responsible to a neutral minister did not mean the creation of a new secretariat, as the feminists thought, but simply the transfer of the original secretariat of male bureaucrats from the Department of Education – who were unsympathetic to an integrated approach – to Children's Services. The two feminists placed temporarily in the Secretariat found themselves outmanoeuvred. The big winners were the pre-schools.

By March 1975 the children's services programme had committed most of its funds to pre-schools. The legislation to establish the Children's Commission was awaiting promulgation on 11 November 1975, when the Whitlam government was dismissed. Had it been established, the Commission in the first instance would not have delivered an integrated Children's Service Programme, for the pre-school lobby was too strong. This feminist programme failed because of feminist bureaucratic inexperience and male bureaucratic intransigence. However, child care had by now come to be seen as a responsibility of the state, and the incoming Fraser government provided opportunities for more experienced bureaucrats to restructure the programme. Child care remained the litmus test of the state's response to women's issues.

The International Women's Year Secretariat 1975

The International Women's Year Secretariat (IWY) of about twenty people was established in November 1974 to service the National Advisory Committee (NAC) chaired by Elizabeth Reid. She selected feminists from within the bureaucracy to work with feminists specially recruited from outside on temporary appointments who had expertise in areas like the media, women's health, child care and education, to advise the NAC on funding, sponsoring conferences and producing the final report. Reid also hoped that the Secretariat could become a prototype feminist bureaucracy. Headed by two sympathetic male public servants from the Department of the Special Minister of state, the Secretariat had a budget of $3 million – small in comparison with the $75 million allotted for the children's services programme. Reid's plan was to persuade government departments to slot a range of feminist projects that had been solicited and/or funded by the NAC into existing funding programmes. An example was the interim NAC funding to feminist community initiatives like women's refuges, while the Secretariat and the Women's Affairs Section sorted out the appropriate long-term funding agency. Others were one-off projects, like the national research project on manuscript sources relating to women.

The attempt to place feminist decision-making processes inside a traditional bureaucratic structure became fraught with difficulty. Many feminists in the IWY Secretariat found they did not have the independence to operate as they wished. Reid was often out of Canberra attending to IWY business both interstate and overseas and many of her ideas and instructions got lost in the panic to keep control of everything. Out of the chaos a system of favouritism developed, which was often more oppressive than the traditional structures. The staff simply had no time to sort out these issues and as the fortunes of the Whitlam government waned, so did IWY. By the end of August 1975, the Secretariat was under siege. Reid resigned in October 1975 when her position was transferred from the Prime Minister's Office to the Prime Minister's Department, heading an upgraded Women's Affairs branch. In becoming a public servant Reid would have lost her independence. So ended the interim period of feminist policy advice to government.

Many of the projects the IWY Secretariat recommended for funding were innovative and Reid always hoped that the year and the projects would have a spin-off effect. Reid may also have envisaged the secretariat as an embryo Department of Women's Affairs, although she was concerned that a separate women's affairs department would become isolated from the mainstream of bureaucracy. Reid and Dowse had quickly discovered that unless a feminist policymaking body was placed in the sphere of the Prime Minister then women would not be at the head of the wheel or have credibility. Indeed the experience of the IWY Secretariat confirmed their view. Reid and Dowse were always thinking of ways to raise the consciousness of other government departments to women's issues. The answer came in two forms; the decision implemented in October 1975 to establish an Equal Employment Opportunity (EEO) Section in the Public Service Board, the policymaker and implementer of employment practices for the Commonwealth Public Service; and the recommendation to establish women's units in key government departments. The first came into effect before the fall of the Whitlam government in November 1975. The second was implemented by the Fraser government in 1976. The first director of the EEO Section, Gail Radford, had been the driving force in Canberra WEL. Her brief was to write an EEO policy for the Public Service Board and to devise means for its implementation in all government departments. Her appointment became a trailblazer for other bureaucracies in Australia.

The First Fraser Ministry 1975–1977

The dismissal of the Whitlam government appeared to place feminist bureaucratic initiatives in jeopardy. But, as Sara Dowse has pointed out, the incoming conservative Prime Minister, Malcolm Fraser, was uncertain of his mandate in many areas. He did promise to retain the Women's Affairs Branch in his department, to appoint women to boards and statutory authorities and to 'integrate women's affairs within individual portfolios'.[6] A number of key women within the Liberal Party supported EEO and the appointment of women to government boards and commissions, while the Liberal government in Victoria had recently appointed a women's adviser. There was also the view that Australian conservative parties would follow the precedent of their counterparts in other Western democracies, of opposing reform while out of government but then administering and extending reforms already made upon return to government.[7] From a feminist bureaucratic perspective there was room for manoeuvre. International Women's Year, including the NAC and the International Women's Year (IWY) Secretariat, was coming to an end. This allowed the two permanent bureaucratic structures to survive, the Women's Affairs Branch, and the EEO section of the Public Service Board. In the midst of immediate post-election uncertainty Dowse was able to save IWY funds earmarked for a film project that Germaine Greer had been unable to get off the ground, to establish the Women's Film Fund.

In Fraser's first term as Prime Minister, from December 1975 to December 1977, Sara Dowse was able to persuade him to establish women's units in a range of key government departments, to establish the Office of Child Care headed by Marie Coleman, the only woman to hold First Division status in Commonwealth Public Service at that time; to extend women's refuge funding; to establish an Inter-Departmental Working Group (IDWG) on Women's Affairs; to support the moves by women in the Liberal Party to prepare a report to establish a National Women's Advisory Council; and to introduce family allowances in the 1976 budget. Fraser gave increased recognition to the area by appointing a Minister assisting the Prime Minister in Women's Affairs in June 1976. The Labor Opposition did not allocate a shadow portfolio to this area until 1979.

The ten new women's units in Health, Environment, Housing and Community Development, Social Security, Education, Attorney General's Department, Immigration and Ethnic Affairs and Aboriginal Affairs as well as in statutory authorities like the Schools Commission and the Australian Development Assistance Bureau, were designed to provide a feminist input into departmental policymaking and to stop androcentric policies from being generated. They were also designed to enable younger feminist bureaucrats to gain experience in policymaking. The units were criticized for not containing more senior appointments, for most consisted of one or two women, mid-way up the third division, not sufficiently senior to gain acceptance by their senior male colleagues. But the Women's Affairs Branch was fearful that unsympathetic women would fill posts at a higher level. At that stage there was only one feminist in the Second Division in the entire Public Service. The units participated in the IDWG on Women's Affairs, which also included the EEO Section of the Public Service Board and the Women's Bureau from the Department of Employment and Industrial Relations, and thus provided the opportunity for training cadres and developing a system of feminist networking. Finally, the women's units provided a counter to the usual socialization that women were getting in the service at their level. There were no women's units in Treasury, Trade, or Primary Industry, traditionally powerful and conservative departments.

The establishment of the IDWG on Women's Affairs had been encouraged by the permanent head the Department of the Prime Minister and the Cabinet, John Menadue, and could only effectively operate with his support. Indeed Menadue had opposed the establishment of a women's unit in the Treasury because he was fearful of giving any leverage to the Treasury's claim to be the major co-ordinating department. When a new permanent head was appointed to the Department of the Prime Minister and the Cabinet late in 1976 who proved unsympathetic to women's issues, the Women's Affairs Branch lost significant support. But with the introduction of anti-discrimination legislation in three States and the appointment of women's advisers in four others, feminists in the Canberra bureaucracy could justifiably promote EEO within the Commonwealth Public Service and convene meetings of women's advisers to develop co-ordinated action in areas like child care and women's refuge funding.

While the children's services budget did not increase in real terms, between 1975 and 1977 there were some important reallocations away from pre-schools and into long-term day care, away from capital expenditure and into recurrent expenditure (on salary subsidies) and away from 'basic care' into a range of innovative programmes. This diversification included the funding of vacation care, out of school care, Aboriginal children's services, child care in women's refuges, Children's Services Development Officers and the youth services scheme.

Another change in 1977 was the conversion of the Supporting Mother's Benefit into the Supporting Parent's Benefit – a recognition of the parenting role of fathers. However, this was countered by the abolition of paid paternity leave for Commonwealth Public Servants. This proved the zenith of feminist bureaucratic success in the first Fraser government.

Downgrading of Women's Affairs 1977–1983

The Women's Affairs Branch was transformed into the Office of Women's Affairs in 1977, indicating that it could no longer necessarily be seen as an integral part of the Department of the Prime Minister and the Cabinet. Following the 1977 federal election, the Office was transferred to the Department of Home Affairs and Environment, one of the most junior ministries. Sara Dowse resigned in protest, thus making the transfer of the Office into a political issue and helping to pave the way for its eventual return to the Department of the Prime Minister and the Cabinet after the change of government in 1983.

Dowse laid the groundwork for the future of feminism in the bureaucracy. On the dilemma of the relationship between feminists and the state, she argued:

> We have to decide whether we are going to change society or whether we are going to develop small enclaves of alternative ways of living which will eventually self-destruct through depletion of energy. If we want to be in a position to help all women who need to free themselves from domestic tyranny we have to devise strategies for extending services on a scale large enough to have a genuine impact.

Other Women's Liberationists argued that in joining patriarchal bureaucratic structures and engaging in masculine decision-making processes feminists lost their identity and autonomy. Dowse felt that progress could be made from within, but she never denied the difficulties 'femocrats' encountered in the bureaucracy and their ability to initiate structural change.[9]

With the transfer of the Office, Kathleen Taperell, Dowse's deputy, became head, a position which she held until December 1983, thus becoming the longest serving head of the Office in the most difficult period of its history. Taperell maintained a low profile, for her goal was to keep the Office and the women's units alive, to develop networks outside the bureaucracy, to liaise with feminist bureaucracies in the States, to promote sex discrimination legislation, to promote Australia's role in relation to women in the international sphere and to support the extension of EEO in the Commonwealth Public Service. This low profile was a boon and a curse. A boon because the feminist bureaucrats could do things without attracting attention from the Right – or giving credit to the Fraser government; and a curse because no-one knew what the femocrats were doing. As a result many femocrats became isolated and felt that they had lost their political base.

The relocation of the Office to such a low-ranking ministry made it very difficult to gain automatic access to Cabinet submissions. It also meant that the co-ordinating role of the Office became dependent on personal relationships established between the head of the Office and key decision-makers in functional departments. Once moved away from a central co-ordinating department to a peripheral one, the Office was no longer able to play such an effective role as the hub of the women's affairs wheel, so the IDWG gradually became moribund.

Despite predictions that the Office would disappear, it flourished and had some resounding successes. Firstly, it established the Women's Shopfront in the centre of Canberra and provided information in the service delivery area. Secondly, it supported the upgrading of the EEO

Section in the Public Service Board to a Branch, and Gail Radford developed new programmes for Aborigines, disabled people, migrants and women. Radford spent much of her time conducting seminars in regional offices, collecting statistics on public service workforce participation and convincing the permanent head of the Board that EEO was good for the public service. In this, she had remarkable success. At a time when the public sector was suffering a barrage of abuse for its size and inefficiency, Radford provided the statistics on employment practices that the Board could cite at the private sector.[10]

Thirdly, in July 1978 the National Women's Advisory Council (NATWAC) was established; Beryl Beaurepaire, a Liberal Party feminist, was the first convenor. Members were appointed by Cabinet partly on the advice of the Office of Women's Affairs. They served part-time and were chosen so that there was a woman from each State who was also informally representative of major women's organizations and important sectional interests. The first Council included an Aboriginal woman, a migrant woman, the leading industrial female advocate from the Australian Council of Trades Unions (ACTU), the president of the Family Planning Association (also a leading member of WEL), and a key member of the Country Women's Association (CWA). NATWAC's brief was to report and to make recommendations through the Minister for Home Affairs and Environment on matters of concern to women, and to act as a channel of communication between women in the community and the government. It was provided with a small secretariat that was part of the Office of Women's Affairs and a travel budget. It produced important reports on the need for anti-discrimination legislation and on migrant women and in 1979 lobbied support against the Lusher amendment in the federal parliament, which sought to withdraw medical benefit funding for abortions.

As a Liberal government initiative with independence, NATWAC also played an important role in Australia's participation in the mid-decade UN conference on women in Copenhagen in 1980. NATWAC was so successful in gaining support from more traditional women's organizations like the CWA and in raising a public profile for the Office of Women's Affairs that New Right women's organizations emerged in reaction: the most important, Women Who Want to be Women (WWWW), was established in 1979 as an offshoot of the Right to Life. In utilizing church networks and following the tactics of US counterparts such as the Moral Majority, WWWW made inroads among Liberal and National Party politicians and their influence was felt most keenly after the 1980 federal election, when the membership of NATWAC became more conservative.

In 1981 the fortunes of the Office of Women's Affairs fluctuated as the small government faction within the Fraser government gained influence. In the Review of Commonwealth Functions cuts of November 1981, most of the women's units were abolished and it took some fast footwork by Taperell to keep the unit in the Australian Development Assistance Bureau as well as the women's bureau in the Department of Employment alive. An unsympathetic Minister for Home Affairs frustrated the work of the Office. The removal of Marie Coleman in 1982 as Head of the Office of Child Care was the high point of the small government lobby. Child care funding was further threatened by the Spender Report which proved so embarrassing to the Fraser government that it was never tabled. However, in 1982 the appointment of a new minister responsible for women's affairs, who proved receptive to women's issues, enabled the Office's recommendation for the appointment of an Aboriginal Women's Taskforce to go ahead. In the international arena Australia was elected to the UN Commission on the status of women on the basis that Taperell would be the representative. In recognition of this international success, the name of the Office was changed in late 1982 to the Office of the Status of Women.

The small government faction had a brief but bloody reign in the women's affairs area. However this period of reaction did see the formation of a national child care lobby, the adoption of equal opportunity policies in the trade union movement, and the commitment by the Labor Opposition to anti-discrimination legislation. Ironically, by June 1982 there were twenty-seven permanent women officers in the Second Division whereas there had been two in 1975, while women made up a quarter of the Third Division and fifty per cent of the Fourth Division.[11] By the change of government in March 1983, feminists had made extraordinary inroads into the federal bureaucracy, not only in terms of jobs and numbers but also in developing networks of survival and in initiating and promoting policies for women. The success of the Office in maintaining funding can be gauged in the increase in women's refuges from twenty-one in 1975 to ninety-six in 1980, and from one women's health centre in 1974 to six in 1980.

The period 1973–83 saw the entry of several hundred feminists into a range of bureaucratic structures in the Commonwealth and the States. It was a pioneering decade which confirmed for the majority of feminists in Australia the need to develop a carefully worked-out relationship to the state. In Australia the state has not only been considered neutral, but as the initiator of change. While it is undoubtedly a patriarchal structure, its potential to liberate women from dependency on husbands and fathers is enormous. There is no doubt that the rise of the New Right in Australia has to a large degree been a response to the success femocrats have achieved in initiating major policy changes in the delivery of services for women. This pioneering decade enabled the femocrats to understand the possibilities as well as the limitations of change.

Notes

1. J. Mercer (ed.), *The Other Half: Women in Australian Society*, Penguin, Ringwood 1975, pp. 396–7.

2. Ibid, p. 400.

3. A. Summers, 'Mandarins or Missionaries: Women in the Federal Bureaucracy' in N. Grieve and A. Burns (eds), *Australian Women: New Feminist Perspectives*, Oxford University Press, Melbourne 1986, pp. 59–69.

4. P. Wilenski, 'The Whitlam Bureaucracy' in S. Encel, P. Wilenski and B. Schaffer (eds), *Decisions*, Longman Cheshire, Melbourne 1980, pp. 40–55.

5. R. Pringle, 'Feminists and Bureaucrats: the Last Four Years', *Refractory Girl* 18–19, 1980; R. Pringle and A. Game, 'Women and Class in Australia: Feminism and the Labor Government' in G. Duncan (ed.), *Critical Essays in Australian Politics*, Edward Arnold, Adelaide 1978, pp. 114–34; see also Summers, pp. 1–15.

6. Liberal Party Platform, 1975.

7. Wilenski, p. 54.

8. S. Dowse, 'The Bureaucrat as Usurer' in Dorothy H. Broom (ed.), *Unfinished Business*, Allen & Unwin, Australia 1984, pp. 139–60.

9. S. Dowse, 'The Transfer of the Office of Women's Affairs' in *Decisions*, pp. 3–20; S. Dowse, 'The Women's Movement Fandango with the State: The Movement's Role in Public Policy since 1972' in Cora V. Baldock and Bettina Cass (eds), *Women, Social Welfare and the State*, Allen & Unwin, Australia 1983, pp. 201–22.

10. G. Radford, 'Equal Employment Opportunity Programs in the Australian Public Service' in Marian Sawer (ed.), *Program for Change*, Allen & Unwin, Australia 1985, pp. 51–71.

11. J. Clarke and K. White, *Women in Australian Politics*, Fontana/Collins, Melbourne 1983, p. 140.

PART II

On the Field

7

Femocrats, Official Feminism and the Uses of Power

Hester Eisenstein

The theme of women and power has been a constant element in feminist theory since the resurgence of the women's movement in the second wave of the 1960s. In this chapter I draw on my experience in Australia from 1980 to 1988 in the world of the 'femocrats' to reflect on this larger issue for feminism. I see this chapter as part of a larger enterprise, being carried out internationally, to assess the impact of a wide variety of feminist interventions. A preliminary categorization of these might be as follows:

(a) Bureaucratic/individual: entering the bureaucracy of state or national government at a policy-making level as a self-identified feminist.

(b) Bureaucratic/structural: creating new structures within government or university administrations to benefit women (for example, women's policy units; Women's Studies programmes; Ministries for Women's Affairs).

(c) Legal reform: introducing new legislation, or revising existing legislation to benefit women (for example, changes in the law regarding rape, now called sexual assault, in New South Wales; anti-discrimination legislation).

NOTE: This chapter was originally presented in a slightly different version to the Feminism and Legal Theory Conference, Institute for Legal Studies, University of Wisconsin, Madison Law School, 27 June–2 July 1988. A revised version will also be published in a special issue of *The Yale Journal of Law and Feminism*, in 1989.

(d) Political participation in a leadership role: running for some form of political office (broadly defined) as a self-proclaimed feminist (for example, the Ferraro vice-presidency; seeking to become a mayor, or member of a legislature; seeking to join the executive arm of a labour union).

(e) Alternative structures: creating a feminist organization outside the mainstream of existing political and administrative structures (for example women's refuges or rape crisis centres).

Obviously it is a matter for debate among feminists as to whether any of these interventions has really helped to improve the status of women. In entering the debate and seeking to make such an assessment, a number of variables need to be taken into account. The set of variables most vivid to me, given my recent experience, is the significance of national differences in shaping feminist interventions. First, there are the national political differences between any two countries. For example an important difference between the United States and Australia is the difference in the role of unions in the two countries. In Australia, the workforce is more than 50 per cent unionized, and the powerful trade unions and their national organization, the ACTU, have an important voice in state and national politics. This is in sharp contrast to the US, where union membership has dropped below 20 per cent and where the influence of organized labour has waned significantly in the Reagan years.

Second, there are national differences in the character of the women's movements, as these have been shaped by – of perhaps more accurately, as these have developed in the context of – each country's political structures. Thus, the campaign for equal pay for work of equal value has a different configuration in Australia from that of the US, because the structure that determines salaries and wages is completely different (there is a centralized industrial arbitration system in Australia whereas collective bargaining takes place in the US).

Finally, there is the particular mix of feminist theory and practice that has emerged in each country. I enter a caveat here, as my data base is idiosyncratic, as someone who moved from the world of Women's Studies in the US to the world of the femocrat in Australia. I maintain, however, that at least some of the differences I have experienced stem from the 'national character' of the feminist theories most current in a given culture, and the effect of this upon the explicit and implicit objectives of local feminist activity. Overall, then, Australian feminists appear to me to operate on the basis of a socialist-feminist praxis linked to the politics of the welfare state. This gives rise to campaigns and objectives that centre upon the protection of the economic rights of women: as mothers, whether or not they work outside the home; in terms of welfare rights, child support payments, protection of women through the unions, and so on.

In contrast, American feminists working in the area of legal reform often draw upon the tradition of radical feminism with its basis in gender theory, concentrating on the debate over equality and difference. This gives rise to campaigns and objectives that centre upon the extension of legal rights to women as women, for example, in the campaign to extend civil rights legislation to cover pornography.

Obviously all strands of feminist theory are present in both the US and in Australia, and there is overlap in the range of activities and commitments connected to these. But it is crucial to observe the interaction between local feminisms, in all of their varieties, and the structures of power within which they are compelled to operate. For feminists seeking to assess the impact of feminist interventions, it is very important to see clearly what strands of feminist theory and practice are picked up by and articulated into the structures of power, and what are the implications of this for the outcomes.

Equal Employment Opportunity Legislation in New South Wales and its Impact on the Department of Education, 1981–1987

When I first got to Sydney, I was dazzled by the highly political feminists I met there. They seemed utterly at ease with the structures of power at state and national levels. They understood the mysteries of submission writing; of applying for senior-level positions in government, including the magic language that unlocked the gates of appointment; of committee procedure, and how to chair a meeting in order to control the outcome; of lobbying at endless winesoaked luncheons and dinner parties; and of the (to me utterly impenetrable) rules of standing for preselection as a candidate for Parliament. These feminists were intensely practically minded, and they were immersed, too, in a kind of detail that I found overwhelming and mystifying.

These women, I was to find out, were mostly 'femocrats'. The term was first introduced to me by Jozefa Sobski as one in current usage that often connoted 'sell-out' or co-option; the 'femocrats' were contrasted with the true believers in boilersuits who inhabited the lesbian separatist communities of Glebe and Balmain, where the true heart of feminist revolution lay. The opposition, then, was between revolutionary feminism on the streets, outside the corrupt system of power and prestige, and the official feminism of the state, which created bureaucrats in its own image, painted birds whose role it was to generally contain and dissipate the energy of feminism.

The strategy of creating a femocracy has gone hand in hand with a strategy of alliance with the Labor Party, which resulted in a strong voice for women in the Labor Government of New South Wales, and subsequently in the national Labor government under Hawke, although the latter appears to be waning in the late eighties (a symptom of this is the resignation of Hawke's feminist Minister of Education, Susan M. Ryan, in 1987). In NSW, there are women's units in the Department of Industrial Relations, the Health Department, and most significantly in the Premier's Department, with the responsibility, *inter alia*, of preparing the so-called women's budget each year; a second round of the budget process announced on International Women's Day with special allocations for women's affairs.

By the time I entered the New South Wales public service, femocrats had become a significant force for change. A whole generation of feminists had taken this route, for a mixture of reasons including financial and professional ambitions, feminist and other political commitments, and blockage in other careers, especially in the academic world, which had not (in contrast to the US) created a world of Women's Studies positions to welcome, or at least make some grudging room for, feminist academics.

For me, what was striking about the femocrats was their undisguised commitment to feminism, and the acceptance of this within the bureaucracy. This was not a generation of women who, to win senior positions in government, had had to conform to the reigning ethos and disguise their personal convictions. Indeed, the requirement of a demonstrated commitment to feminism, in the form of some experience in an activist area, had been, with some help from the Equal Employment Opportunity (EEO) programme, incorporated into job descriptions. The spectacle of very traditional-looking male bureaucrats, in pin-striped suits and conservative ties, reading over the credentials of women candidates and discussing seriously their respective claims to authentic feminist commitment and political experience, is one that stays with me as a testimony to the effectiveness of the femocratic strategy, at least as a way into the ranks of the bureaucracy.

By the 1980s, there were sufficient numbers of femocrats at least in New South Wales, to be divided into specializations. There were health, child care, welfare, legal reform, and education femocrats, and there were also femocrats edging their way into very 'male' areas such as the Treasury and the Water Board. One element that accelerated the progress of femocratization of the bureaucracy was the impact of the EEO programme.

The EEO legislation in New South Wales was introduced in September 1980, as an amendment to the Anti-Discrimination Act of 1977. The legislation established the Office of the Director of Equal Opportunity in Public Employment (DEOPE), to oversee the implementation of the law, and required all authorities scheduled under the Act to submit an Equal Employment Opportunity Management Plan to the Director for her approval. The plan was to be statistically based and to establish targets for the increased hiring and promotion for members of the target groups, originally women, migrants of non-English-speaking background, and Aborigines. People with physical disabilities were added as a target group under Part IXA in 1983.

The legislation in New South Wales was based on US experience in the implementation of affirmative action, but with a distinctive Australian flavour. An elusive concept, this meant generally an avoidance of what were seen as the excesses of the American experience. Specifically, the legislation avoided any provision for what was termed 'hard' affirmative action in the form of quota hiring, that is, direct preferential hiring for members of the target groups. Rather, it was intended that the exercise of preparing a statistical analysis of the workforce in each authority, and then of developing targets for increasing representation of the target groups, would have the effect over time of improving the profile of the organization by a process of slow organizational change – both in attitudes and in organizational procedures – without the requirement of imposing a fixed number or percentage of target group members for recruitment or promotion.

In September 1981, the DEOPE appointed Alison Ziller as director. Ziller had a background in sociology, had worked in the New South Wales public service in a number of capacities, and had been a colleague of Dr Peter Wilenski on the review of the New South Wales Public Administration which had given rise, among other reforms, to the EEO legislation. She had written the report for the Review on EEO entitled *Affirmative Action Handbook*, published in 1980, and had worked at the Anti-Discrimination Board and the Public Service Board. She was thus well qualified to take up the position of Director, although her appointment was delayed by the opposition of the head of the Premier's Department, Gerry Gleeson, on the well-founded suspicion that she was likely to be an effective implementer of the legislation.

I joined the Office of the DEOPE in March 1981, as the first Senior Adviser. I was thus part of the early years of the implementation of Part IXA, when the question was still open as to whether or not this piece of law would have any real impact on practices within the New South

Wales public service. The crucial variable here was the attitude of the New South Wales Premier, Neville Wran. Wran had been elected to office in 1976 on a platform that included a promise of equal employment opportunity legislation. In his first year in office he had established the Anti-Discrimination Board, with legislation that provided for complaint-based discrimination on the grounds of sex, race, and marital status, (physical and mental disability and homosexuality were added later). Wran was a powerful and charismatic figure, who had led Labor to victory in New South Wales the year after the traumatic defeat of Labor nationally in 1975. The coalition of constituencies that Wran put together – including trade unions, progressive inner-city yuppies, business people, women, Aborigines, and members of the migrant communities – was to become a model for Labor leaders in the decade that followed, culminating in victories for Labor in Victoria, South Australia, Western Australia, and in 1983 the national government of Bob Hawke.

One secret of Wran's power within the party was his balancing act between the Right and the Left. This he maintained, in part, in a complicated partnership with Gleeson, his head of department, whom he used to attack policies and persons who were perceived as too left-wing. The struggle between Left and Right often took the form of his allowing Gleeson some victories, but then vetoing or overriding him on some other issues. On the appointment of Alison Ziller, Wran overrode Gleeson, thus giving a first indication that he intended to take the EEO legislation seriously.

The first act in implementation was the requirement that the departments and authorities submit their EEO management plans by a set date, namely, 1 September 1981. In order to do this, organizations had to hire an EEO officer, called a Co-ordinator. The role of DEOPE under the legislation was to advise and assist organizations, and this we did in the first instance by helping them find appropriate personnel to prepare the plans and by providing seminars on data collection to assist Co-ordinators in carrying out the statistical survey to establish a profile of their workforce. We also answered questions and gave moral, political, and emotional support to the Co-ordinators who, as the first of their breed in the New South Wales public service, were invariably viewed with enormous suspicion by everyone including those who had hired them. By a familiar bureaucratic mechanism, the EEO Co-ordinators were rapidly placed on the defensive.

The organization is required – by some external or internal force – to take on board a programme that it basically perceives as unnecessary, stupid, wasteful of resources, or subversive. It hires the person who will preside over the programme, and then proceeds to marginalize and disempower that person by placing the responsibility and the blame for the idea of the programme on the poor soul who has agreed to run it. The new Co-ordinators were thus in a state of bewilderment, and required enormous support and encouragement.

Under the 1979 Public Service Act, another reform following the Wilenski report, departments had been given a great deal of freedom to manage themselves, especially in the area of recruitment and promotion of staff above the entry (base grade) levels. Authorities already had such freedom by virtue of operating under their own legislation. All government organizations viewed the passage of Part IXA as a form of window-dressing. The initial letters to heads of departments, and the dutiful visits of the Director to meet with each of them, were greeted with derision. The first months of the operation of the DEOPE were therefore a kind of phony war, with all players in effect waiting to see what position the Premier would take.

When it became clear that organizations were dragging their heels and showing no intention of meeting the deadline, the Director decided to draft a memo for the Premier indicating his support for the legislation. I was asked to draft two memos, one indicating mild dismay at the delays in lodgement of the initial EEO management plans, and the other forceful, using phrases like 'I view with grave concern ... '. After her meeting with the Premier Alison Ziller returned in triumph, reporting that Wran had pushed aside the weaker memo, and signed the tough one.

The effect of the memo was magical. The EEO plans began to appear in our office. It was evident that the Premier had come down on the side of the Director and of the legislation, and that people understood that this meant business. The DEOPE had the backing of the Premier, and so power flowed to us in an invisible but palpable stream.

But the power, such as it was, was not exerted equally. The organizations making up the New South Wales public administration were very individual and distinct, and so, too, were their attitudes to the EEO legislation. In the first phase of the legislation, the authorities scheduled under the act were the departments and the declared authorities, some seventy-five in number. These included enormous operational bodies such as the Department of Main Roads, the Water Board, and the State Rail Authority, varying in size from 5,000 to over 50,000 employees throughout the state. Their employment practices had gone without scrutiny for many years, and were based on seniority, controlled by powerful trade unions, and in some cases on nepotism and local networks.

The Department of Education was an especially tough nut to crack. This was, and is, one of the most powerful of the state agencies, controlling approximately twenty-five per cent of the state's budget each year, employing some 46,000 teachers and 12,000 administrative staff to run 2,300 schools across the state. While organized into ten regional administrations, the real power of the Department remained at the centre, controlled by Head Office. As I was to learn, any measure which could be depicted as threatening the orderly conduct of the schools, and especially of the Higher School Certificate exam, could be ruled out of court without much difficulty.

The progress of the legislation, then, was uneven. In the departments where some reform to personnel practices had already taken place – particularly where selection by merit rather than on seniority had been introduced – EEO principles were easier to implement, and the atmosphere was more receptive. Other factors in this included what service the department provided, the professional make-up of the staff, the organizational ethos, and perhaps most crucially, the senior executive officer of the organization, and his or her politics and commitments.

The progress of implementing EEO in New South Wales can be traced through the annual reports of the Director, which were lodged each year in Parliament as a chapter of the Annual Report from the Anti-Discrimination Board. The first stage for each organization was lodging the EEO management plan with the DEOPE. The initial plans were superficial, and easy to pick apart. The statistical analysis of the workforce was in some cases incomplete. In others the tables were adequate but the interpretation was astounding. We read each one and graded it as though it were a term paper, sending back a letter to the head of the organization which read, in effect, 'B- for effort, and D for content; do it again, please.' We later learned that these letters from the Director, which we spent hours gleefully composing, and which were written in a style very far from the convoluted prose of public service correspondence, were passed from hand to hand by heads of organizations at their monthly meetings. It became a matter of prestige to have received a letter that praised your organization for some EEO initiative or other, and a matter of shame if you had once again been rapped over the knuckles. I believe that the harsh judgements passed by the DEOPE on the initial plans were received at first with anger and astonishment by the heads of organizations. But the support of the Premier for the Office had been made public, visible, and continued, and so the disapproval of the Director had considerable weight. Most of the plans were sent back to be redone, and eventually the fact that one's EEO plan had been found satisfactory by the Director was incorporated into the public sector as a sign of good management. This effect must, in part, have depended on the close-knit community of the public service, where reputations and the opinion of peers counted in the balance.

Some organizations resisted the pressure. Foremost among them was the Department of Education. That the EEO management plan of the Department remained unsatisfactory for longer than that of almost any other organization appeared to leave the Department unmoved. The Director-General of Education composed letters back to the Director that were equal to hers in bureaucratic power although couched in more traditional language. The heart of the EEO issue for the Department of Education was the imbalance in the distribution of women teachers. In the clear majority of the service as a whole, some fifty-seven per cent overall, women teachers over the years had been under-represented in the promotions positions that gave power and prestige in the schools and that led, via the position of inspector, to power in regional and central administration. The male domination of the teaching service at senior levels (as with school systems elsewhere) had been critiqued and documented via reports of the Anti-Discrimination Board. The EEO legislation was the perfect vehicle to overcome this, at least in theory. But this required agreement among the DEOPE, the Department, and the powerful teachers' trade union, the Teachers' Federation of New South Wales, as to the dismantling of the system of appointment by seniority that had shaped the system for many years.

The stand-off between the Director and the Director-General on the EEO legislation took the following form. The Department had proposed an initial break with seniority in its EEO management plan in two parts. Ten per cent of promotions positions were to be allocated for selection by merit rather than by seniority. Forty per cent of the positions were to go on affirmative action to women, in a system of direct preference to qualified women teachers. The remainder of the system would stay intact, with positions allocated on seniority alone.

This was the plan that the Director vetoed in the first instance, for a series of complex reasons. One of these was her fears about the extent of the power of the provisions of Part IXA. The legislation authorized the setting of goals and targets, but not 'quotas'. The forty per cent provision appeared to be a stronger form of affirmative action than had previously been authorized under the Act for other EEO management plans. And it was clear that there were activist male teachers who were prepared to take court action immediately any affirmative action measure was brought in. It appeared safer for 'our' legislation to ask the Department to amend its own Act, as it had done previously in the case of Aboriginal teachers. This amendment, following a five-year exemption under the Anti-Discrimination Act, provided for absolute preference to be given to Aboriginal teachers in recruitment for an indefinite period. But from the point of view of the Department it would be a much harder row to hoe to convince the Cabinet of the need for affirmative action on behalf of women. (Aboriginal teachers, male and female, comprised 53 of the more than 46,000 teachers in 1988).

Another factor was the vagueness of the provision for a ten per cent merit slice, as it was termed colloquially. What positions would be covered by this provision, and how would they be selected? The Director took the view that the introduction of a system of promotion on merit should have a logic to it. For example, it would make sense to do this at the level of Principals, as the chief leaders in schools.

The possibility of resolving these differences was diminished by the souring of relations between the Office of the DEOPE and the Director-General. Each felt aggrieved. The Department considered that it had taken enormous steps toward meeting the requirements of the legislation, yet the Director appeared to give little credit for this and refused to approve the plan. The Director, who envisaged a reform to the promotions system that would remove seniority altogether, saw the forty per cent provision as a stop-gap measure that preserved some of the worst features of seniority. This was in a context where the DEOPE had succeeded in convincing other, equally tradition-bound branches of the public service such as the Police Force to progressively abandon seniority in favour of merit promotion. The situation was not improved when the Minister and the Director-General decided to launch the EEO Management Plan at a very public occasion without having received the approval of the DEOPE. She attended, but the atmosphere at the launch was icy.

In the middle of this stand-off, I was recruited by the Department to take up the newly created position of Leader of their EEO Unit. In effect I had been poached by the Department to act as a bridge or mediator between my former boss and current employer. The Director-General, the Director of Industrial Relations, the EEO Co-ordinator and myself commenced a year-long campaign to sell a revised version of the EEO strategies to the DEOPE, the Minister, and the Teaching Service itself. The Department proposed a three-part reform, which became known as the 'package'. Part One was the promotion of principals by comparative assessment. The system of placing principals in school according to their number on the seniority list was to be replaced by a system of recommendations and interviews, which gave rise to a merit list, where candidates were rated according to a series of criteria. The system of interviews was elaborate, organized in each of the ten regions, with the rating list then 'moderated' by a kind of supercommittee at the centre. But the net effect was to open the positions of principal to candidates who might have been assessed as eligible for promotion in the last one or two years, whereas under the old system, those taking positions had been waiting patiently on the list for up to fifteen years.

Part Two was the affirmative action for women teachers for forty per cent of promotions positions below the level of principal. The women on the relevant promotions list for each category of appointment were constituted as a subset of the seniority list, and of each ten positions, four´ (one, four, seven, ten) were 'first offered' to the most senior women. (This mechanism was designed to allay suspicions of favouritism among male teachers, some of whom had manipulated the old system for years to ensure promotion to the best located schools).

Part Three was the provision to remove the 'service undertaking' which had been a requirement for permanency under the system. EEO statistics had shown that many women had refused to sign the under-taking – which pledged their readiness to serve anywhere in the state – due to domestic responsibilities. To forfeit permanency meant also to forfeit the right to promotion, to superannuation, and to job security. The rationale of jettisoning this provision was that in practice the Department went to enormous trouble to accommodate the geographi-cal requirements of teachers. In any case the Education Commission Act empowered the Director-General to move teachers with or without their having signed a pledge. This measure would permit a significant number of temporary teachers, eighty per cent of them women, to become per-manent.

The package won Cabinet approval and was signed into law in May 1987. The story of the coalition forged to 'sell' the package is the story of the extraordinary alliance of femocrats and bureaucrats, each bringing to the campaign a particular and not necessarily shared set of objectives. The DEOPE wanted to reform the promotions system of the Education Department along the lines of other EEO reforms in the state, and to have her authority recognized by the Department, without weakening the legislation. The Director-General wanted to accommodate to the requirements of the EEO legislation without threatening the centralized control over the running of the schools that he saw as key to maintaining the standard of public education and the power of the centre as against the regions, the schools, and the local communities. The Director of Industrial Relations wanted a progressive reform that would not disrupt the smooth industrial relations he had achieved with the Teachers' Federation. And the EEO officers wanted to ensure that the reform to the promotions system benefitted women teachers in a concrete and measurable way.

The motives of the Minister are harder to summarize. The Minister for Education, Rodney Cavalier, was a complex character. A classicist and student of history, he was fanatical about watching and playing cricket, and notorious for his public animosity to feminism and feminists. In a battle within the Labor Party before the affirmative action to increase the number of women standing for Parliament and holding senior positions within the Party, Cavalier had resolutely opposed these measures, coining the term 'gender fascists' to refer to their proponents. He was thus an unlikely Minister to sympathize with, let alone preside over the introduction of, providing for affirmative action for women teachers.

But Cavalier had as staff members several feminists very committed to the longstanding campaign in New South Wales for women's educational opportunities. While Cavalier enjoyed mocking his feminist advisers, he was capable of grasping the importance of their advice on the need for female role models, for excellence in the leadership, and for flexibility in staffing. Among his more admirable qualities were a capacity to listen and absorb an argument, and the ability to change his mind, and his policies. He was a very tough player in the Caucus and in the Parliament, and committed, as were most of his colleagues, to winning. Once he made up his mind, he was unshakeable. This firmness turned out to be an enormous asset.

Cavalier presented the proposed reform to Cabinet, which referred it to a subcommittee where, some assumed, the measure would die. In fact the subcommittee, convened by the Minister of Health, duly invited the Minister to speak to his proposal. He, in turn, invited the team that had been 'selling' the package, namely, the Director of Industrial Relations, the Leader of the EEO, and the EEO Co-ordinator, to address the committee and to answer their questions. The Ministers present appeared to be sympathetic to reform. One mentioned the problem of 'dead wood', namely, people appointed as principals so far toward the end of their careers that they were in effect retiring on the job. None opposed the idea of taking some direct measure to ensure a greater representation of women in promotions positions.

We presented the statistics on the current distribution of women and their likely future distribution given the retirement and loss of seniority due to time out for child rearing. And we explained the forty per cent as a minimum figure that would begin to redress the balance. One of the Ministers posed the question that came up repeatedly: would it not be fairer simply to establish two lists, one of men, one of women, and take each name off the top of the lists in alternation? Whenever this question was asked, I would simply pause, until the questioner exclaimed, as this one did: 'Hang on, that's fifty per cent!' Nothing more needed to be said; the laughter in the room expressed relief that we were not asking for a majority share of the positions.

When the tea was brought in by a tea lady, the Chair of the committee remarked, looking embarrassed, that they had equal opportunity and there were also tea men on duty. I answered with a smile that there was no need for the Minister to be defensive. This produced a roar of laughter all around. The Director-General later told me that this was probably a turning point. At that level, he said, they are basing their decisions as much on who is bringing the proposals forward as on the content. My willingness to laugh reassured them that I and my team were not fanatics seeking the defeat of a Labor Government and they were willing to trust us.

The subcommittee approved the proposal, and then returned the matter to Cabinet. Weeks went by, with agonizing phone calls to the Premier's Department to find out if the measure had been put on the agenda. The fear was that the head of department who controlled the agenda would simply arrange for the measure to die through delay. Finally, we heard that it was on the agenda, and then that it had been passed. There was a last-minute attempt by the Labor Council to dissuade the Premier from approving the measure. But this failed, and the amendments to the legislation were officially gazetted in May, 1987, to take effect as of the staffing operation on 1 July 1987.

Soon after the measures came into effect, a very vocal group of right-wing male teachers began a campaign against the forty per cent. They gathered signatures in schools, pressured women teachers against accepting positions, and influenced some teachers to isolate and harass women who were to benefit from the measure. A public debate began in the press. There seemed to be general acceptance at least for the principle of what had been enacted. But the Liberal Party considered the forty per cent to be an excess caused by Labor Party ideology, and signalled very loudly that should they come to power, the forty per cent would have to go. Meanwhile, the projected figures of how many women teachers would actually benefit from the measure turned out to be low. The EEO research had indicated that forty per cent would be a high estimate, and that some women would reject the positions, either for reasons of geography, or out of reluctance to take a promotion not 'won on merit'. But of the fifty-one deputy principals' positions offered to women under the forty per cent measure all but one were taken up. The year-long debate about affirmative action, and the long years of campaigns on behalf of women teachers, had had their effect, and there was a generation of teachers who were happy to accept the measure of redress that had been won on their behalf.

The victory, however, was shortlived. On 19 March 1988 the Labor Party lost power to the Liberal–National Coalition. Within a week of winning the election, the new government announced that the forty per cent measure would be withdrawn. Privately the new Minister assured the Department of his support for EEO measures, but said that the government had been obliged to get rid of the forty per cent as they had made a very public campaign promise. At this writing the forty per cent provision has been withdrawn, the selection process using coparative assessment has been extended to the level of Deputy Principals, and the EEO Unit in the Department has been reduced from twenty-three officers to three. The future of the EEO programme in the New South Wales public service would appear to be in doubt under the Greiner regime.

Implications for Feminist Theory and Practice

The account I have given is a bare-bones narrative. I have left out chunks of the history as they are both painful to recall and politically unwise to make public. But some general remarks can be made on the basis of the tale as recounted here. The first is about the pull of institutional loyalties and socialization on women, and the impact of this upon ideals of behaviour governed by feminist solidarity. In becoming a femocrat one is inevitably drawn into the politics and the ethos of the organization for which one is working. This seems a truism, yet it is crucial to understand. The EEO officers in the Department of Education had two choices. If they gave their allegiance wholeheartedly to the organization then inevitably their behaviour and their decision-making favoured the interests of the organization, at the expense, therefore, of the ability really to offer inside information to femocrats located elsewhere (in DEOPE or in the Minister's office). If they gave their allegiance to DEOPE, then they were viewed with intense suspicion, and treated in effect as members of a fifth column, to whom delicate and sensitive matters of high policy could not be divulged. In effect, they were rendered powerless. The navigation of these shoals was a constant matter of judgement, and thus no interaction with one's 'sisters' inside or outside the organization was free of calculation. All transactions were subject to the same editing and caveats about confidentiality and deniability – 'You never heard this from me'. As with other bureaucratic transactions, communication among femocrats was carefully managed and the degree of trust was at best partial.

The second remark concerns forms of feminism. There was a continuing debate during the decade of EEO activism as to whether or not this was 'really' feminism. EEO and affirmative action were seen as imports from the US, and were therefore suspect. In addition, the structure of the EEO legislation placed it squarely within a tradition of liberal-democratic reform. To the extent that the emphasis was on reform to procedures such as selection criteria, it was seen as reformist, limited in scope, and having little to do with the needs of women as a group. The forty per cent affirmative action measure for women in the Department of Education tested this, as it was an out-and-out measure of redress specifically to women teachers. The reluctance of DEOPE initially to espouse it opened that office to a charge (unfair, in my judgement) of betraying feminism, or more broadly, never having been really feminist in the first place.

Thirdly, there is the issue of linking feminist aspirations to the fortunes of political parties and leaders. The EEO initiative in New South Wales was linked to Wran and to the power of the Labor Party. The fragility of this alliance is indicated by the outcome of the story. The Labor Party in New South Wales and nationally has committed itself in policy terms to a range of feminist objectives, from affirmative action to child care (although not to equal pay for work of comparable value), as a frank exercise in increasing its electoral margin. The women's movement in turn has taken advantage of this to claim its dues for women's issues. This is a risky fate for feminism. Yet what other path forward is there?

Finally, what kind of power do 'femocrats' have? In an early discussion with my boss at the Department of Education, he remarked that in his first year as Director of Industrial Relations he had made perhaps hundreds of phone calls to his colleagues, the Regional Directors of Education (RDEs), with requests for them to take action of some kind. Often they were most reluctant to comply. Technically my boss was exactly at the same bureaucratic level as the RDEs. Yet it was known that he was close to the Director-General, and often was phoning at the D-G's request. In only one case during the year had he had to phrase the phone call more strongly than saying 'Look, Ralph, I wonder if you'd mind doing X?'

This style of wielding power was very far indeed from that to which I was accustomed in the Office of DEOPE, where, even with the derived power of the Premier behind us, we wrote stern letter upon stern letter before getting action. Was this a function of the gender difference? Or the bureaucratic response to the outside change agent versus the inside keeper of the rules? It ran through my mind that each male bureaucrat, whatever his style or his location in the hierarchy, had a tradition of ten thousand years of bureaucratic power behind him, stretching back to Babylon. The senior women groped for an appropriate style, eschewing a nurturing role for fear of being treated as a mother, but unable really to use the male style (especially the Wran male style) of exerting authority through rage, as this evoked a particularly deadly form of rage in return.

What was effective, in my experience, was a form of alliance between femocrats and traditional bureaucrats, where our interests ran parallel.

In this context one's authority as a feminist expert was recognized, and even sought: one's gender was legitimate. Speaking as an advocate for women, arguments had weight. In a curious way the power of femocrats stemmed from their explicit orientation and role. This provided some freedom to manoeuvre. But the power thus wielded was limited. It was hedged about by the priorities of the organization as a whole, and the degree to which one's own feminist projects could be fitted in. The struggle was always to extend the areas within which one's gender experience and expertise was recognized by the men who continued, overall, to set the agenda.

By way of conclusion, on some questions in the context of the EEO experiment in New South Wales, there has been a widespread expression of disillusionment with femocrats. What is our expectation of women, and especially feminists, with a degree of power? Why does the political among women get so personal? In considering this question, I found myself thinking back to the experience of consciousness-raising, and to some of the comments by Adrienne Rich about the difficulties of mother–daughter relationships in the generation of feminists growing up in the 1940s. At least among white feminists there was an experience of finding within feminism relationships among women that were free of the conflicts and ambivalence that had characterized those among women within the family and in friendships. Feminism seemed to promise a world of nurturance and acceptance, a redress of the hurts suffered by women at each others' hands in an era when female solidarity was impossible culturally. The entry of women into positions of significant power, even when this is accompanied by a feminist programme and personal commitment, has meant that relations among women of this kind cannot, structurally speaking, partake of the quality of nurturance and mutual acceptance that was part of the feminist utopia. Is this why conflicts among femocrats, or other professional feminists such as Women's Studies scholars or feminist politicians, have such a painful quality?

The path followed by Australian feminists has been reliant upon an alliance with the Labor Party, and on a decision to take up positions within state and federal bureaucracies, in order to further the interests of women using the power of the state. This strategy relies upon a willingness to accept the constraints of what is politically expedient, that is, saleable to the electorate and to the Party. Is this an acceptable model? Is it even a feasible model? In the US, the Democratic Party seems an unreliable ally for women. But there are many avenues for feminist interventions at local and state levels. In the late 1980s it seems futile to argue that feminists should not where possible be seeking to use the political process to further our ends.

Lastly, has gender theory become a kind of feminist Tower of Babel? The deconstructionists seem barely able to speak to the empiricists, and vice versa. To some extent this is a result of success, and of specialization: feminists have infiltrated the academy, and as moles within the disciplines are shaping, and being shaped by, the discourses that reign in each. The experience of feminist interventions in what we refer to as the real world, as filtered through the lenses of the various disciplines, gets fragmented and distorted. Feminism becomes a series of disparate phenomena: women as political leaders or voters in political science data; women as bearers of difference in literary theory: women as the embodiment of an alternative morality in psychology; and feminism as epistemology in philosophy.

Meanwhile a generation of feminists has been reshaping the meaning of gender through their lived experience as political actors in a wide range of different settings. I have the persistent impression that theory lags radically behind practice, and that the experience of these women – the 'first woman' fireperson, union president, and so on – provides data for a reconsideration of a lot of what has been said in the first round of theorizing about gender difference, and its relation to organizational structures, socialization, and work experience. This chapter has been an attempt to contribute some experiential data to the investigation. I imagine that much more of this kind of work is needed to rethink our theoretical framework about the relationship of women – and particularly of feminist women – to power.

8

Government Action Against Employment Discrimination

Chris Ronalds

The Affirmative Action (Equal Employment Opportunity for Women) Act became legislation in Australia in 1986. Its significance was that it was the first legislative attempt to require private sector companies to institute affirmative action programmes for women. The final title of the Act, containing both affirmative action and equal employment opportunity (EEO), reflected a number of the conflicts and compromises that had occurred prior to its Parliamentary passage.

The legislation was the result of demands over ten years from the women's movement that governments respond to inequalities in the workforce by making discrimination against women unlawful and by requiring employers to develop programmes addressed specifically to the employment needs of women. Feminists had, since the early 1970s, been involved actively in the political process at both a state and federal level, making demands on governments to address a particular issue. One of the primary and continuing focuses was in the area of employment, and this covered access to jobs and promotions, equal pay, provision of child care and links between education and employment opportunities.

The social reform climate of the federal Whitlam Labor government from 1973 raised expectations among previously ignored or disenfranchized groups, such as women and Aborigines, that reform through government action was not only theoretically possible but was a practical and feasible option. The Whitlam government's recognition of the United Nations' proposal for International Women's Year, by the provision of funds for women's organizations and individual women's activities during 1974, encouraged that view.[1]

Late in 1974 the Prime Minister wrote to Federal Ministers and State

Premiers outlining the type of programmes which would be in line with
the overall objectives of the Year and which would improve the status of
women. Generally he asked that Ministers and Premiers ensure the
integration of women in society by emphasizing their responsibility and
role in economic, social and cultural development and called for the
removal of discrimination against women and promotion of equality of
opportunity between women and men.[2]

Though by the early 1970s women were a third of all workers, job
segregation did not decrease.[3] The vast majority of women were
employed in eight occupational classifications: clerk, saleswoman, typist,
stenographer, domestic worker, process worker, nurse and teacher.[4]
There were unequal pay rates and women were denied access to a
number of skilled, better-paid positions. Public campaigns over the
refusal to allow women to be tram drivers in Melbourne, or bus and
train drivers in Sydney, and the right of married women to work in
certain isolated mining towns highlighted the many different barriers
women continued to face in the workforce.

In 1974 and 1975, the women's movement increased its pressure for
legislation to prevent employers from denying women jobs or promotions on the basis of their sex. The federal government introduced legislation to make racial discrimination unlawful in 1974. A United Nations
Convention provided the necessary constitutional basis for this legislation, but at that time there was no equivalent convention for women.
In mid 1975, the federal Labor government proposed a form of national
anti-discrimination legislation to cover women, but it was removed from
office before this could be achieved.

Unlike the limitations facing a federal government, there were no
constitutional or legal limitations on the actions of state governments, so
the women's movement transferred its focus to them. One state passed
legislation proscribing sex and marital discrimination in employment and
other areas, such as education, accommodation, and access to goods and
services, in 1975. Two other state governments followed in 1977.[5] The
conservative federal government made several announcements of its
intention to bring a minor form of sex discrimination legislation to cover
the territories it administered, but not the rest of the country; but no
legislation was introduced.

Sex Discrimination Bill 1981

Demands for federal legislation to cover all women in Australia
continued, as three conservative state governments had made it clear
that they saw no necessity for such legislation. The National Women's

Advisory Council held a major national conference on anti-discrimination legislation in May 1979, which recommended to the federal government that such legislation should be immediately introduced to cover the Australian Capital Territory and federal government employment.[6] There was considerable opposition in the conservative government as the ultra-conservative rurally based minor coalition party presented the proposal as an attack on the family and as undermining the role of women who did not work outside the home.

By 1980, the federal Labor Party was developing new policies to revitalize the party after the substantial electoral defeats of 1975 and 1977. Women's issues and policies directed towards eliminating the perceived inequalities of women became a priority. The Opposition spokeswoman on status of women issues, Senator Susan Ryan, used her position to raise the multiple issues relating to the status of women and the actions needed to eliminate discrimination.

In December 1981, she introduced a private member's Bill, the Sex Discrimination Bill 1981, and committed a future Labor government to passing similar legislation. The Bill covered the definitions and areas to eliminate discrimination on the grounds of sex and marital status and followed the pattern of existing state legislation. However, it went further than the state legislation and incorporated provisions to require both private and public sector employers to introduce affirmative action programmes for women. The proposed sanction against private sector employers for failing or refusing to follow the legislation was that any contract with the federal government worth more than $50,000 could be cancelled, terminated or suspended. The United Nations Convention on the Elimination of All Forms of Discrimination Against Women was to be its major constitutional plank.

While there was some media and business interest in the Bill its contents were not seriously or thoughtfully debated publicly. Even if it had been passed by the Senate, the Bill would not have passed in the House of Representatives, as the conservative government opposed the use of international conventions as the basis for national legislation. In the political climate of 1981 and 1982, the prospect of the early return of a national Labor government was not seriously considered by most sections of the media or the business community.

Sex Discrimination Bill 1983

The seemingly unimaginable occurred in May 1983 with the election of a national Labor government, led by Prime Minister Bob Hawke. Susan Ryan was appointed Minister of Education and Minister Assisting the

Prime Minister on the Status of Women. One of the early bureaucratic moves of the new government was to reinstate the Office of the Status of Women to the prime central bureaucratic department (Prime Minister and Cabinet) from the most minor status department (Home Affairs), where it had been moved by the conservative government. Anne Summers, a feminist academic and journalist, was appointed as its head. One of the first major pieces of legislation introduced, in June 1983, was the Sex Discrimination Bill. This was represented as 'the initial step towards the fulfilment of the government's major election commitment to women'.[7]

The Bill proposed to make discrimination on the grounds of sex, marital status and pregnancy unlawful in employment, education, accommodation, provision of goods, services and facilities, the disposal of land, the activities of clubs and the administration of Commonwealth laws and programmes. It was the first Australian anti-discrimination legislation to address specifically the issue of sexual harassment, defining the concept and making it unlawful in the workplace and in educational institutions. The position of Sex Discrimination Commissioner was created to administer the legislation and to receive and conciliate complaints; the Human Rights Commission had the power to conduct quasi-judicial inquiries where conciliation was unsuccessful. Decisions of the Commission were made enforceable in the Federal Court. The Bill contained two further important initiatives. Provision was made for representative (or class) actions, enabling one or several complainants to represent a larger group where there were similar issues of law of fact.[8] The Australian Council of Trade Unions demanded that individual trade unions be given the right to lodge complaints on behalf of their members and the government agreed. It was anticipated that the combination of trade union complainants and representative actions would provide a powerful tool for women in eliminating discrimination in the workplace.[9]

The conservative parties, still reeling from the election loss, saw the 'Sex Bill', as it unfortunately became known, as a major focus to attack the new 'socialist' government. They united with some right-wing women's 'pro-family' and church organizations to lead a public debate which misrepresented and distorted the aim and content of the Bill. The legislation was represented as a major attack on the family. Mrs Doug Anthony, the wife of the leader of the rural National Party took a high profile public role in opposing the Bill. She argued:

> What all women long for is equality of personal worth, which is not something you can legislate for. They want to be listened to, recognized, and valued for their talents whatever they do have, but this bill makes it impossible for a housewife to value herself. She feels there is a subtle message in the bill which

tells her she is wrong to stay in the home.... The breakdown of the family unit would only be encouraged by legislation that made mothers and housewives feel inadequate.[10]

An organization called 'Women for the Family' organized a rally outside Parliament House during the debate on the Bill, and advertised in all major newspapers for people to come to Canberra to 'Stop Ryan! Australia's feminist dictator'.[11] The advertisement called for a stop to Ryan's 'ruthless juggernaut', 'Anti-female-Sex Bill', and 'Anti-Family UN Convention'.

The Opposition Coalition split, with some members of the Liberal Party strongly supporting the Bill and rejecting the assertions being advanced by National Party members, including the leader, and by other public opponents of the Bill.[12] The government accepted some minor amendments, mainly relating to the employment practices of religious schools, but the major content remained unchanged. The Opposition had a conscience vote on the legislation, with a number of Liberal members of both Houses voting on opposite sides. The Bill was passed in March 1984 and became operative in August 1984.

Green Paper on Affirmative Action for Women

When the Minister introduced the Sex Discrimination Bill, she noted that the provisions covering affirmative action which had been in her private member's Bill were not included:

> The Government will issue a green paper setting out options for further legislation providing for the introduction and implementation of affirmative action programmes in employment. Recognizing the need for employers, employees, unions and the community generally to be better informed, the Government has decided that it is more appropriate to generate public discussion and understanding of its proposals and to have wide ranging consultations in advance of the introduction of legislation.[13]

Some women's organizations saw the government's refusal to legislate immediately on affirmative action as a backdown and as a compromise to the business sector. There was some opposition within the government to affirmative action, particularly by ministers who were working closely with business representatives. The concept of a green paper to advance discussion, and reduce opposition, was seen by supporters of affirmative action within the government and the bureaucracy as the only feasible means of furthering the possibility of legislation. As the debate on the Sex Discrimination Bill raged, it was realized that the inclusion of affirmative action at that stage could have led to the entire proposal being lost because of the ill-informed nature of the debate. The government decided that the green paper should not be released until the Sex Discrimination Act was passed by the Parliament and the community concerns stirred up by opponents to the legislation had subsided.

There was a recognition in the government and the women's movement that anti-discrimination legislation by itself would not be sufficient to break down the rigid sex segregation that operated in the Australian workforce. As the legislation requires individuals or groups to initiate an action through the confidential complaint process, the result may benefit only that individual or group of individuals rather than the whole workforce or others in the same or similar occupations.

The Green Paper, *Affirmative Action for Women,* contained several key proposals for community debate.[14] The major proposal was for legislation to cover the private sector, with some tentative views on size of employers to be covered, minimum legislative requirements and the timetable for implementation.[15] The Green Paper defined affirmative action as:

> A systematic means, determined by the employer in consultation with senior management, employees and unions of achieving equal employment opportunity for women. Affirmative action is compatible with appointment and promotion on the basis of merit, skills and qualifications. It does not mean women will be given preference over better qualified men. It does mean men may expect to face stiffer competition for jobs. This is not discrimination.[16]

At the time of its release, two other elements of the policy were announced. The Prime Minister obtained the co-operation of the chief executives of twenty-eight Australian major private sector companies and three higher education institutions to participate in a twelve-month voluntary pilot programme to test the principles of affirmative action as they were to apply practically in the workforce, and particularly the right-step programme detailed in the *Affirmative Action Implementation Manual.*[17] The companies covered all major occupational classifications and products or industries and were in major cities, large rural areas and small country towns.

While a minority of women's organizations criticized the government for not immediately implementing legislation and for delay in fulfilling an election commitment, there was widespread support for the pilot programme across business, trade unions and most women's organizations.

The government established the Affirmative Action Resource Unit, within the Office of the Status of Women. The Unit was mainly staffed with women from the private sector, on twelve months' secondment, and provided detailed assistance and advice to the pilot programme participants. The Unit also provided advice to the government, and undertook many public speaking engagements to explain the programme and the aims, objectives and content of affirmative action to seminars attended by business representatives, trade union organizers, women's organizations and other organizations and individuals.

The second element, a Working Party on Affirmative Action Legislation, was established, with the usual tripartite members of government, business and trade unions. In an important break with the long tradition of such arrangements, women representatives were included. Management of higher education institutions and, in a late compromise, a member of the Opposition were included also. The trade union movement nominated two women as their representatives, Senator Susan Ryan chaired the meetings, and the business and higher education representatives were men.

The Working Party met during the course of the pilot programme, and after nine months, they had a one-day meeting with the pilot companies and institutions so they could present their views on the progress and limitations of the voluntary programme.[18] In September 1985, the Working Party released its *Report*,[19] which recommended that there be legislation covering all private sector companies with more than eight steps for an affirmative action programme which the Working Party supported, and recommended the establishment of a separate statutory authority to administer the legislation and the nature of employers' reports which were to be provided to that agency. The only sanction against employers for failing to report, or report adequately, on the content and progress of their programme would be named in Parliament. The legislation eventually passed mirrored the Working Party's recommendations.

The views of each member organization of the Working Party, listed in the *Report*, clearly demonstrated that the recommendations were reached by consensus with the women's organizations and trade union movement trading their higher demands and expectations to reach a legislative compromise against the opposition of business and the conservative parties to the notion of legislated affirmative action programmes. The ACTU considered that all employers should be covered and that sanctions and penalties should apply where there was non-compliance. The National Women's Consultative Council strongly supported the legislative proposals, but criticized the coverage and called for effective sanctions and an earlier starting date.[20]

Some women's organizations criticized the legislative proposals as being weak and a 'sell out' to business, mainly because they felt that the single sanction of being named in a report to Parliament was a weak and ineffective penalty for companies who refused to co-operate in implementing the legislation. They argued that the government was again sacrificing the interests of workers, and this time women workers, to the interests of business. Many women's organizations, particularly those representing middle-class women, strongly supported the legislation.

Business representatives argued that being named in Parliament was a powerful tool, especially as the concepts of EEO and affirmative action were now so widely accepted and supported in the business community and the economic benefits of such programmes were now recognized. This argument would seem to hold more weight for large corporations which promote themselves as model corporate citizens. It is too early to tell whether smaller companies will feel bound by the same business ethic and effectively implement affirmative action, particularly as there are some on-costs that they need to absorb before any real economic benefit will accrue. Also, it is too early to judge whether the business rhetoric of strong support for the issues of affirmative action and EEO are translated into meaningful programmes that actually break down the barriers currently operating to keep women in a limited range of occupations and at the lower end of promotion and pay scales.

The business community endeavoured to undermine the proposals contained in the *Report* in a late move, by establishing a Council for Equal Employment Opportunity which would promote EEO in the business sector on a voluntary basis. They strongly opposed legislation, and pushed for an extension and expansion of the voluntary programme.[21] The business sector opposed the use of the term 'affirmative action', on the ground that it had a 'bad reputation' because of programmes and court cases in the US, and that the term 'EEO' was more acceptable. The government refused to drop the term, and presented it as the means to achieve the long-term goal of EEO.

The business sector had underestimated the government's commitment to legislation. To some extent, this was not surprising. By late 1985, The Hawke Labor government had gained a reputation for pandering to the interests of 'big business' over the interests of their traditional constituency, and a number of government proposals had been dropped or watered down after business opposition. The government prided itself on the consensus model of tripartite negotiations on issues such as tax reform. However, it had introduced some reforms which were strongly opposed by the business sector and affirmative action became another.

The unanimous endorsement by the Working Party of the recommendations considerably strengthened the government's hand, despite the considerable reservations of the various member organizations. The Prime Minister had been, and continued to be, a strong and public supporter of affirmative action and Susan Ryan was a high profile proponent of the principles and aims of the legislation. The Cabinet accepted the recommendations for legislation. There was some opposition within the government that there would be a business backlash, but this was overridden by concerns that affirmative action legislation was by then seen as a long-standing commitment to women workers and that any moves to further delay or avoid its introduction would cause a significant backlash from women Labor supporters as well as from many sections of the trade union movement.

There was some ministerial opposition to the expenditure of government funds on staffing and resourcing an agency during a period of government expenditure restraint. They were of the opinion that such programmes were a waste of public resources, and refused to recognize the equity and efficiency principles on which the programme was based.

Affirmative Action Act

The legislation was introduced in early 1986 by the Prime Minister, the first and only Bill he has ever introduced into Parliament.[22] The tenor of public debate was considerably more reasoned and informed than the debate over the Sex Discrimination Bill, mainly because of the considerable media exposure to the principles of affirmative action over the previous two years and the by then muted business opposition.

The emerging 'New Right' were the main opponents of the legislation and they sought to confuse the public debate by insisting that the legislation would require the introduction of quotas. This would mean that employers would be forced to employ or promote unqualified or under-qualified women over properly qualified men. They misrepresented the programmes being conducted in the US, and used scare tactics to frighten women into believing that the legislation would undermine their real work potential. They claimed that the legislation would destroy the principle of merit, and sex would be the sole or major determining factor in all employment decisions. While they generated considerable support during the Parliamentary debate from the National Party, the majority of the Liberal Party rejected their propositions. Their long-term effect has been minimal and there is still considerable broad support within business for the legislation, which is now accepted as being reasonable and not onerous on large companies in particular.

The Act sets out the broad framework for affirmative action

programmes, through an eight-step programme, and details the cover-age of employers and establishes the statutory agency to monitor the implementation of the legislation.[23] One step in the affirmative action programme is the requirement for consultation with trade unions, which has caused continuing employer concern and resistance. It is really a form of industrial democracy, which does not have widespread support or practice in the Australian business community. The union movement opposed the consultation with employees outside of the union structure; but the government considered that as there were many women workers who were non-unionized and some workplaces where there was no union representation, or weak representation, if this was not included then women would still be denied the access that the legislation was endeavouring to create for them.

The setting of objectives and forward estimates, particularly the latter, is where the most serious and long-term opposition to the actual content of the legislation is arising. Forward estimates are defined in the Act as meaning a

> quantitative measure or aim, which may be expressed in numerical terms, designed to achieve equality of opportunity for women in employment matters, being a measure of aim that can reasonably be implemented by the relevant employer within a specified time.

This continues to be the most controversial aspect of the Act, as, while the debate about the supposed hidden agenda of quotas has largely subsided, many employers are resisting the notion of putting numbers or percentages on such matters as recruitment, promotion or training targets for women. This is despite the fact that they put numbers and percentages on all usual business objectives such as profit margins, profit increases and production levels.

The public report is the first time that such detailed information on the employment profile and practices of private sector companies will be available publicly, and any person or organisation has a statutory right to have a copy made available by the Agency. The confidential report was a concession to the business sector, as the government accepted their argument that business secrets such as proposals for expansion or reduc-tion should not be exposed to competitors in the affirmative action programme.

Potential or Affirmative Action Legislation

Affirmative action and EEO have always been perceived, by their supporters and the government, as only one component of the campaign to eliminate discrimination against women in the workforce and to promote EEO for women. However, it has been promoted as a major tool and was the primary government action for several years. The legislation itself is more far-reaching in its coverage and in programme content than any equivalent overseas legislation.

The primary focus is on employers recognizing and acting on the perceived inequalities for women, after they have undertaken the basic research through analysis of employment statistics and formal and informal policies and practices. Therefore, the focus of each individual employer's programme appears to be completely within their control and, on the face of it, there is little Affirmative Action Agency control. In reality, there are industry profiles or 'norms' against which to measure the progress of individual employers, which are based on employment data collected in the census and in national industry surveys. Also, other individual employers engaged in the same or a similar business or enterprise lodge reports on their activities and so a 'norm' can be established from these to ascertain an expected or anticipated level of programme action.

The programme is based on a certain amount of voluntary goodwill and co-operation from employers. While the government has some control over higher education institutions, as the major funder, it does not have the same control over business. The business community's representatives gave a commitment that co-operation would be forthcoming and would continue and the government has indicated that if this is not the case, it is prepared to re-examine the available sanctions. Presumably, if there was large-scale avoidance of the legislation or resistance to lodging any reports or reports that contained the required information, the government would be forced to devise other forms of more effective sanctions. At this early stage, there is no indication that there is any such widespread resistance or subversive intentions.

Special educational programmes to broaden career choices for young women continue, aimed at young women, teachers, parents and the community. The previous media fascination with the one young woman working as a car mechanic or welding apprentice has decreased as there are a small, but increasing, number of women entering such jobs.

Some sections of the women's movement continue to argue that women, and women's organizations, have been co-opted by government into accepting affirmative action as a major panacea for existing inequalities in the workplace. They argue that the only women who are benefitting and will continue to benefit from such programmes are middle-class, tertiary-educated women who would have 'made it' through the promotion system anyway. The contention is that the majority of women workers, in low-classified and low-paid jobs, will not be part of the programme as they are unable to articulate their demands. Similarly, unemployed women who are outside any formal employment structure cannot and will not benefit as they are not able to be consulted about their needs or requirements.

These arguments confuse the role of affirmative action, and assign it a broader objective than could possibly be achieved or was ever intended. Affirmative action has resulted in some examination of major employment concerns such as barriers preventing keyboard operators from moving into other jobs, the limitations imposed through rigid and unnecessary requirements of certain formal qualifications to gain access to particular jobs, training or transfer. The matters being addressed through the programme will continue to develop, although the recognition and dismantling of some barriers will be a long, slow process requiring significant restructuring of some work practices and job classifications and designs.

Those in support of affirmative action have never suggested that it would be the sole 'cure' for the disadvantage and discrimination which women confront in the workforce. However, it can, and is, assisting in the analysis and dismantling of the barriers which deny women full participation. It has also placed women's employment back on the Australian political agenda, from which it had been displaced during the late 1970s and early 1980s. The legislation itself demonstrates that traditional notions of women's role in the workforce are not acceptable by the majority of people. It is now recognized that there are structural barriers created and maintained by managers which have prevented or inhibited the potential and possible contribution of women to the workforce, and to the economy as a whole.

Appendix: Affirmative Action (Equal Employment Opportunity for Women) Act 1986

Coverage: The Act requires all private sector employers with a hundred or more employees and all universities and colleges of advanced education to develop and implement affirmative action programmes for women. The legislation is being phased in over three years, with each group of employers (depending on their size) given twelve months to prepare their first reports. The last group, employers with between 100 and 499 employers, will be covered from 1 February 1989 with reports due in 1990.

Programme contents: An affirmative action programme is required to cover the following eight steps:

1. issuing a policy statement
2. appointing appropriate staff
3. consulting with trade unions
4. consulting with employees
5. analysing the employment profile, including statistics
6. analysing the employment policies and practices
7. setting objectives and forward estimates
8. monitoring and evaluation

Reporting: All employers are required to lodge two reports with the Affirmative Action Agency. The public report contains the employment profile, through statistics, of all employees by sex and job undertaken or occupational classification and an outline of the processes undertaken to implement the programme. The confidential report contains the detailed analysis of the programme.

Sanctions: The only formal sanction against an employer for failing to lodge one or either report or for failing to provide further information where a report does not meet the minimum legislative requirements is for the Director of Affirmative Action to report to the appropriate Minister. The Minister is required to lodge that report in Parliament. As the Act has only been in operation for a short period, it is too early to judge the impact of its operations, and the power to name has not yet been used.

Administrative agency: The legislation establishes the position of Director of Affirmative Action, and she has a staff of approximately twenty to assist her in the administration of the legislation. Some of the staff are designated to assist companies and institutions in the development of their affirmative action programmes; one person works with trade unions in their response (or lack of response) to the requirements of the legislation and employer demands, and some deal with the analysis and evaluation of employers' reports and the preparation of public education material.

Notes

1. The Australian National Advisory Committee for International Women's Year was appointed in September 1974 and its aims and objectives were focused in three major

areas: change of attitude, areas of discrimination and creative aspects. The Committee stated: 'There can be no doubt that there was widespread recognition throughout the Australian community of the fact that 1975 was International Women's Year' (*Report*, p. 19). There was considerable adverse reaction in the media and a backlash occurred, particularly during the Women and Politics Conference held in Canberra in September 1975.

2. Australian National Advisory Council on International Women's Year, *Report*, pp. 152–3.

3. The number of women in the workforce more than doubled from 1947 to 1973, compared with a fifty per cent increase for men, see Ryan and Conlon, p. 174.

4. 'A survey taken in February 1972 showed that 2 per cent of all female wage earners were in managerial, executive and administrative positions, compared with 6 per cent of males'. Ryan and Conlon, p. 174.

5. The South Australian Labor government passed the Sex Discrimination Act in 1975, and the New South Wales Labor government and the Victorian Liberal government passed similar legislation in 1977. All three Acts followed the model of the English Sex Discrimination Act 1975 in the definitions of unlawful discrimination and the areas covered.

6. National Women's Advisory Council, First Annual Report, p. 50.

7. Senator Susan Ryan, Second Reading Speech to the Sex Discrimination Bill, 2 June 1983.

8. Class actions had not been operative in Australia, and there was considerable business opposition to the concept as understood by the experience in the US. The terms of the legislation were based on the New South Wales Anti-Discrimination Act 1977, which in turn had adapted the principles established in US legislation. The important difference was that in Australia it is not possible for lawyers to defer their costs and then receive a set percentage of any damages awarded at the successful completion of an action, as occurs in the US.

9. In fact, this has not occurred; there has been little use made of the legislation by trade unions in the first four years of its operation and there have been no major representative actions. One action under the New South Wales Act has been fought by a group of women, many of whom are migrants, against a subsidiary of Australia's biggest company, BHP, on access to jobs and promotions in a steel mill in Wollongong. The women have won a major appeal and the damages are estimated to be several million dollars.

10. 'Why Mrs Doug Anthony is Against the Sex Bill: Is it Wrong to Stay at home?', *Sydney Morning Herald*, 16 September 1983.

11. See illustration, *Sydney Morning Herald*, 8 October 1983.

12. 'Macphee Attacks Nationals over Sex Bill', *The Australian*, 19 September 1983; 'Equality Bill Divides Liberals', *The Australian*, 21 September 1983; 'Macphee's Talking like a Feminist – and Losing', *Sydney Morning Herald*, 23 September 1983.

13. Senator Susan Ryan, Second Reading Speech to the Sex Discrimination Bill 1983, 2 June 1983.

14. Department of the Prime Minister and Cabinet, *Affirmative Action for Women*, AGPS, May 1984. The government separated public and private sector employment, and passed amendments to the Public Service Act in mid 1984 which required all federal government departments to have an EEO programme for women, Aboriginal and Torres Strait Island people, migrants whose first language is not English, and people who are physically or mentally disabled. The programme involved a six-stage approach, similar in design and intent to the eventual private sector legislation.

15. *Affirmative Action for Women*, pp. 53–4.

16. Green Paper, vol. 1, p. 3.

17. Office of the Status of Women, Department of the Prime Minister and Cabinet, AGPS, 1984.

18. Affirmative Action Resource Unit, *Affirmative Action for Women: A Progress Report on Pilot Program*, AGPS, May 1985, contained much of the material present during the case study day and was published to enable further debate on affirmative action.

19. AGPS (Australian Government Printing Service), 1985.

20. Working Party, *Report*, p. 23, p. 26.

21. The Confederation of Australian Industry, represented on the Working Party and one of the two major employer representatives, stated that: 'Affirmative action legislation is unnecessary, undesirable, will add to employers' costs and will have counter-productive effects. The Government should not introduce such legislation but should leave the field to voluntary programs' (Working Party *Report*, p. 25). The other employer representative, the Business Council of Australia, stated that it was 'concerned that superimposing compulsory programs onto this voluntary activity will have a negative effect on the attitude of corporate managers and risks a serious backlash against these initiatives and the cause of women ... The Business Council ... strongly opposes the view that legislation is either appropriate or necessary to achieve Government's objectives of equal employment opportunity for women. This view is shared by the whole business community (and, indeed, many in Government) and the Council believes there would not be widespread community support for the creation of a new agency ... it is disappointing that the proponents of legislation are not prepared to reconsider their approach in the light of enlightened self-regulation by the business sector' (Working Party *Report*, p. 25).

22. Traditionally, Prime Ministers only introduce legislation which proclaims that the nation is at war. Some pundits suggested that this was a form of war, and so it was proper that he should do so.

23. For further details on the content of the legislation, see the Appendix to this chapter.

9

Women in Trade Unions in Australia

Anna Booth and Linda Rubenstein

Women make up one third of all trade unionists in Australia and 48 per cent of women are in the paid workforce. Women are increasingly active participants in their unions at all levels and over recent years have had significant success in placing feminist issues within the mainstream of the trade union movement. This chapter analyses the emergence of women as a force in Australian trade unionism and the strategies employed to achieve results.

For much of their history Australian unions were branches of their British equivalents. It was not until the 1960s that the Amalgamated Engineering Union (now the Amalgamated Metal Workers' Union) finally cut its ties to the 'motherland'. Their character also derived from the specific nature of the country. The strong Australian Workers' Union had its roots in the pastoral industry (particularly sheep shearers); the maritime and land transport, mining and building unions were almost exclusively male and, together with the traditionally militant craft unions, provided the movement's industrial and political leadership.

At the first Inter-colonial Trades Union Conference (later to be the Australian Council of Trade Unions – ACTU) in 1897, the major concern was to protect jobs and employment standards through industry protection (to prevent the importation of cheaper goods), immigration control (to prevent cheap labour, particularly from Asia) and conciliation and arbitration to prevent labour 'sweating' and to set fair wages and conditions. It was the Melbourne Tailoresses' strike in 1882 against 'sweating' which resulted in the establishment of a Wages Board to set standards and prevent gross exploitation.

The Australian workforce has had a high level of union membership and, through affiliation to the Australian Labor Party, (ALP), a significant political presence. The ALP was formed by the trade unions and its union affiliates hold a majority of votes for conference and executive delegates. The unions which are affiliated to the ALP tend to be blue collar with a traditional male leadership which is then reflected in the various party bodies. The ALP's adoption of an Affirmative Action policy in most internal elections has put some pressure on the unions to nominate female delegates in recent years.

Since the famous 'Harvester' decision in 1907 the centralized wage fixing system, based on the Conciliation and Arbitration Commission, provided for a 'family wage', a minimum which would allow a man to provide for a dependent wife and family. This notion legitimized paying women half to three-quarters of the male wage. While the trade union movement had a policy commitment to equal pay for women ('one rate for the job') this was as much motivated by a fear of men's jobs being taken by cheaper female labour as by notions of equality. The chief priority was to ensure that women received equal pay in industries where men also worked, to prevent undercutting.

During the Second World War unions insisted that women entering industries or occupations which had previously employed only men (such as metal and other trades, munitions, aircraft, tram conductors) receive 'male' rates of pay. They presumed that once male labour was available, women would not then be kept on. There was less concern with equal pay in jobs in which few men were employed, and an under-valuing of female-dominated occupations with comparable skills.

Since the 1930s there has been a strong left influence, particularly in the industrially strong unions led by officials who were members of, or close to, the Communist Party of Australia (CPA) and who generally worked in alliance with left members of the ALP. This was reflected in industrial militancy around wages and in policies opposing capitalism and the arbitration system (the 'bosses' court') and in campaigns on international issues such as peace, anti-colonialism, support of the USSR and various revolutionary movements. Although members of these unions were overwhelmingly male, the officials expressed a politi-cal commitment to equal rights and, through the CPA, had links with progressive women's organizations such as the Union of Australian Women (UAW) and the Council of Action for Equal Pay (CAEP). The UAW was formed in 1946 (originally named the New Housewives Association and re-named in 1950) by communist women some of whom had been involved as auxiliaries in the miners' and other male unions. The CAEP was established in 1937 following a conference called by the Clerks' Union. The CAEP argued vigorously not only for equal pay but for the right of women to economic independence. In some cases CAEP activists were employed in left-wing union offices, represented the unions in meetings on women's issues, and promoted women's issues in their own union.

By the late sixties there had been marked changes in the structure of female employment and trade union participation. This coincided and was clearly linked with the emergence of a women's liberation movement, and reflected similar developments throughout the industrialized world. Women's workforce participation increased from 25 per cent in 1947 to 36 per cent in 1966 and 48 per cent in 1986. Much of this is due to the growth of the clerical and services sectors and the rapid increase of part-time employment encouraging the mothers of young children into the workforce. Blue-collar unions, particularly, have been concerned that the growth in part-time work would undermine opportunities for full-time employment. In the service industries and the public sector, unions have negotiated agreements for 'permanent' part-time work giving equal pro-rata benefits. The big growth in female membership has resulted from increased unionization in the public sector, in professions such as nursing and social work, and from 'closed shop' agreements in service industries such as retail, banking and insurance.

Five parallel developments formed the springboard for women's issues to be taken into the mainstream of the trade union movement. First, the increase in female labour force participation. Second, the restructuring of the Australian economy towards female-dominated industries. Third, the growing unionization in the public sector and in white collar and service industries. Fourth, increased militancy and an identification of these unions with the broad trade union movement. This resulted from the general radical climate of the 1960s and 1970s and was reflected in the mergers of the ACTU with the Australian Council of Salaried and Professional Associations (ACSPA) in 1979, the Council of Australian Government Employee Organizations (CAGEO) in 1981 and the state public service associations in 1985. Teachers, nurses, public servants and insurance workers, with many feminist activists, were thus brought into the ACTU structure. Fifth, the emergence of the women's liberation movement brought many feminists into these industries and unions. At the same time a number of left women who were involved in the trade union movement became key activists in the early women's liberation movement.

The ACTU congresses, at which there was little female representation, remained an important focus in the campaign for equal pay. Women demonstrated, canvassed delegates and held women-only conferences to discuss employment and trade union issues. In 1967 the ACTU took a test case to the Conciliation and Arbitration Commission which resulted in the awarding of 'equal pay' for 'equal work' where

men and women did identical jobs. A further test case in 1972 led to
'equal pay for work of equal value' but the principle was not utilized in
more than a handful of industries.

The election of the first post-war federal Labor Government in 1972
gave a focus to the emerging group of young feminist trade union
officials and activists. Some were involved in the expanding public
service and professional unions, while others worked in blue-collar
unions, frequently employed as research officers after completing
tertiary education. The more traditional blue-collar unions were being
confronted by new challenges – industrial restructuring, international
finance policies and complicated legal approaches to conciliation and
arbitration. They realized that officers with a tertiary education, who had
not necessarily come through the ranks of the union, could complement
the abilities of officials with industry backgrounds. A number of the new
officers were young women who had entered previously male-dominated
university courses such as economics, industrial relations and law.

These research officers, along with the women activists from the
public sector and white-collar unions, and the long-standing activists in
blue-collar unions, worked with the women's liberation movement to
make a major impact on Australian trade unions. They were assisted by
federal government funding to unions. Activities which male officials
had been reluctant to pursue, often because of a lack of resources, such
as the 'special needs' of migrant women, became more attractive when
government funding was made available. Women employed in funded
positions often sought further funding, became involved in policy
development and implementation and continued to be employed within
the trade union movement. In 1975 ACSPA established a Working
Women's Centre (WWC) in Melbourne with a federal grant and
contributions from a number of individual trade unions. In Sydney an
International Women's Year grant was obtained to establish the
Women's Trade Union Commission which was run by women unionists
but outside the formal structures of the union movement. The WWC
provided a framework for women to intervene through official trade
union structures and at the same time link up with women's movement
groups concerned with employment issues.

The effectiveness of these links was evident in the adoption by the
WWC of a Charter for Working Women (based on the British Charter)
and the establishment of a Working Women's Charter Campaign. The
charter covered such issues as the right to work, one rate for the job,
equal employment and education opportunity, child care, maternity and
paternity leave, birth control and abortion and flexible working hours.
The aim was to have the Charter adopted by the ACTU and as many
unions as possible, and to develop strategies to implement its various

The NSW Women's Advisory Council cover for a pamphlet on sexual harassment at work

demands. Feminists working in areas such as workers' health, rape crisis, domestic violence, child care, family planning and housing combined with women trade unionists to develop the Charter. Women trade union and women's liberation activists set up Working Women's Charter Campaign groups throughout Australia, and convened a number of conferences between 1975 and 1977. Although the Labor Government had been replaced by a conservative Liberal National Party coalition, many of the funded women's programs were retained.

The WWC played an important role in shaping the debate within the ACTU. Central to this debate was the family wage and the 'mother's allowance'. The extreme right unions representing clerks and shop assistants argued that women should not be forced to work by economic necessity and that the general wage should be adequate to support a dependent family and eliminate the need for dual incomes. In 1975, the ACTU Congress adopted a policy which was described by Edna Ryan, a feminist trade union activist and historian as 'something for everyone, from Laurie Carmichael [a communist Metal Workers' Union official] to the Festival of Light [a group sharing the policies and concerns of Mary Whitehouse]'. That is, it combined the progressive policies of the women's movement with the demands for a mother's allowance.

Activity around the charter brought pressure on the ACTU for its adoption. In 1977 the ACTU circulated a Draft Charter for Working Women which was adopted at the Congress later that year. It picked up the major issues of the WWC Charter, although its demands were more moderate. The adoption of the ACTU Charter marked the end of one era and the beginning of another. A broad coalition of trade unions and women's liberation activists had united to achieve the adoption of a comprehensive women's policy by the premier trade union movement organization. Subsequently the emphasis shifted to implementation as well as, at later Congresses, improvement.

In 1978 an ACTU Special Unions Conference was held to discuss the implementation of the Charter, and the ACTU Executive, then an all-male body, established a specialist subcommittee to make recommendations. Responsibility for day-to-day work on the charter fell to Jan Marsh, then ACTU Research Officer. The most notable success was the Arbitration commission test case argued by Ms Marsh which resulted in 1979 in twelve months' unpaid maternity leave for all female workers. This set a new standard in the private sector. The public sector had achieved paid maternity leave under the federal Labor Government. One week's paid paternity leave had also been awarded, but was withdrawn by the Fraser Government in 1978.

Between the defeat of Whitlam and the election of the Hawke Labor Government just over seven years later there was a notable shift in general trade union consciousness and activity around women's issues. This was reflected in a range of initiatives:

- the development of policies on issues of specific concern to women by individual trade unions and by the ACTU

- the incorporation of the Working Women's Centre into the ACTU when ACSPA merged into the larger peak body in 1979

- support by unions for Working Women's Centre projects such as the multilingual newspaper 'Women at Work'

- the establishment of work-related child care projects sponsored by unions and the entry of trade unions into the child care policy and funding debate

- the support (although limited) for programmes to break down the gender segmentation of the workforce by encouraging women into non-traditional jobs

- promotion of state and federal Anti-Discrimination, Equal Employment Opportunity and Affirmative Action legislation

- focus on migrant women's needs such as English as a second language training

- concern with occupational health and safety issues such as Repetition Strain Injury

- trade union education courses specifically aimed at women unionists

- establishment of State Working Women's Charter Committees in the state branches of the ACTU (the State Trades and Labour Councils)

- the establishment of women's groups and caucuses within individual trade unions, particularly in white-collar organizations, and encouragement of women to play a more active role

- the appointment of women's officers by some unions and trades and labour councils.

Recent Developments

Despite gains in terms of level of debate, consciousness and representation, in only a few areas such as maternity leave and equal opportunity legislation had the goals of the charter been realized by the time Labor was re-elected. Limited progress had been made on equal pay and child care. Women were still employed in a narrow range of occupations and industries, with the majority in clerical and sales work or teaching and nursing.

Women were pushing against a great wall of apathy from male unionists, with some active support from a minority of left unions and opposition from the extreme right. Policy debates at ACTU Congress became notable for the inattention of most delegates as feminists slugged it out with the 'pro-life, pro-family' supporters of the National Civic Council, an extreme right political/industrial organization. The trade union movement itself had been quite embattled during seven years of conservative government. Centralized wage fixing was failing to maintain real pay values. A series of industrial disputes brought gains to the stronger areas of the workforce, particularly in the area of over-award payments. This was especially discriminatory against women, who were mostly restricted to the award rate. High unemployment hit women the hardest (10.7 per cent compared to 9.5 per cent for men, in March 1983). Cuts in welfare expenditure and the 'social wage' (government services) had the effect of making Australia a less fair society while women were disproportionately represented amongst the poor and low wage earners.

In the early eighties a strategy was considered necessary in the ACTU to ensure that the benefits of economic recovery and growth were distributed equitably and to improve the relative position of the low paid. It was recognized that the wage gains of the industrially strong sections of the workforce disadvantaged less militant sections and, more importantly, that the gains could be whittled away by government policies on taxation and provision of services. Senior ALP politicians also believed that their only chance of sustained economic recovery, if they were elected, would be via a centralized wages system preventing a growth/inflation cycle. Discussions around the need for an incomes policy led to an Accord between the ACTU and the ALP launched during the successful 1983 election campaign.

The Accord has provided the framework within which the trade union movement has operated since the election of the Hawke Government. Not surprisingly it has caused considerable debate within the women's movement. Criticisms have been raised first that the Accord was negotiated primarily by men (reflecting the composition of political and industrial leadership). Second, that the document did not deal specifically with women's issues. Third, that because the centralized wage fixing system maintained existing relativities between particular occupations and industries there was no scope to implement equal pay. Supporters of the Accord argued that in a free collective bargaining situation, as proposed by an odd coalition of militant unions and conservative politicians, women would fall to the bottom.

We believe that the centralized wage system plus reforms in the social wage area have had significantly redistributive effects which have benefitted women. These have included the introduction of universal health insurance, tax cuts, increases in the real value of social welfare benefits, especially for families with children, increased government spending on services such as health and education, strong employment growth and a doubling of the number of child care places. The unprecedented close relationship between ACTU officials and the Federal Government has given the union movement a strong voice in the development of legislation governing sex discrimination and affirmative action. The Accord period has seen a real commitment from the ACTU leadership to improve the relative position of low paid workers and specifically that of women.

There have been tensions between some trade union women and the ACTU leadership over the politics of the Accord process. This crystallized around issues concerning the role of the Working Women's Centre, which had experienced difficulty in defining its role within the ACTU and had had its resources run down. The ACTU Women's Committee was divided on factional lines with no side satisfied with its functioning. Extreme right- and left-wing women spent meetings sparring with each other rather than exploring ways of improving ACTU activity for women. The question was no longer one of policy development, as most of these battles had been won, but rather one of implementation. The 'oppositionist' stance of some feminists was a barrier to properly integrating the Working Women's Centre's work with the general policy direction of the ACTU, without which it was impossible to operate effectively. Our policies were marginalized and ignored when major decisions were made about the direction of the trade union movement. Women activists were not included in key decision-making forums and nobody seriously raised women's concerns when matters like wages policy, employment policy, education and so on were debated.

In late 1984 the ACTU revitalized its women's activities by adopting an Action Program for Women Workers and appointing a co-ordinator directly responsible to the Secretary, Bill Kelty. Based on the Working Women's charter and the ACTU Women's Policy, it sets out the priorities of the ACTU and a proposed strategy to achieve each priority. These include leave and flexible working arrangements for workers with family responsibilities, improved provision of child care, equal pay, Equal Employment Opportunity and Affirmative Action, and increased involvement of women in the trade union movement. It thus sets women's issues firmly within the general strategy of the trade union movement and integrates them into the work of most of the ACTU's officers. The comparable worth case fought in the Arbitration Commission resulted from this, as did the case examining awards in low paid industries.

The ACTU has identified a range of reasons for the differentials between men's and women's earnings. First, youths who earn less than adults are a higher proportion of employed women than employed men. Second, part-time work is more prevalent amongst women than men. Third, women work less overtime than men. Fourth, women are concentrated in a small range of occupations and industries where earnings are relatively low, and around the lower grades of any occupation. Fifth, payments made by the individual employer in excess of the award, known as over-award payments, are lower for women than men. Finally, jobs done by women have attracted lower rates of pay than jobs done by men. That is, comparable worth whereby a worker's pay is based on factors such as the knowledge, skill, effort and responsibility required, regardless of whether the work is undertaken by a man or a woman, has not been fully applied in Australia.

It was to this latter source of pay inequity that the comparable worth case was directed. The ACTU sought to reaffirm the 1972 Equal Pay decision which determined the principle of equal pay for work of equal value, allowing a comparison of female wage rates with male and female wage rates in other awards. It also sought to establish that the Wage Fixation Guidelines did not preclude the application of this principle. The ACTU won on both grounds, though the Commission rejected the use of the term comparable worth. There has subsequently been limited flow-on of this decision to nurses' and teachers' aides.

The case concerning low paid awards was overtaken by the introduction of a new set of Wage Fixation Principles in March 1986. The ACTU sought and achieved a principle providing for the introduction of a 'Supplementary Payment' into an award. This is a pay increase which is paid to those workers who do not earn payments over the award rate or if they do, those payments are less than the amount of the Supplementary Payment. This means low paid workers get an increase which higher paid workers do not. Clothing workers, 95 per cent of whom are women, are currently seeking a Supplementary Payment, and it is generally recognized that skill levels are undervalued because it is a female industry. Machining, for example, is not an apprenticeship trade.

The expansionary macroeconomic policies of the Federal Labor government which were outlined in the accord had the effect of increasing demand in the economy. Australia has historically exported agricultural and mining commodities and imported manufactured products. A boom in consumer demand and demand for capital items in response to new investment sucked in imports and the balance of trade deficit rapidly escalated. The financial sector, including the exchange rate, was deregulated and the world marked the currency down with huge falls in the value of the Australian dollar. Interest repayments on foreign debt (foreign debt had increased during the life of the conservative Federal Government which supported overseas borrowings to finance resource sector expansion) increased because the value of our dollar had fallen and our balance of payments deficit skyrocketed with the burden of an increased invisible account deficit. The devaluation, whilst improving our international competitiveness, was inflationary because imported goods cost more.

In response the Federal Labor Government reversed its expansionary strategy in favour of contractionary monetary and fiscal policies and retreated from the commitment of the Accord to full indexation of wages for movements in the cost of living. The mainstream employer groups and an emerging radical right group of employers, politicians and academics (dubbed the New Right) were calling for a wage freeze and abandonment of centralized wage fixation in favour of a 'flexible' system of free collective bargaining between workers and their employer without the 'interference' of trade unions. Moves to raise the real wages of those without the industrial muscle to win gains in the field faced severe difficulties. Despite stated equal pay principles, there have been few real gains. Female average earnings have remained at two-thirds of male earnings essentially because women tend to work part-time in low-paid industries and have little access to over-award payments, overtime and promotion. The difficulties associated with overcoming the gender segmentation of the labour market highlight the general dilemma of legislative change which has done little so far to alter the structural nature of discrimination against women.

Affirmative Action is useful for women with definite career paths particularly in the public sector. It enables small numbers of women in the private sector to receive reasonable consideration for appointment to professional and managerial positions. But it has done little to assist women locked in unskilled and low paid occupations in the manufacturing and service industries. It has yet to be taken up in a serious way by trade unions in those areas. The Amalgamated Metal Workers' Union and the Textile, Clothing and Footwear Unions (TCF) are restructuring their awards – broadbanding a multiplicity of occupational classifications into a small number of groups and providing career paths within their industries for production workers. This offers the opportunity to build on the Affirmative Action legislation and open up new options for women. Time will tell if these unions take up the opportunity.

Equal opportunity legislation has certainly had an effect on the

community consciousness of women's right to work. The focus on individual complaints limits its impact and provisions for representative
complaints (similar to American 'class actions') have greater potential.
The most notable example was a case against Australian Iron and Steel
in the industrial town of Wollongong, New South Wales. Women fought
a long battle to achieve employment opportunities in the steelworks.
Thirty-four women finally won a case in which they argued that the use
of 'protective' legislation which limited the weights women are allowed
to lift to 16kg could not be used as a reason for not employing them.
They also argued that the generally accepted system of 'last on, first off'
in retrenchments (i.e. those with least seniority are sacked first) was
discriminatory since women's lack of seniority derived from past discriminatory practices. Although the women were supported by their own
union, the case elicited a hostile reaction from the New South Wales
Labor Council which opposed the use of equal opportunity legislation in
an industrial relations context. They were concerned that the long-
standing principle of 'last on, first off' was being undermined even
though the principle resulted in discrimination.

There has been a growing recognition that to be effective, feminists
have to move beyond the traditional 'women's issues', and influence the
macroeconomic factors which affect the underlying structural causes of
discrimination. This means intervening in the mainstream debates to
ensure that they are informed by considerations of women's employment and remuneration. For example, in 1985 the Federal Labor
Government held a 'Tax Summit'. The favoured option for tax reform
was to introduce a broadly-based consumption tax with complementary
reductions in personal taxation. The women's movement considered that
this regressive form of taxation would impact negatively upon women
and organized an alternative Tax Summit prior to the official one. They
succeeded in placing women amongst the key negotiators with the
government during the summit, and in pushing the ACTU to argue
forcefully against the consumption tax. The trade union movement's
superannuation campaign provides another example, at the same time as
highlighting the difficulties of achieving measures to improve the relative
position of women workers. Superannuation is generally made available
to full-time, higher paid employees in the more profitable sectors of
private industry and to permanent employees in the public sector. Both
categories are disproportionately male. Only one in two Australian
workers and one in four women workers have occupational superannuation.

In recent negotiations with the government for support for a wage
increase based on productivity (separate from consumer price index-
related increases), the ACTU proposed that it be in the form of extend-

ing superannuation to those not already receiving it. This would have benefitted women and other low paid workers by bringing them closer to the level of the more privileged half of the workforce. Improving conditions in existing superannuation schemes, which discriminate against part-time and low paid workers, and against those (often women) who do not stay in the same job until retirement was also discussed. As debate continued it became clear that the support of the whole movement for the claim would require equal sharing in the benefit. The success of the campaign depended on the industrial sectors of the workforce, most of which had some form of superannuation. Thus the final agreement was that an additional 3 per cent of wages paid as superannuation would be negotiated by the unions and employers in each industry. Though the ACTU heavily promoted the particular concerns of women in the debate leading up to the agreement, and in the general campaign for the specific industry agreements, there are still large gaps between the treatment of men and women. It is likely (as early experience of the campaign bears out) that the initial gains will be made by the strongest sections of the workforce and, ironically, those who already have some superannuation coverage.

Feminist trade unionists are also attempting to intervene in the industry policy debate concerning revitalization of our industrial base in manufacturing. A range of tripartite consultative mechanisms called Industry Councils have been established to examine particular industries and plans have been agreed for the shipbuilding, steel, heavy engineering, textiles, clothing, footwear and computer industries. These plans are blueprints setting out goals for improvements in international competitiveness, increased exports, and the raising of skills.

Industry policy is relevant to women in two main ways. First, it is areas of women's employment such as textiles, clothing and footwear which are particularly subject to structural changes. The industry policy approach must be designed to maximize opportunities for employment in areas where women are already employed and must recognize the special features of the workforce in these industries when designing labour market policies. For example, the TCF Plan provides income support which is not means-tested so married women are able to receive it; it also provides English language tuition for non-English-speaking migrants. Second, industry policy can be used to broaden the range of occupations and industries where women work, breaking down the gender segmentation of the workforce. Hitherto the main negotiators of industry policy agreements, male trade union officials, have failed to put these concerns forward.

Women in the trade union movement have brought these issues to the attention of our male counterparts through seminars organized by the

ACTU Women's Committee, by liaison with the all-male ACTU Industry Policy Committee, through the ACTU Executive (the decision-making body in between biennial ACTU Congresses) and finally at the 1987 Congress. Here the trade union movement focused on the internal reorganization necessary to face the challenge of an increasingly complex and damaging economic and political environment. The amalgamation of our 326 unions into twenty broad groupings was seen to be a priority. Three new positions on the ACTU Executive were allocated to women, while another two women were elected. Since then one more woman has been elected which means that six of the thirty-eight members of the ACTU Executive are now women.

Women are far more visible in the trade union movement than they were fifteen years ago. We have achieved formal policy positions which reflect most of the major concerns of the women's movement. Some concrete gains have been made in areas of maternity leave, child care and equal opportunity legislation. There has been a recognition of the need for special measures to ensure representative female participation in unions. These include women's trade union training courses, formal or informal affirmative action within individual unions, the employment of women's officers and the establishment of women's positions on the ACTU Executive. Women's movement groups (such as the Working Women's Charter Campaign) have played a major part in achieving these policies and in the preparing of women to participate in the formal structures of the trade union movement. With a significant number of feminist officials, such groups have perhaps become more marginal, although the lack of actual campaigning on issues such as equal pay by unions demonstrates the need for continued pressure from feminists. The Council of Action for Equal Pay which has been active around the comparative worth case is one such example.

Feminist participation is more prevalent amongst the younger generation of trade union officials, who have better education, a concern with broader social issues and a commitment to democratic processes within the unions. It is strongest in the professional and public sector unions. It could not be said that a great deal of change has taken place in private sector workplaces. There has been little progress in ameliorating the situation of the non-English speaking migrant women who predominate in manufacturing industry, or the part-time workforce in service industries. Recent victories in the regulation of outwork in the clothing industry and in the provision of English as a second language classes on the job are, however, important developments for migrant women. It is our strong view that women gain most from a strategy which aims at influencing the economic mainstream in areas of wages, tax, budgetary policy, social welfare, employment and industry policy. Further, that a social agreement between a Labor government and the trade union movement is the best vehicle for this. The Accord has been far from fully implemented, although for five years since March 1983 it has protected the position of the low paid and the industrially weak. This would not have been possible without the centralized wage system upon which the Accord is based. However, the government has retreated from the wage commitments of the Accord. It has adopted deregulatory and quasi-monetarist policies in response to the economic crises. In the face of this retreat the trade union movement has had to carefully examine the options for wage policy. It is significant that the Australian trade union movement has recently collectively determined to pursue an approach which holds back the unions which could achieve gains in a free collective bargaining situation, so that all workers can be protected by centralized wage fixation. In late 1986 we retreated from the brink of a wage free-for-all in favour of the Two-Tiered Wage System which provided across-the-board increase for all workers expressed as a flat dollar amount and a further increase available via a number of principles. This system has been more beneficial for women than a wages free-for-all would be.

At the time of writing the trade union movement is developing a proposal for a new wages system which will maintain the current value of real wages against inflation. Consideration is also being given to restructuring awards to provide for clear career paths and recognition for skill, training and experience, a process which would assist women to break out of the lowest paid, 'dead-end' classifications. There is ongoing debate on issues of vital concern to women such as taxation, welfare and the proposed tax on higher education.

Despite some major conflicts, the effectiveness of the trade union movement will depend to a great extent on the survival of the Labor government. The recent conservative victory in the New South Wales state election has already seen the beginnings of industrial confrontation and reactionary social policy which can only have disastrous consequences for women's employment and living standards.

10

Making Industry Work for Women

Kim Windsor

By the 1980s, the country once said to be riding on the sheep's back was in danger of being trampled by it. The growing trade imbalance, reflecting Australia's heavy dependence on mineral and agricultural products, has left it with a massive balance of payments deficit. Few would argue against the need for a major restructuring of the economy. The low value-added products that were once the mainstay of our exports face shrinking markets and declining prices. The greatest growth potential is in the more sophisticated, high value-added specialized end of the market, which is least developed locally. The transition requires a wholesale restructuring not only of what is produced, but how and who produces it. More sophisticated and flexible skills are the necessary basis of an efficient and competitive industry sector. The traditional organization of work, and training arrangements that have constituted structural barriers to equality for women in the workplace, are under change.

This chapter reviews the major approaches to improving employment opportunities for women. It then links strategies for promoting women's employment with the changing environment of industry and company level debates, policies and initiatives. Under a Labor government tripartite industry structures have been established, giving expression, at least in principle, to a commitment to consultation. At the same time, a number of unions, led by those in the metal industry, are embarking on a process of award restructuring, job redesign and training reviews. The outcome of these exercises will be critical in determining whether the majority of women will have access to more skilled, well paid positions or remain even more securely locked into low skilled jobs at the bottom end of employment hierarchies. Finally, this chapter raises some of the issues that need to be tackled for women in restructuring, training arrangements and company level agreements.

One of the sharpest measures of labour market inequality between men and women in Australia is the extent of occupational and industrial segregation. That women now comprise 43 per cent of the workforce reflects an expansion in traditionally female jobs rather than any dilution of the structures, values and attitudes that rigidly define men's and women's work. Work and management practices maintain and reinforce these divisions. For example, even though men and women may both be classified as clerks, the work and experience they are allocated will either provide a stepping stone to further promotion or cut off further opportunities.

The breadth of opportunities within the same occupation was once clearly delineated in award structures which made specific reference to 'mens' and 'women's' jobs. After the Equal Pay decision of 1972, these more blatant distinctions were removed, often being renamed as separated streams. For example, a clerical job involving mainly keyboard work, employing predominantly women, could be Stream 1, while a job introducing administrative and other office skills, employing a higher proportion of males, may be Stream 2. While the label has changed, the legacy of prejudice, expectations, values, has been slow to change.

The implications of the narrow concentration of working women are reflected in differential opportunities and rewards, which by now are only too familiar. In August 1987, women were six times as likely to work in part time jobs, were less likely to have any post-school qualifications and on average, received only eighty per cent of the salaries and wages paid out to their male workmates and colleagues for a full working week. Because the majority work in non-career, dead-end jobs and have no training base on which to build further skills, the jobs they leave at the end of their working lives vary little in terms of pay, status and opportunities from those they entered on joining the workforce.

Improving Employment Opportunities

In the face of marked and persistent discrimination against women, the major gains have been achieved through legislative reform. The first round of anti-discrimination legislation was initiated by a number of State governments in the mid 1970s, followed by the Commonwealth government in 1984. By the early 1980s a second round of legislation had put the onus for equal opportunity on the employer, rather than on an individual complainant in the public sector via EEO programmes. The principle affirmative action in 1986 was extended to the private sector with the introduction of the Commonwealth Affirmative Action (Equal Employment Opportunity for Women) Act. Experience in the public service suggests that the greatest impact of the Act is to promote opportunities for women at the middle and senior levels. This partly reflects the statistically driven approach to identifying discrimination. Targets for action are identified by the under-representation of women in particular occupations. Small changes in numerical terms can translate into impressive statistical improvements. While affirmative action strategies allow some women to jump the hurdle of base grade jobs to enter employment or gain promotion to higher status, better paid positions, they do little to improve the nature and opportunities offered by jobs at the bottom of the ladder, where the majority of women continue to work.

A range of other government initiatives aim to improve employment opportunities for women. In education and training, the emphasis is on altering the subject choice of girls and providing targetted programmes of assistance to increase the number of young women entering courses where they have been under-represented. In the area of assistance to industry, the Victorian government has established the precedent of refusing to let government contracts or industry assistance go to any Australian-based company that fails to comply with affirmative action legislation.

While these initiatives represent important developments for women, it would be naive to suggest that they are adequately resourced and effectively integrated into overall government spending. The reality is that these programmes are poorly funded and remain separated from industry development. There is a resistance in the mainstream programmes to accepting women's participation targets, which results in a kind of Orwellian doublespeak that runs through government policy and programmes. The preambles typically contain all the trimmings of equal opportunity commitments, but fall short of clear undertakings when it comes to carving up the resources.

A third group of government initiatives concerns improvements to employment conditions, including child care, wage equity, availability of non-exploitative part-time employment, superannuation and long service leave entitlements. The structure of employment and payment of related benefits often assume a full time, permanent pattern of employment with no provisions for having children or caring for them and other family members. This has massively disadvantaged women and often excluded them from the workforce. The major role for governments on these issues is to review conditions of service for its own employees. It can also support industrial cases brought before the Australian Conciliation and Arbitration Commission (ACAC).

The ACTU is currently preparing such a case in support of paternity and parental leave and leave to care for sick children. This is in line with the government's moves towards ratifying the International Labour Organization's Convention 156 on 'Equal Opportunities and Equal Treatment of Men and Women: Workers With Family Responsibilities'. The Case being put before the ACAC aims to extend provisions granted as a result of an earlier test case for Maternity Leave in 1979, in which the ACAC determined that women would be entitled to take up to fifty-two weeks unpaid maternity leave with a guarantee that this would not adversely affect their employment status on returning to work. The Case currently being prepared is to extend eligibility for unpaid leave of up to fifty-two weeks to both parents with greater flexibility so that it can be taken any time up to the child's second birthday. It would also provide a minimum period of unpaid leave to allow workers to meet short term and emergency child care demands without jeopardizing their jobs.

A common feature of the initiatives outlined is that they aim to influence the gender mix within existing education training and employment structures, but overlook the discriminatory nature of the structures themselves. Improving employment opportunities for women needs to go beyond strategies to reshuffle the existing jobs; what must be questioned is the fundamental design of a work process that divides job opportunities into primary positions – offering job security, promotion and skill development opportunities, job satisfaction and favourable pay and conditions – and secondary positions, which are often part time or casual, which involve few opportunities for developing, applying or rewarding skill, which have no career prospects and which are highly vulnerable to redundancy in restructuring processes. The dynamics that shape work organization, job design, training and the gender-based allocation of these differ between and within industries and enterprises.

Changes in the basis of competitive and efficient performance are increasingly characterized by the introduction of new management techniques and the more innovative application of technology which requires greater workforce co-operation and 'flexibility'. At the heart of current industrial debates is the question of how that 'flexibility' should be defined. Women have faced substantial barriers in attempting to influence economic and industry policy. Women's involvement in the process of policy formulation and implementation is important to establish issues relevant to women on industrial agendas. Rapid changes in production processes and training requirements create an industrial climate in which award restructuring of company-level agreements are the order of the day. This provides an unprecedented opportunity to intervene in reshaping industrial and training structures to ensure that patterns of labour market segregation are not maintained.

The Policy Framework

The formulation of industry policy has undergone some significant changes under the Labor government. A range of tripartite economic and industry policy committees and councils were established, providing a recognized channel for direct union involvement in policy development. The government's failure to deliver on key aspects of the Accord, particularly on the social wage, has put enormous strains on the agreement. Nevertheless, the fundamental premise of a consensus approach between unions, government and employers has survived. This orientation was strongly endorsed by a recent delegation of ACTU and government officials to Western Europe. The report of the mission, *Australia Reconstructed* (1987) draws on European experience to argue that the full involvement and commitment of all parties is integral to a successful economic policy.

The central aim of economic and industry policy at both macro and local levels, is to address the structural weakness of Australia's industrial base. Abundant natural resources have provided the basis of Australia's export capacity. Throughout the century, manufacturing policy targeted import replacement. The major form of industry support was the blanket application of high protection levels virtually dictated by employers. The sector that developed was diverse, unspecialized, and often uncompetitive. With little incentive to develop greater efficiencies or innovation in either product or process, the sector stagnated. The devaluation of the Australian dollar and the resurgence of economic growth in the early 1980s quickly outstripped the capacity of the local manufacturing sector to respond as imports flooded the market to fill the shortfalls.

The massive task of restructuring Australia's ailing industrial base has been recognized by all parties as both a political and economic imperative. Labor came to power supporting a targetted, interventionist industry policy as the basis for building a more competitive, export-oriented manufacturing sector. A central feature of this approach has been the development of sectoral plans to provide a comprehensive package of assistance to industries facing major structural adjustment. To date, such plans have been developed for the steel, automotive, heavy engineering and textiles, clothing and footwear industries. In theory there was to be full union consultation and involvement at company and industry levels.

Such involvement is reflected in the Textile, Clothing and Footwear (TCF) and Heavy Engineering packages which make specific provision for labour adjustment programmes to assist those displaced by the restructuring process. Assistance is also directed to encourage employers to reassess training programmes and increase investment in skill development. However, unions are increasingly critical of the government's failure to give some real teeth to an interventionist approach to industry policy. Far from being a condition of providing assistance, some unions report bureaucratic barriers to even finding out which of the companies in their industry are receiving support.

The issue of intervention to promote the employment interests of women is even more fraught. While the ACTU has embraced the potential of a consultative approach to industry policy, frequently citing develpments in Sweden, there has been scant regard paid to women's issues. Yet in Sweden extensive efforts have been made to target the expanded participation of women in all occupations. This feature has been all but ignored in the Australian debates over industry development policy. A further barrier is the low priority and support given to women's industries. Employment patterns in Australia's manufacturing sector mirror those of other developed countries. The stagnating industries such as the TCF, relying on labour intensive work processes, employ predominantly women. Those industries attracting most government support and assistance employ predominantly men. Where women are employed in male dominated industries, they form the occupational base level, starting and finishing somewhere below the first rung on the career ladder.

Work Organization

Increasingly, the basis of competitiveness is determined as much by non-cost factors such as quality, efficient inventory control, reduced equipment downtime, delivery and service reliability as by the cost per unit figure which has been the focus of traditional approaches. The need to make rapid, flexible responses makes the Taylorist approach based on high volume, and standardized runs with the associated costs of maintaining and storing costly buffer stocks, a cumbersome and often inefficient form of work organization.

Companies vary widely in their response to these developments. Some resist restructuring pressures. Some are selecting elements of a different approach such as Just-In-Time and a range of quality improvement programmes, slotting these into the existing work arrangements. As the available technology becomes fairly standard, competitive advantage depends more on the development of creative forms of work organization and job design. This shift places a premium on a highly skilled, flexible workforce. The rigid divisions between skilled and unskilled jobs and the highly specialized nature of tasks performed that characterized traditional manufacturing are ill suited to meeting these emerging labour requirements.

The changing requirements of the production process itself challenge the entrenched demarcations between skilled and unskilled work. Features of predominantly female jobs such as lack of skill development and career opportunities, or opportunities or training to perform more than a narrow range of tasks and high labour turnover, potentially conflict with emerging skill needs. These developments will not automatically benefit women. Ensuring that women occupy their fair share of positions and have equal access to new jobs will only be achieved through direct intervention in shaping and allocating those opportunities.

Far from providing a panacea to workforce segregation, overseas experience illustrates some of the pitfalls for the labour movement and particularly for women, in the drive towards a more highly skilled, more flexible workforce. The often cited advances in productivity and efficiency achieved in Japan, for example, provide secure, well paid employment for a primary, predominantly male labour force. This is premised on a peripheral and often female workforce who enjoy few of the benefits but shoulder most of the costs of this growth. The rise of contract labour and outwork is a worldwide phenomenon. Part-time, casual and home-based work are the forms of labour flexibility most familiar to women. While a degree of numerical flexibility may be legitimate to take account of seasonal or cyclical production patterns, the progressive marginalization of employment opportunities will continue to have a devastating effect on women and undermine the employment security of all workers.

As long as work opportunities divide along the lines of relatively secure, well paid, satisfying work, compared with insecure, highly specialized and poorly paid work, women will remain overwhelmingly concentrated in the latter area. Debates over functional flexibility go to the heart of the industrial and training structures that define the boundaries of employment opportunities. How far these structures go towards addressing training opportunities and the industrial status of workers presently described as 'unskilled' will be a key determinant of whether and where women fit in in emerging employment structures.

While theories differ in emphasis there is general agreement that the notion of 'skill' is central to explaining employment patterns and opportunities. Some feminists argue that socio-economic factors, such as poor access to relevant education and training, the unequal distribution of domestic responsibilities, and employer discrimination, have largely confined women to unskilled jobs. This assumes that jobs can be defined by some objective, technical measure of skill, and that initiatives such as affirmative action should reallocate jobs and opportunities within the existing framework. A second approach argues that there is nothing inherently 'unskilled' about speed, dexterity, intense concentration and repetition, except that they characterize women's work. The concept of skill says more about the ability of men to mobilize their industrial bargaining power than it does about some inherently more valuable work ability.

That industrial bargaining power is central in creating the classifications which provide a structure for defining and rewarding 'skill' is illustrated in many awards. For example, the Metal Trades Award lists hundreds of classifications, many describing highly differentiated and often obscure tasks. The majority of women covered by this award fall into just two categories – process worker and machine operator. These classifications describe a range of vastly different jobs which share the common characteristics of being performed often by women who have lacked industrial strength, whose demands have been constrained by the interests of more highly paid male workers to maintain pay and status relativities and who have no trade or technical qualifications.

Central elements to defining skill, in addition to industrial power, are the ability to perform a range of tasks and the way that ability has been developed. For example, it is not enough to perform some of the same tasks as a tradesperson without knowing how to perform all aspects of the trade. Harnessing the formal training system to support a male dominated concept of skill further distinguishes skilled and unskilled by enabling the skilled worker to point to the objective difference in the way those skills are acquired. A young man enters an industry and acquires on-the-job experience and knowledge under the umbrella of a formally recognized apprenticeship. A young woman enters an industry and learns to perform various tasks. This learning may be of the 'sitting next to Nellie' and copying kind or it may involve more organized in-house training. Either way, it will not provide a basis for further formal training, and it is likely that the woman would continue to be described as un- or semi-skilled worker according to award classifications.

The Flexible Solution

While government policies pay lip service to the need to promote improved employment and training opportunities for all employees, the skill flexibility debate remains focused on those workers who are already regarded as 'skilled'. This in part reflects the employers' agenda which has seized on the issues of labour efficiency and flexibility to attack restrictive work practices, and particularly trade demarcations, as the primary cause of inefficiencies. Productivity-based wage bargaining has provided the arena for these debates. Most women are not formally recognized as skilled, and have been largely absent from the scene. This absence has suited both unions and employers. Each has a vested interest in restricting the concept of 'skill'. Its connection with the apprenticeship system of training has provided the basis for union strategies which relied on distinguishing and accentuating the differences in training, job content and pay, between skilled and unskilled workers and defending those relativities. Employers have been able to expand the job functions and responsibilities of process workers while ignoring the associated issues of improving training opportunities, job status and pay.

The use of low skilled workers to absorb the tasks that remain as a by-product of skilled jobs is an old and familiar practice. What is new is the pace and pervasiveness of these changes. There is frequently a reallocation of tasks between skilled and unskilled workers with subtle changes in the nature and responsibilities attached to low skilled jobs. An emphasis on improved efficiency and quality, often implemented through management techniques such as Just-In-Time or Total Quality Control programmes can alter the nature and responsibilities attached to process work. For example, responsibility for quality assessment may be relocated from specific test and check points at specific stages of assembly to be integrated into the assembly process itself. Few would argue against the benefits of incorporating quality control into the production process, thereby minimizing the amount of unproductive time devoted to fault finding and reworking. What is not as readily acknowledged is the change in content of process work. The new emphasis on quality will not be offset by a reduction in additional and often conflicting pressures such as speed. Poor quality may well become a basis on which a bonus earner has his or her earnings reduced but it is highly unlikely that output targets will be adjusted in recognition of this increased pressure.

Responding to Change

Industrial responses that fail to come to grips with changes occurring at the process work level will ultimately undermine the potential for building a strong and united labour movement. More is required than negotiating a few additional training and career opportunities for the low skilled. Unions must reassess strategies premised on the protection of an apprenticeship based system of training and the maintenance of pay and conditions relativities between skilled and unskilled workers.

If the work process is to become more sophisticated, how can the relatively low skilled tasks be incorporated into mainstream production process to avoid the development of a peripheral labour market? How can the production process be designed to provide opportunities for workers in base level occupations to upgrade skills, experience and career opportunities? And what are the most effective strategies for ensuring that those currently classified as 'low skilled' have access to different kinds of jobs? These issues are central to informing an industrial position relevant to women. Despite some incremental gains in the numbers of women represented in negotiating forums, the key mechanisms for developing and implementing an industrial response to workplace changes, including award provisions, training arrangements and company level agreements, remain largely determined by men. There are some important industrial precedents such as negotiations in the textile, clothing and footwear industry to establish financial assistance for women to undertake training which was not subject to a family income means test. However, the increased unionization and active participation of women is a fundamental prerequisite if changing industrial and training structures are to reflect the interests of all workers.

Changes in work processes have outpaced the capacity of many industrial awards adequately to describe the range of occupations and their connections with career structures. Comprehensive reviews of industrial awards are underway in a number of industries, lead by the metal industry unions which have initiated a review of the largest manufacturing sector award. This review will be a major industrial pacesetter emphasizing a structured career and training path. In theory it should be possible to enter at the current equivalent of the process worker level and move through trade and technical jobs with the further option of going on to professional engineering, or managerial positions. Greater skill flexibility will be achieved through a process of broadbanding the hundreds of job classifications into nine main groups.

It is impossible to predict the final content of the new award or its outcome for women. The changes will most dramatically affect workers at the bottom of the scale and, without specific initiatives, are unlikely to benefit women to the same extent as men. New training provisions being developed alongside award changes provide for all workers to at least receive base level training. While more progressive companies may upgrade skill and training provisions, experience suggests that without strong affirmative action measures these entry points could well be dominated by men. The barrier to women's advancement would then be lowered from where it currently sits, at the trade and technical training level, to the basic entry training level.

As awards establish industry wide standards, they can provide an important mechanism for recognizing differences in skill levels and responsibilities that have been largely unaddressed in occupations dominated by women. The trend towards broadbanding to provide greater flexibility across what are often outdated job demarcations makes sense for highly differentiated trade and technical classifications. At the other end of the scale, the problem is the reverse. Process workers treated as homogenous in their lack of skill, are undertaking an expanding range of tasks and responsibilities requiring different levels of training and skill development. It is not appropriate to treat the electronics process worker with forty weeks' worth of in-house training in the same way under the award as the process worker in a metal fabrication shop who, if he or she is lucky, may go through an eight-hour induction.

The same pressures for review of industrial awards are present in relation to training structures. Subject prerequisites, sex-biased entry tests, age restrictions, the requirements of an unbroken training period, typically of four years' duration, curriculum design and delivery are just some of the features which make apprenticeships inaccessible and/or unattractive to most young women.

Training structures are coming under closer scrutiny, not for their failure to cater for women, but for their inflexibility in responding to changing skill requirements of industry. Differences in the training experience of men and women demand different strategies to address the shortcomings. The present debate remains preoccupied with trade and technical level training structures. Trade qualifications have emphasized broad skill acquisition, allowing for maximum job mobility. A relatively flat career structure for trade workers within the company has often necessitated changing employers as the only means of promotion. As greater sophistication and specialization are demanded, this arrangement, which encourages relatively high labour turnover, is less appropriate. A number of companies are developing internal career structures and providing further in-house training opportunities to promote and retain their skilled workers.

The training experience of 'unskilled' workers and the issues that emerge from it follow a different pattern. Their only opportunity to undertake training is usually provided by the company and extends only as far as immediate skill needs to perform the task at hand. Without a grounding in the production process overall, skill development is often disjointed, company specific and highly specialized. The lack of broad-based skills development and the substantial variation between companies in the provision and quality of in-house training, undermines job mobility for workers with no formal trade or technical qualification. There is no mechanism for acknowledging or accrediting skills acquired in-house. In contrast to the trade qualified worker for whom changing employers is often the only way of getting a raise, a change of employers for women is often synonomous with starting back at the same level as someone who walks in off the street. The training received by many women in base level jobs does not provide a basis for further skill development. Access to more extensive in-house training does not guarantee improved pay, conditions or future career opportunities in the way that a trade qualification does.

As new approaches to manufacturing further blur the boundaries between 'skilled' and 'unskilled' work, there is a need for a comprehensive, integrated training response at both industry and company levels. Issues of training, quality recognition and accreditation of skills acquired in-house, and the articulation of training so that in-house learning is accredited towards other formal training qualifications, are central to a training response that is relevant to women.

The industry-wide nature of training arrangements and industrial awards limits the capacity of these mechanisms to respond to specific arrangements at the company level. The pace and nature of structural industry adjustment varies substantially from one company to another. This establishes a role for company level negotiations and agreements. In the same way that peak level union bodies are becoming more involved in industry debates at company level, shop stewards' committees could be taking on broader issues of work organization and job design, training and skill enhancement, payment systems, technological change and health and safety. As with all industry bodies, shop stewards' committees remain male dominated, and it will be important to increase the participation of women members.

It is necessary to locate and prioritize issues of particular relevance to women, within industrial strategies and negotiations at the company level.[1] A recently conducted industrial democracy project provides some practical possibilities here. Conducted by shop stewards at a large telecommunications company, supported by their union organizers and a consultant from the Labor Resource Centre, the project involved an extensive study of in-house payment systems, the major type being piece-rate bonus payments. They found that rates of over-award payments were heavily dependent on managerial discretion. While production quantity and quality were the objective criteria on which process workers were paid, this could be adjusted upwards or downwards on the basis of considerations ranging from legitimate issues such as flow of work supply to vaguely defined concepts such as work attitude or appropriate appearance. These adjustments were usually left to the discretion of the supervisor. The most favourable adjustments were made in sections where both male and female process workers were employed. Where the majority of workers were women, discretionary judgements were less generous, compounding the considerable pay disadvantages already experienced by workers with no recognized skill qualifications.

A further finding was that the pay-by-results system was in funda-mental conflict with the changing skill and work organization needs of the company. Bonus payments, designed to reward high speed and accuracy, encourage a high degree of individualized skill specialization. This conflicts with the prerequisites of a more flexible manufacturing approach which relies on the interest and preparedness of workers to expand the range and application of their skills. The interlinking of previously discrete aspects of the work process required greater com-munication and co-operation. As changes in work content and process proceeded in tandem with an increasingly irrelevant bonus system, the differential ability of different sections to accurately measure and reward work varied substantially. This produced widening anomalies, which were a source of considerable tension and dispute amongst workers. Once again, the male process workers were concentrated in the 'easy' bonus earning sections while work pressures were maintained or intensified for women.

On the basis of their work, the shop stewards' committee proposed a set of principles to guide the review and design of internal wage systems. These included:

- that criteria for applying wage systems should be fair and equitable, clearly explained to all workers, consistently applied across the workforce and determined through company/union negotiations

- that wage systems should encourage all workers to expand their skills and undertake training and that the company should aim to protect their investment in labour by developing a career structure that specifically promotes opportunities for the largest occupational group; i.e. process workers and machine operators, to upgrade their position

- that wage systems should not contribute to a widening of pay differ-entials between skilled and unskilled workers

The opportunity to examine the overall impact of company level arrangements rather than responding to problems related to specific components allowed the shop stewards' committee to develop a broad policy perspective on the wages issue. The investigation highlighted the extent of discrimination against process workers, particularly women. This influenced company level industrial strategies in two important ways.

First, it challenged the priority given to negotiating improvements in pay and conditions for skilled workers on the basis that these benefits would trickle down to workers at the bottom of the pile. This was clearly not happening. Not only had process workers failed to gain comparably from movements further up the pay scale, but the focus on trade and technical workers detracted attention from the sliding position of those at the bottom of the scale. The allocation of over-award payments further exaggerated pay differentials on the basis of gender.

Second, the project drew attention to a significant gap in the knowledge and experience of the shop stewards' committee. For many committee members, most of whom were male trade and technical workers, the problems and barriers faced by process workers were issues they were hearing about for the first time. The project provided an opportunity to examine these problems and respond to specific concerns of this group. This was important in winning the support of better organized male workers for issues most relevant to women. It also underlined the need to encourage the increased involvement of these workers who comprised around two-thirds of the company's production workforce.

Negotiations on the company's response to issues raised by this work are still proceeding. How thoroughly the findings of the project are reflected in ongoing union strategies to give greater priority to process workers remains to be seen. This will in part depend on establishing basic preconditions to ensure that women can become involved.

A number of unions are actively promoting affirmative action strategies to increase womens' involvement in their representational structures. At the company level involvement of shop stewards' committees in consultative arrangements requires the greater provision of paid leave to allow shop stewards to undertake this work and to be involved in developing a union position on an expanding range of issues, as well as assurances that supervisors will not penalize workers for their involvement. Meetings need also to occur during work time. The specific issues to be addressed will vary from one company to another. The establishment of some broad principles, such as those developed in the project described, and a range of practical examples of approaches to tackling industrial isues in ways that incorporate rather than exclude women, will provide an important stimulus for parallel developments at both an industry and company level.

The review of industrial and training structures presents a critical opportunity for women to intervene in shaping the new arrangements. Women have traditionally been locked out of economic and industry policy debates in the same way as they have been largely excluded from skilled jobs by the existing industry and training structures. Changes in the process of policy development and implementation under the Labor government which recognizes a legitimate role for union involvement and at least adopts the rhetoric of equal opportunity for women should provide greater potential to raise issues of priority for women.

At the company level the extent to which the agenda reflects women's interests will largely rely on their direct involvement. This will only be achieved where unions prioritize the recruitment and involvement of women members and establish clear rights and entitlements for shop stewards. The strength of an industrial response to meet the dual objectives of promoting a more dynamic and efficient industrial base and improving employment standards and opportunities will rely on its relevance to all workers.

Notes

1. Labor Resource Centre, *Working Report of The Industrial Democracy Project Team on the Wages System*, 1987. Publication of the Working Environment Branch. Department of Industrial Relations.

11

Feminism and Law Reform: Matrimonial Property Law and Models of Equality

Regina Graycar

Feminists in Australia, as elsewhere, have devoted considerable energy to law reform campaigns to improve the status of women. The use of law as a feminist strategy remains problematic as it involves engagement with the state and its agencies, considered by some to be the very centre of women's oppression. This chapter starts from the (perhaps questionable) premise that the law reform process is an important and integral part of women's quest to change society. Thus, the prior question of whether this is an appropriate avenue is left for another time and place.[1] This chapter outlines some of the key issues with which feminists have been involved and then focuses on one major area: the debate on matrimonial property law reform. The final section examines some of the more theoretical questions concerning 'equality' raised by feminist lawyers and others in order to consider the extent to which the matrimonial property debate reflected recent understandings of the role of law in the subordination of women.

In Australia, there are a number of law reform processes.[2] As a federation, Australia has nine major jurisdictions: the national (Commonwealth or federal) level, six states and two territories. Each of the six states has a law reform commission or committee, though not all of these have full time staffed secretariats. In addition, the Australian government established a permanent Law Reform Commission (ALRC) in 1975 which, for constitutional reasons, makes recommendations only on matters of federal law or the law of the Australian Capital Territory. Governments have also come to rely increasingly on the task force model. In New South Wales, this has been used in a number of areas of particular significance to women, such as domestic violence, rape and sexual assault, child sexual assault and women in prison.

Over the past two decades feminists have engaged with the state through law reform processes on issues such as violence in the home, rape and sexual assault of women and children, abortion law reform, prostitution, women in prison and more recently, reproductive technologies. In addition to these areas of so called 'private' life, women have also campaigned for the enactment of anti-discrimination laws and affirmative action measures, designed to secure equal employment opportunity for women in the public sphere of the work place and the market, and for publicly funded child care and maternity leave. Most of these issues directly involve women and children.

Feminist mobilization around issues of particular concern to women and to children has been not only tolerated, but indeed facilitated by, for example, the basing of law reform task forces in the women's units in government. Women's involvement in other reform activities has generally not fared so well. A notable exception was the Women's Tax Summit of 1985 at which some 200 women's organizations met to campaign against a government proposal for the adoption of a broadly based consumption tax, which it was argued, would be regressive and affect women particularly badly. This intervention into the 'Tax Debate' triggered the opposition, resulting in the government's abandoning this option at the Tax summit which followed the women's meeting.

The Matrimonial Property Debate

One of the issues most vigorously debated in the early 1980s was the question of how the law should deal with the distribution of property upon the breakdown of marital relationships. While property distribution might appear to be a 'private' issue, its public significance lies in the fact that Australia has one of the world's highest levels of private home ownership, with some seventy per cent of people owning or paying mortgages on their own properties. There is a very meagre public housing sector, characterized by massive waiting lists, and a largely unregulated, insecure and expensive private rental market.[3] In this context, the disposition of matrimonial property is important in welfare provision for sole parent families. Thus the 'private' law regulation of property distribution on divorce has been very much a matter of public debate amongst feminists and social policy analysts.

The matrimonial property debate brought about a much publicized split in the major Australian women's organization, the Women's Electoral Lobby, a split which has never properly healed. It also raised difficult theoretical problems about the meaning of 'equality' and the value of reliance on this notion as a practical and rhetorical reform mechanism for women. Two competing models were at issue: a 'rule' or 'formal' equality model characterized by the proponents of community of property, or 'equal rights to marital assets';[4] and a 'result equality' model, based upon a recognition that women were economically and structurally disadvantaged by marriage and divorce and that it was inappropriate to ignore these disadvantages by treating them as equal 'partners'.

Constitutional and Legal Framework

Australia's federal system has significantly limited the government's capacity to establish a national family law regime. The 'founding fathers' who drafted Australia's constitution in the late nineteenth century saw the need for a national law on marriage and divorce, but did not anticipate the changes in domestic arrangements that would occur during the twentieth century. As a result, the national law-making power extends only to marriage, the divorce of people who have been legally married, financial adjustment, and the custody of the 'children of a marriage'. Until the recent references of legislative powers from four of the six states [5] to the Commonwealth, the national parliament was unable to regulate aspects of relationships not formalized by marriage. These were left to be dealt with by the various state and territory laws. This has created some anomalies, such as disputing parties having to go to separate courts, for example, in a custody case involving a 'blended family' with children of the marriage, and children of other relationships.[6] Thus the debate about matrimonial property has been concerned only with what should be the proper approach to property disputes between parties who had been legally married.[7]

Australia made a number of major reforms to divorce law and related matters when it enacted the Family Law Act in 1975. The most significant was the establishment of 'no fault' divorce, available upon irretrievable breakdown of marriage, evidenced by twelve months' separation. The 1975 divorce law reforms heralded a new era for Australian law and received considerable support from feminists. While the Act transformed not only the grounds of divorce, but also custody, maintenance and property, contemporary public discussion of these latter issues was notably lacking.

Divorce and related matters, previously dealt with under the Matrimonial Causes Act 1959, had been inextricably tied to fault standards. Divorces were granted to the innocent party, who was required to specify some blameworthy conduct on the part of the previous partner. Significantly, consideration of the parties' conduct flowed through to the ancillary matters of custody, maintenance and the division of property. Although the welfare of the child was the paramount consideration, conduct, particularly adulterous conduct on the part of women, was given considerable weight by the courts in determining the very broad question of the child's best interests.[8] The welfare of the child was by no means considered by courts to be the *sole* consideration. Under the 1959 legislation, the position on maintenance was more explicitly fault-based: the court was empowered to award 'such maintenance as it thinks proper, having regard to the means, earning capacity and *conduct* of the parties to the marriage and all other relevant circumstances' (section 84). The distribution of property was very much within the discretion of the court: it could order 'such a settlement of property ... as the court considers just and equitable in the circumstances of the case' (section 86).[9]

Dissatisfaction with these divorce laws became evident in the late 1960s and early 1970s. Concern was expressed from a number of different quarters about the difficulty of ending unsatisfactory relationships, as the only no-fault ground required a demonstration that the parties had been separated for five years. The frequent use of adultery as a ground gave the tabloid press considerable opportunities for reporting prurient details of divorce cases, a factor which, combined with the expense involved in securing a divorce, no doubt discouraged a large number of separated couples from formally ending their marriages.

The nascent women's movement, through organizations like the Women's Electoral Lobby, supported the reform proposals which received broad endorsement from the Australian community, despite some conservative opposition from church groups and others wedded to a notion of preserving 'the family' at any cost. During its seven years of office (1976–1983), the conservative Fraser government made no serious attempt to repeal the Act. If anything, subsequent amendments and inquiries have been directed at broadening rather than narrowing its reach, culminating in the Family Court's acquiring (from 1988) extended powers to deal with matters concerning ex-nuptial children in four of the six states.

During the period of public debate surrounding the introduction of the Act, the principle focus of discussion was the ground of divorce itself. The parliamentary debate was similarly oriented: a Senate Committee established to report on the clauses of the Family Law Bill [10] gave only minimal attention to matters of custody, maintenance and property. Yet one of the most unsatisfactory aspects of the old divorce law was the way in which these ancillary questions were all determined within the shadow of the finding of fault. This failure to give detailed consideration to the ancillary matters related to divorce, while consistent with the history of divorce law reforms elsewhere,[11] is nonetheless surprising given the radical alteration of the rules governing custody, maintenance and property effected by the Family Law Act.

This legislation, adopted by the reformist Whitlam government and drafted by progressive Attorney General and later High Court judge Lionel Murphy, changed the situation dramatically. Spouse maintenance (though rarely awarded)[12] is available on the basis of two criteria: need, on the one hand, and capacity to pay, on the other. The general philosophy of the Act is that women and men should, to the extent possible, be financially independent after divorce. There is also a clear intention that the relations between the parties be finalized so that parties can effect a 'clean break' (see Family Law Act, s.81).[13] The Act establishes a close relationship between the related financial provisions areas of property and maintenance. It provides, for example, that lump sum awards of property may be made to deal with future maintenance needs.

Under section 79, which deals with property orders, the court has a broad discretion to 'make such order as it thinks fit' if, 'in all the circumstances, it is just and equitable to make the order'. With a few limited exceptions, this has not been used by the Family Court as a back door way of reintroducing considerations of marital fault into determinations about the allocation of matrimonial property.[14]

Matrimonial Property Law under the Family Law Act

The shift away from purely legal and equitable principles of property ownership to reliance on the broad discretionary powers of the court has been widely debated within the women's movement. The rule equality proponents argue that the contributions of husbands and wives should be presumed to be equal when it comes to property division and the future needs of the parties should not be taken into account. Others, the result equality side, do not believe it possible to secure economic equity for women without reference to their past contributions to the marriage and the economic disadvantages of marriage to women, as well as consideration of post divorce needs.

Section 79 of the Family Law Act currently provides:

79(1) In proceedings with respect to the property of the parties to a marriage or either of them, the court may make such order as it thinks fit altering the interests of the parties in the property ...

(4) In considering what order (if any) should be made under this section ... the court shall take into account

(a) the financial contribution made directly or indirectly by or on behalf of a party to the marriage or a child of the marriage to the acquisition, conservation or improvement of any of the property of the parties to the marriage or either of them ...

(b) the contribution (other than a financial contribution) made directly or indirectly by or on behalf of a party to the marriage or a child of the marriage to the acquisition, conservation or improvement of any of the property of the parties to the marriage or either of them . . .

(c) the contribution made by a party to the marriage to the welfare of the family constituted by the parties to the marriage and any children of the marriage, including any contribution made in the capacity of homemaker or parent;

(d) the effect of any proposed order upon the earning capacity of either party to the marriage;

(e) the matters referred to in sub-section 75(2)[15] so far as they are relevant; and

(f) any other order made under this Act affecting a party to the marriage or a child of the marriage.

Prior to 1983, section 79(4)(b) had included both indirect financial contributions and contributions 'made in the capacity of homemaker or parent.' This led to arguments (which did not generally find favour with the full Family Court) that homemaker contributions could be valued only where these were clearly linked to the acquisition, improvement, and so on, of the marital property. In its present form, the Act makes it quite clear that the contribution as a homemaker or parent warrants valuation in its own right.

The purpose of the homemaker's contribution provision has been described by the High Court of Australia as to 'give recognition to the position of the housewife who, by her attention to the home and the children, frees her husband to earn income and acquire assets'.[16] This rationale appears to be firmly based on liberal equality notions which presume to establish an equivalence between contributions, different in nature, but arguably of equal value. The enactment of section 79 (and its many overseas counterparts) appears to have been influenced by earlier feminist debates about the value of housework.[17]

Given the broad discretionary nature of both section 79 and section 75, it was inevitable that the case law would reflect some diversity of view by Family Court judges. Prior to 1984, the full Family Court had held, in a number of cases, that the appropriate *starting point* for a property determination in a marriage of significant duration, including in a case where one party's contribution was not financial, was a fifty-

fifty division of those assets associated with the marriage.[18] In *Mallet*,[19] the High Court rejected this on the basis that to adopt such a 'principle' or even, 'rule of thumb'[20] was inconsistent with the broad discretion contained in section 79. This judgement gave considerable ammunition to the rule equality proponents. However, well before this decision, matrimonial property law had already been subjected to some official scrutiny.

A Joint Select Committee on Family Law (the Ruddock Committee)[21] constituted by government and opposition members from both houses of parliament, was established in 1978 to review the Family Law Act in respect of the grounds of divorce, the rules and practices concerning custody, maintenance and property and the operation of the Family Court and its counselling service. The committee recommended that a spouse's contribution to the welfare of the family should be separately recognized 'to remove any possibility of an interpretation requiring a nexus between a spouse's contributions to a specific item of property' (para. 5.136). Before any full matrimonial property regime was established, there was to be a comprehensive survey of community attitudes, coupled with a full law reform commission study of the implications of such a scheme and a comparative assessment of community of property regimes in other countries (para 5.158). The committee also suggested that parties of the marriage should be presumed to own the matrimonial home in equal shares, both during the subsistence of a marriage, and upon its dissolution (ibid.).

The committee expressed concern about the 'need to ensure that the law does not give the appearance that it acts in an arbitrary and capricious way to divest a person of property' (para 5.151). On the one hand, some men had made submissions that the broad discretionary nature of section 79 'operated as an asset stripping device'. On the other, women's organizations had demonstrated 'a sense of injustice at not receiving recognition for their contributions as homemaker or parent' (ibid). Not until 1983 did the Federal government formally act on the recommendation to establish an enquiry into matrimonial property. In the meantime, the Women's Electoral Lobby began a vigorous campaign to secure a regime of 'equal rights to marital assets', or community of property.

The Women's Electoral Lobby (WEL) Campaign

In February 1981, WEL published its first discussion paper on 'Reform of marital property laws in Australia by means of a system of community of property'. It aimed to promote discussion in the community, the legal profession and the Family Court and was widely distributed to women's organizations, government law reform bodies, law schools and the community generally. The writers argued that the present system of separate property, subject to a broad discretion in the Family Court to reallocate the property upon divorce, was unsatisfactory:

4.6   The law should ensure, as far as possible, that in marriage there is a democratic husband and wife relationship with both parties having equal status and equal economic power within the family unit ...

4.11   Spouses should be entitled to share equally in the management and assets (marital property) of the family created by their marital relationship.

The paper canvassed two alternatives. Under the first, a full community of property scheme, all marital property would be equally owned and managed *during* marriage. In a deferred community of property scheme, the spouse who contributed the particular property to the marriage would retain ownership and control through the subsisting marriage, but upon breakdown, all the marital assets would be shared equally by the parties (para 2.6). The question of which of these systems should be adopted was left open.

It was argued that this proposal would enable the parties to know just what their rights were in the event of breakdown of the marriage. This would avoid expensive and unnecessary litigation. Social security expenditure would be reduced because women would secure a share of the property currently denied to them under the discretionary system (para 5.6). The main argument was that a clearly defined legal entitlement to ownership of half of the marital assets was a precondition to equality between women and men in marriage. The authors claimed widespread community support for the proposition that a 'fifty-fifty' split is a fair and just principle upon which to base the division of marital assets.[22]

This paper formed the basis for a protracted, and at times acrimonious, debate within WEL and the wider women's movement. At the WEL national meeting in July 1981, some members expressed disquiet at the assumption that a fifty-fifty split of marital assets would ensure equality for women during and after marriage. After intense debate, it was resolved that papers putting forward alternative viewpoints should be prepared and circulated. A staff lawyer of the Office of Women's Affairs, Elizabeth O'Keefe, prepared a paper canvassing the arguments for and against community property,[23] while the National Women's Advisory Council also commissioned an academic lawyer, Rebecca Bailey, to outline the regimes operating in a number of overseas jurisdictions.[24] Bailey concluded that a community of property scheme was not likely to be an improvement on the discretionary system then in operation. O'Keefe argued that WEL had ignored the broad discretion of the Family Court to make adjustments to what would otherwise be the legal ownership of property, and particularly, to take into account non-financial contributions made in the capacity of homemaker or parent. She stressed that as a matter of practice, the Family Court started from a premise that assets were to be equally divided, departing from this starting point only where the particular circumstances warranted it (though, as noted, this practice was later expressly dis-approved by the High Court in 1984, in *Mallet*).

O'Keefe argued that the proposals favouring full community of property, particularly *during* marriage, went beyond what was provided for in most overseas jurisdictions which had similarly amended their laws. The elimination of all discretion in the process of determining property rights might well rebound against women, particularly those who had been sole breadwinner or who had otherwise been responsible for the acquisition of all, or the substantial part, of the matrimonial property. A presumption of equal ownership of all the property could pave the way for income splitting in a tax system which has always been based on the individual, rather than the family, as the unit of assess-ment.[25] For women who work both outside and in the home, equal shares might not sufficiently recognize the financial *and* non-financial contributions involved. Women from low income families could be left liable for half of the marriage's accumulated debts, including those incurred solely by the husband. And as O'Keefe pointed out, the sugges-tion that both parties be required to sign their consent to dealings with family property still would not prevent overbearing and coercive force being applied to secure that consent. The legal requirement would not *of itself* significantly alter the inequalities in bargaining power.

WEL continued to campaign vigorously about its chosen model, but within the organization, dissent was growing. One critic was feminist and activist Eva Cox, whose paper circulated at the 1981 national meeting had influenced the decision to debate the issue further before adopting community property as national WEL policy.[26] In October 1981, the Family Law Action Group (FLAG: WEL's community of property lobby) circulated a detailed refutation of this paper. A key difference was the effect such a regime would have upon securing equality in areas other than family property. Cox argued that a fifty-fifty split of assets presumed that in other respects, such as in their access to paid work, women and men were similarly situated. She preferred a system of property allocation which acknowledged the unequal division of child care responsibilities and could compensate women for the economic disadvantages accrued through marriage. For women who had been unable to undertake paid work, or who had done so only on a part time basis, such a scheme, by including a compensation element, could result in their receiving more than half of the property.[27] Cox also pointed out that the community of property debate had little relevance to those who owned no property at all. By contrast, FLAG's argument was that it was not appropriate to use the context of matrimonial property law reform to effect other broad structural changes in the position of Australian women.

So vigorous did this debate become that in 1983, the *Australian Journal of Social Issues* published a special issue on family law with three articles specifically focused on it.[28] The two major proponents of 'equal rights to marital assets' were lawyer Jocelynne Scutt and activist Di Graham. Together and separately, they published papers, submissions, press releases, and a book addressed at the need for community property. In *For Richer, for Poorer*,[29] edited accounts of various Family Court decisions were used to demonstrate the unsatisfactory manner in which the Family Court was exercising its discretionary jurisdiction. Despite sharp criticism of the methodology and its general argument,[30] the book received wide media coverage giving its authors considerable opportunity to present 'the' feminist position.

The ALRC Reference on Matrimonial Property

The Law Reform Commission commenced an inquiry into matrimonial property in 1983. To assist it in its task, the Commissioner in charge, David Hambly, arranged for the Australian Institute of Family Studies (AIFS) to conduct an exhaustive empirical study of the economic consequences of divorce. Like its Californian counterpart,[31] the AIFS study demonstrated starkly the gross disparities in post-divorce living standards between women and men. Women living alone or as single parents experienced a vast decline in living standards, while men, including those who became sole parents, experienced improvement. Significantly, women, especially those who were custodial parents, were likely to receive more than fifty per cent of the basic assets,[32] usually somewhere around a sixty-forty division in their favour.[33] In a large number of cases women with custody were enabled to stay in the matrimonial home with their children. The Californian study had demonstrated that a strict regime of equal division led more often than not to the house being sold and the proceeds divided down the middle, leaving neither party, particularly a woman with limited or non-existent work experience or skills, in a position to purchase another property.[34]

With the preliminary results of the AIFS study available, in 1985 the ALRC published a discussion paper proposing a three stage model. The first stage was to identify the pool of property (including superannuation and 'financial resources') and assess the shares by reference to contribution, with equality of contributions to be presumed except in cases of substantial disparity. Secondly, shares should be adjusted where there was any disparity in the parties' capacity to achieve a reasonable standard of living after separation. This required a consideration of child care responsibilities during and after the marriage and the effect of the marriage on the respective income earning capacities of the parties. Thirdly, future maintenance needs were to be assessed in light of the property arrangement.[35] The Commission made it clear that it did not favour the establishment of a community of property regime, but preferred to focus on 'result equality'.

> Recognition of the different economic effects of the presumptively equal contributions made by the spouses to the marriage partnership may require unequal division of their property at the end of the marriage.[36]

They did, however, acknowledge that a greater degree of certainty was required as a basis on which the parties could negotiate.[37] Such a presumption had been rejected by the High Court in *Mallet*.

The publication of the discussion paper refuelled the debate. The commissioner debated community of property advocate, Jocelynne Scutt, on national television. It was put to her by one interviewer that a rigid division of fifty-fifty may leave women disadvantaged, as they did not have the same access to paid work as their ex-husbands. Scutt responded by saying that those matters were best dealt with by government training programmes, not by adjustments of property as between individuals.[38] By pitting a publicly identified feminist against a male law professor/bureaucrat, an impression was created that the positions lined up crudely as 'for' women's interests and 'against' them. Yet the real issue was one's view of 'equality', or more specifically, formal equality versus real, practical or result equality.

The ALRC's final report in 1987 endorsed the proposals for the three-stage division. The commission stated explicitly the principles upon which a matrimonial property regime should be based: the equal status of the spouses in marriage; the irrelevance of fault to a consideration of the parties' economic relationship; and a fair sharing between the members of the family of the economic hardship arising from the breakdown of marriage. For the commission, the central issue was not judicial discretion versus fixed entitlements, but rather, whether post-separation circumstances ought to be taken into account by matrimonial property law as opposed to social security or maintenance law.[39] The report pointed out that overseas, the enactment of 'equality' regimes had initially been seen as an advance for women, but empirical studies suggested that such a regime 'would aggravate the economic inequality that often arises from the differing effects of marriage and childrearing on the spouses'. It would change the direction of Family Court decision-making, 'primarily to the detriment of custodial parents and women whose earning capacity has been impaired by their marriage' and would 'conflict with the overwhelming weight of public opinion'.

> All the evidence leads to the conclusion that equal sharing of property at the end of a marriage is not necessarily fair sharing. A just sharing of property should be based upon a practical rather than a merely formal, view of the equal status of husbands and wives within marriage ... Thus, a just sharing of property should take into account any disparity arising from the marriage in the standards of living reasonably attainable by the parties after separation (para 273).

Matrimonial Property and Models of Equality: An Evaluation

The original divorce law reform moves in Australia shared with their overseas counterparts a failure to discuss divorce law within a context which took account of the deep-seated gender inequality between women and men.[40] While with hindsight it is sometimes assumed that no-fault divorce resulted from campaigning by the women's movement, informed by a commitment to equality based upon a notion of gender neutrality, in fact discussions of such issues came only later to this debate. Not until the new divorce laws had been operating for some time did evaluations of their impact on the relative circumstances of women and men begin to be made, in Australia as elsewhere. The matrimonial property issue was able to crystallize these concerns in a way that the earlier public discussion about the grounds of divorce had not.

In the US, Martha Fineman undertook a comprehensive study of the divorce law reform process and the matrimonial property debate in the state of Wisconsin. She suggested that the two key issues, past contribution and future needs, are related to the competing values of the symbolic notion of rule equality versus the more instrumentally oriented result equality.[41] While feminists have recognized that issues concerning the workplace and the market require the adoption of a result equality model (involving, for example, affirmative action), family law debates have remained largely untouched by such arguments. Fineman has demonstrated that feminists who became involved in the law reform process (well after the initial move toward no-fault divorce) relied upon a liberal equality model, based around the business metaphor of 'partnership'.

She suggests a number of reasons for this. Differential treatment on divorce does not seem to accord with a picture of the 'egalitarian' family during marriage. 'Second, ... result-oriented arguments for different treatment might be transferred to and used to perpetuate discriminatory beliefs already operating to disadvantage women at work'.[42] Third, it cannot automatically be assumed that all result equality (sometimes manifested as gender specific) rules in family law advantage women. Some gender specific rules, such as the 'tender years' doctrine in custody, may perpetuate the notion that biology is destiny.[43] Finally, at a rhetorical level, the recognition that equality does not exist may create an impression that it *cannot* exist. If women need special protective rules, this suggests that as a group women *are* dependent and may well remain so forever. Despite these arguments, Fineman concludes:

> To be satisfied with or to insist upon rule equality in divorce is to overlook the serious toll that an egalitarian ideology may take on women who must function in an unequal world which requires that they meet greater demands with fewer resources. It also elevates a simplified ideal to the status of a rule of decision, and obscures the real issues in divorce. Feminists, consistent with their desire to assist women, should be advocating the need for unequal treatment – for result equality – in divorce.[44]

Fineman's work helps put the Australian debate into broad perspective. The WEL campaign focused on a rhetorical and symbolic notion of rule equality, to the extent that its proponents were forced to reject any recognition of women's future needs by reference to their structurally disadvantaged position in the highly sex-segmented workforce and the unequal distribution of domestic and child care responsibilities. By contrast, women's movement critics and the Law Reform Commission recognized that a formal equality model, assuming equality of contribution to the marriage but ignoring the disadvantages created by marriage, and the future needs arising from that, provided little more than a rhetorical rallying cry.[45]

How did the Law Reform Commission come to reject the formal equality notion inherent in community of property? This can only be a matter of some speculation, but a number of possibilities suggest themselves. By the time Australia came to deal with this issue in comprehensive fashion, the empirical evidence from the US had clearly established the disastrous and unintended consequences of 'equality' on divorce for women and children. The Law Reform Commission personnel paid attention to structural economic issues, including housing and the labour market. A research paper on housing, commissioned by the ALRC as part of the reference,[46] demonstrated the difficulties faced by divorced women in securing alternative accommodation if their needs, particularly those as custodial parents, were not taken into particular account. It confirmed that equal sharing of marital assets would affect women particularly badly when it came to re-establishing a household. The Family Law Council and some members of the Family Court itself also supported the result equality model, or at least, a presumptive rule equality starting point, with provision for adjustments to be made on various criteria. A close working relationship developed between members of the Commission, the Family Court, the Australian Institute of Family Studies, which undertook the empirical research, and the Family Law Council.[47]

Public submissions to the inquiry manifested overwhelming community support for result equality over rule equality. The WEL/FLAG group received little support for its position from other organizations who made submissions. The very vigorous and public WEL campaign, given considerable assistance by extensive media coverage, did not succeed in persuading the ALRC that rule equality was the preferable model.

The National Women's Consultative Committee[48] expressly relied on the idea of result equality in its submission. The Victorian Women's Advisory Council explicitly rejected the New Zealand model of equal sharing since 'the corollary of this approach does not necessarily guarantee equality of results'. It referred to the preliminary findings of the AIFS study as confirming the dangers involved in equating equality of division with equality of result.[49] The Western Australia Women's Advisory Council shared this approach, emphasizing the poverty of women and children after divorce.[50] Similarly, the New South Wales Domestic Violence Committee (established within the Women's Co-ordination Unit of the Premier's Department) expressly rejected community of property, stating that it would undermine women's financial and legal independence and preclude the possibility of compensating women who are substantially disadvantaged as a result of marriage and motherhood. In a submission endorsed by the New South Wales Women's Legal Resources Centre, they argued that the court should retain its discretionary power to allocate property by reference to both past contributions *and* future needs. They stressed that the custodial parent should be compensated for the expenses of housing and rearing children and for their loss of earning capacity.[51]

As stated earlier, the commission's final report was tabled in Parliament in late 1987, but has not yet been implemented. But the matrimonial property debate in Australia provided an important opportunity for feminist law reform campaigners. It enabled feminists to demonstrate that what are acceptable strategies in the workplace and the market, such as affirmative action measures, could be applied equally to the 'private' world of the family and domestic relations, in particular to financial relations between parties to a dissolved marriage. Secondly, it clearly demonstrated the limitations inherent in the symbolic or rhetorical pursuit of formal equality for women in a highly gender-specific world where women do not have equal access to independent income and where domestic responsibilities, despite the increasing media attention given to 'new wave dads', are not shared. It also raised theoretical questions about the complex meaning of equality for women. The two models which were opposed in the matrimonial property debate, rule equality and result equality, are themselves constrained and by no means exhaust the range of possibilities for women seeking to understand the role of the law in the continued subordination of women.[52] But at the very least, the matrimonial property debate furthered discussion of the complex interrelationship between domestic production, the state and the market[53] and the structural and deep-seated nature of inequality between women and men in Australia.

Notes

I should like to thank Michael Chesterman, Eva Cox, Owen Jessep and Sophie Watson for helpful comments on earlier drafts. Justice Elizabeth Evatt and the Australian Law Reform Commission, and the Women's Electoral Lobby provided important background material for this chapter.

1. See, for example, Catharine A. MacKinnon, *Feminism Unmodified: Discourses on Life and Law*, Harvard University Press, Cambridge MA, 1987, especially chapter 9, 'Sexual Harassment: Its First Decade in Court', and her discussion of 'sexual politics as feminist jurisprudence, of possibilities for social change for women through law' (p.103). See also Part III, dealing with the creation of a civil right of action for people harmed by pornography.

2. The legislative focus of law reform in Australia must be contrasted with other countries, such as the US and Canada, where courts are used very much more as agents of change, through, for example, the test case strategy. Courts in Australia have played little part in the progressive development of laws. Indeed, some members of the appellate courts have expressly declined to make decisions which overtly change the law, stating that the doctrine of the separation of powers precludes them from undertaking what is properly the function of Parliament (see, for example, the views of the majority in *SGIC* v *Trigwell* (1979) 26 ALR 67, and *Dugan* v *Mirror Newspapers* (1978) 22 ALR 439). One possible reason for judicial non-activism in Australia is the lack of any constitutional guarantees, such as a Bill of Rights in Australia. This can be contrasted with the high profile of the US Supreme Court and the increasing amount of constitutional litigation in Canada, especially under the equality provisions of the recently enacted Charter of Rights and Freedoms 1982; see for example, the important decisions of *Roe* v *Wade* (1973) 410 US 179, and

Morgentaler v *R* (1988) Supreme Court of Canada, January 28, 1988.

3. Sophie Watson, *Accommodating Inequality: Gender and Housing,* Allen and Unwin, Sydney, 1988.

4. See Jocelynne Scutt and Di Graham, *For Richer For Poorer,* Penguin, Melbourne, 1984.

5. This gave the national parliament law-making power over ex-nuptial children in the referring states of New South Wales, Victoria, Tasmania and South Australia: see the Family Law Amendment Act 1987, which came into operation on April 1, 1988.

6. See Owen Jessep and Richard Chisholm, 'Children, the Constitution and the Family Court', (1985) 8 *University of South Wales Law Journal* 152; and Barbara Guthrie and Maureen Kingshott, 'Children', in R. Graycar and D. Shiff (eds), *Life Without Marriage: A Woman's Guide to the Law,* Pluto Press, Sydney, 1987.

7. For a discussion of legal issues concerning cohabiting couples, or as they are called in Australia, 'de facto relationships', see Graycar and Shiff (eds).

8. See David Hambly and J. Neville Turner, *Cases and Materials on Australian Family Law,* Law Book, Sydney, 1971.

9. See generally Richard Chisholm and Owen Jessep, 'Fault and Financial Adjustment under the Family Law Act', (1981) 4 *University of New South Wales Law Journal* 43.

10. Senate Standing Committee on Constitutional and Legal Affairs, *Interim Report on the Law and Administration of Divorce and Related Matters and the Clauses of the Family Law Bill 1974,* AGPS, Canberra; Senate Standing Committee on Constitutional and Legal Affairs, *Report on the Law and Administration of Divorce and Related Matters and the Clauses of the Family Law Bill 1974,* AGPS, Canberra.

11. See, for example, Martha Fineman, 'Implementing Equality: Ideology, Contradiction and Social Change. A Study of Rhetoric and Results in the Regulation of the Consequences of Divorce', (1983) *Wisconsin Law Review* 789; Herma Hill Kay, 'Equality and Difference: A Perspective on No-Fault Divorce and its Aftermath' (1987) 56 *Cincinatti Law Journal* 1.

12. See Peter J. McDonald, (ed.) and the Australian Institute of Family Studies (AIFS), *Settling up: Property and Income Distribution on Divorce in Australia,* Prentice Hall, Melbourne 1986, p. 315.

13. The recent amendments to the legislation, designed to link the Family Law Act more closely with the social security system by tighter enforcement of both child and spouse maintenance, detract from the 'clean break' philosophy by requiring the Family Court to give priority to periodic ongoing maintenance over any other form, such as lump sums, and making it more difficult finally to resolve financial matters between the parties: see, for example, s.66E, s.80(2) and ss.87(4A)-(4C).

14. Despite eschewing consideration of 'fault', the courts, in evaluating the wife's contribution as 'homemaker and parent' under s.79(4) may make reference to the quality of the wife's services, a matter one of my colleagues describes as the 'lemon meringue pie' test: i.e. 'is she a good housewife, cook etc'.

15. This is the section detailing the matters which may be taken into account in maintenance actions

16. *Mallet* v *Mallet* (1984) 52 ALR 193, 207 (per Mason J).

17. See, for example, Ellen Malos (ed.), *The Politics of Housework,* Allison and Busby, London, 1980.

18. See, for example, *Wardman and Hudson* (1978) 33 FLR 196.

19. *Mallet* v *Mallet.*

20. The phrase 'rule of thumb' originally referred to the thickness of the stick with which it was deemed permissible for a man to beat his wife. Those who used weapons thicker than their thumbs risked criminal liability for this activity.

21. Joint Select Committee on the Family Law Act (the Ruddock Committee), *Family Law in Australia,* AGPS, Canberra. 1980.

22. Women's Electoral Lobby New South Wales, Family Law Action Group (WEL), *Discussion Paper on Reform of Marital Property Laws in Australia by means of a system of Community of Property,* February, 1981, para 4.4.

23. Elizabeth O'Keefe, 'A Discussion Paper on Property Rights in Marriage and Property Distribution on Divorce', Office of Women's Affairs, Canberra, 1981.

24. Rebecca Bailey, 'Community of property', Discussion Paper, National Women's Advisory Council, AGPS, Canberra, 1982. See also Rebecca Bailey, 'Principles of Property Distribution on Divorce: Compensation, Need or Community?', (1980) 54 *Australian Law Journal* 190.

25. The one significant exception to the individual as the unit of assessment in Australian tax law is the dependent spouse rebate.

26. Eva Cox, 'Community of Property: A Step Forward or Back?', paper prepared for the WEL national conference, July, 1981.

27. Cox further developed this 'compensation' model in a review of the ALRC's 1985 discussion paper; see Eva Cox, 'Matrimonial Property Scuttled' (1985) 10 *Legal Service Bulletin* 192. For another discussion of this compensation approach, see McDonald (ed.) pp. 313–16.

28. Jocelynne A. Scutt, 'Equal Marital Property Rights' (1983) 18 *Australian Journal of Social Issues* 128; Elizabeth O'Keefe, 'Property Rights on Marriage and Property Distribution on Divorce: Room for Manoeuvre', (1983) 18 *Australian Journal of Social Issues* 136; Eva Cox, 'Beyond Community of Property: A Plea for Equity', (1983) 18 *Australian Journal of Social Issues* 142.

29. See Scutt and Graham.

30. For an example of a critical review see Deena Shiff and Susan MacIllhatton, 'Review of *For Richer, for Poorer*', (1985) 10 *Legal Service Bulletin* 29.

31. Lenore Weitzman, *The Divorce Revolution: The Unexpected Social and Economic Consequences for Women and Children in America*, Free Press, New York, 1985.

32. It should be stressed that the 'basic assets' usually means only those assets, such as the matrimonial home, closely associated with the marriage.

33. McDonald (ed.), and the Australian Institute of Family Studies, p. 184.

34. See Weitzman. For some comments on this work, which has generated a vast body of literature, see Martha Fineman, 'Illusive Equality: On Weitzman's *Divorce Revolution*', (1986) *American Bar Foundation Research Journal* 781, and, for an earlier discussion of similar issues, see Fineman, 'Implementing Equality: Ideology, Contradiction and Social Change. A Study of Rhetoric and Results in the Regulation of the Consequences of Divorce', (1983) *Wisconsin Law Review* 789; Herbert Jacob, 'Faulting No-Fault' (1986) American Bar Foundation Research Journal 773; Marigold S. Melli, 'Constructing a Social Problem: The Post-Divorce Plight of Women and Children' (1986) *American Bar Foundation Research Journal* 759; and Martha Minow, 'Consider the Consequences', (1986) 84 *Michigan Law Review* 900.

35. Australian Law Reform Commission, 'Matrimonial Property Law', Discussion Paper No. 22, AGPS, 1985, paras. 149–59.

36. Ibid., para 146.

37. C.f. Robert Mnookin and L. Kornhauser, 'Bargaining in the Shadow of the Law: the Case of Divorce', (1979) 88 *Yale Law Journal;* 950.

38. 'Pressure Point', ABC Television, August 1, 1985.

39. Australian Law Reform Commission, 'Matrimonial Property Law', Report No. 39, AGPS, 1987, para 270.

40. See, for example, Fineman; Carol Smart, *The Ties that Bind: Law, Marriage and the Reproduction of Patriarchal Relations*, Routledge & Kegan Paul, London, 1984; and Kay.

41. See Fineman, pp. 791–2.

42. Fineman, p. 825. This argument resonates with concerns about 'protective legislation' in the workplace: see Katherine O'Donovan, 'Protection or Paternalism' in M.D.A Freeman (ed.), *The State, the Law and the Family*, Tavistock, London, 1984; Chris Burvill, 'Women and Protective Legislation', (1985) 28 *Refractory Girl* 27; Frances Olsen, 'From False Paternalism to False Equality: Judicial Assaults on Feminist Community, Illinois 1869–1895', (1986) 84 *Michigan Law Review* 1518.

43. However, it is now well documented that the recent shift toward the 'gender neutral' idea of joint custody may well work against women's interests: see Frances Olsen,

'The Politics of Family Law' (1984) 2 *Law and Inequality* 1; Martha Fineman, 'Dominant Discourse, Professional Language and Legal Change in Child Custody Decision Making' (1988) 101 *Harvard Law Review* 727; Regina Graycar, 'Equal Rights versus Fathers' Rights: the Child Custody Debate in Australia' in S. Sevenhuijsen and C. Smart (eds), *Child Custody and the Politics of Gender*, Routledge, London, 1989.

44. Fineman, p. 826.

45. For some empirical data on single parents in Australia, see Meg Montague and Jenny Stephens, *Paying the price for Sugar and Spice: A Study of Women's Pathways into Social Security Recipiency*, Brotherhood of St. Laurence and National Women's Advisory Council, AGPS, 1985; Judy Raymond, 'Bringing up Children Alone: Policies for Sole Parents', *Social Security Review*, Issues paper No. 3, Department of Social Security, Woden, ACT, 1987.

46. Sophie Watson, 'Housing After Divorce', ALRC Research Paper No. 2, Matrimonial Property Inquiry, 1985.

47. The AIFS and the Family Law Council are statutory bodies established by the Family Law Act and were involved closely in monitoring its workings since it began operation in 1976.

48. National Women's Consultative Committee, Submission to ALRC Matrimonial Property Inquiry, 1985 (on file with ALRC).

49. Victorian Women's Advisory Council, Submission to ALRC Matrimonial Property Inquiry, 1986 (on file with ALRC).

50. WA Women's Advisory Council, Submission to ALRC Matrimonial Property Inquiry, 1986 (on file with ALRC).

51. New South Wales Domestic Violence Committee, Submission to ALRC Matrimonial Property Inquiry, 1985 (on file with ALRC); and see also Women's Legal Resources Centre (NSW), Submission to ALRC Matrimonial Property Inquiry, 1985 (on file with ALRC).

52. See, for example, the explanations of women's inequality which focus *not* on women's differences from or similarities to men, but on issues of hierarchy and subordination: see Catharine A. MacKinnon; and for an example of the application of a broader range of different models of equality in a specific law reform context, see Elizabeth A. Sheehy, 'Personal Autonomy and the Criminal Law', Background Paper, Canadian Advisory Council on the Status of Women, Ottawa, 1987.

53. Frances Olsen, 'The Family and the Market: A Study of Ideology and Legal Reform' (1983) 96 *Harvard Law Review* 1497; Katherine O'Donovan, *Sexual Divisions in Law*, Weidenfeld and Nicholson, 1985.

PART III

Debating Strategies

12

Sex Equality and the Australian Body Politic

Barbara Sullivan

Australian feminist movements have long been preoccupied with obtaining equality for women in the public sphere. Since the emergence of 'second wave' feminism in the 1970s however, demands for 'sex equality' have been inextricably linked to the concept of sex discrimination. Indeed, sex discrimination has often been seen as wholly or largely responsible for a number of specific phenomena including a marked sex-based disparity in wages and wealth, the different participation rates of men and women in higher and technical education and the under-representation of women in the public institutions of political decision-making.[1] Feminists have called upon the state to enact anti-discrimination laws which aim to foster 'sex equality' by outlawing sex discrimination in the public sphere. This approach has, at times, been subjected to radical critique.[2] However, the demand for sex equality legislation has assumed a significant and highly visible position within Australian feminism over the last decade.

This chapter has two main concerns. First it investigates the nature of the sex equality granted to Australian women by the enactment of federal sex discrimination legislation in 1984. A close textual reading of the parliamentary debates which occurred during review of the 1983 Sex Discrimination Bill reveals that a number of significant cultural prohibitions and constraints upon the activities of women were brought to bear on (and incorporated in) the legislation. It will be suggested that these have significantly limited the realization of 'sex equality' in the Australian body politic.

Second it explores some of the categories and concepts produced by framing a more general demand for 'sex equality' within a strategy designed to outlaw 'sex discrimination'. Such an undertaking is perhaps particularly relevant for those feminists seeking to improve the status of women by mobilizing the legal framework of the state. However, as part of a more general evaluation of feminist strategies the focus will be upon the pursuit of 'sex equality' and of measures designed to bring about 'the destruction of gender' in the public sphere. It will be argued that degendering strategies (such as sex discrimination laws) cannot address the often irrational adherence to sex specific identities, behaviours and practices – especially those constitutive of sex discrimination. Indeed, the passage of sex discrimination legislation may be the moment at which the existing boundaries between public and private life are confirmed with issues bearing on (women's) sexual difference being firmly relocated in the private sphere. Moves to degender the public sphere may privatize and depoliticize issues of particular relevance to women such as abortion, maternity and child care.

This is not to suggest that sex discrimination legislation is of no value. While the limitations and advantages of degendering proposals need to be addressed there are some pertinent reasons for continuing to pursue 'sex equality'. When combined with an explicit critique of the public/private distinction, degendering laws may be an important part of a broader political strategy which aims to improve the circumstances of women's lives.

The 1983 Sex Discrimination Bill

This Bill was presented to parliament by Senator Susan Ryan in June 1983, shortly after the election of the Hawke government. Over the next eight months it formed a focus of intense public debate and media interest.

The Bill had three stated objectives:

(1) to give effect to certain provisions of the United Nations Convention on the Elimination of All Forms of Discrimination Against Women

(2) to eliminate so far as is possible, discrimination against persons on the ground of sex, marital status or pregnancy in the areas of work, accommodation, education, the provision of goods, facilities and services, the disposal of land, the activities of clubs and the administration of Commonwealth laws and programmes

(3) to promote recognition and acceptance within the community of the principle of the equality of men and women

The scope of the Sex Discrimination Bill was clearly broad and far-reaching, in contrast to the more limited legislation enacted in the US, Britain and Canada.[3] The provisions in regard to sexual harassment represented the first attempt by an Australian legislature to come to terms with this form of sex discrimination and, like the Bill as a whole, took into account the experiences of three State governments (South Australia, New South Wales and Victoria) with anti-discrimination laws in place for some time. However, the Bill did not constitute a 'blanket' attempt to outlaw sex discrimination. Only *certain* provisions of the United Nations Conventions were to be given legislative force and the aim was to eliminate sex discrimination in the public sphere only 'so far as is possible'. This indicates the presence of intractable sex discrimination in the public sphere. Similarly, couching the fourth or equality objective of the Bill in terms of 'the *principle* of the equality of men and women' must cast some official doubt upon how, or in what way, such a principle could operate in practice.

From its inception the Sex Discrimination Bill encompassed only a limited view of 'sex equality' and of the areas in which sex discrimination was to be illegal. This reflected – in part at least – some of the major political concerns of the new Labor government which, while attempting to implement reforms along the lines suggested by various feminists (including those within the Labor party itself), was concerned about alienating the more traditional sections of the Australian electorate. As the Sex Discrimination Bill sought a selective outlawing of sex discrimination in the public sphere so the areas of non-address, the various omissions and exemptions, as well as the limitations set on the process of anti-discrimination, reflected a set of significant cultural prohibitions and constraints upon the activities of women in Australian society. One clear example was the armed forces exemption which permitted the military to discriminate against women – on the grounds of their sex alone – regarding positions involving combat or combat-related duties.[4] In parliament, members of all major political parties agreed that it was not appropriate or customary practice in Australia for women to perform such duties.

Two quite distinct and competing discourses can be identified. These are what will be termed the 'degendering discourse' and the 'biological discourse'. Each brought different premises and assumptions to bear on the process of review and came to disparate conclusions about the meaning of sexual difference and its relevance to the organization of social life.

As a result of its adoption by the Labor party, the Australian Democrats and significant sections of the Liberal-National party opposition, the degendering discourse dominated debate in parliament and was clearly implicit in the Bill from its inception. Proponents of the degendering discourse argued that the visibly different gender roles adopted by men and women in society were wholly the result of a socialization process instigated at birth. Thus, as one member of the government argued:

> All of us here are the product of a society with discrimination between the sexes deeply entrenched. From the pink and blue baby rugs to manual arts and home economics, *society* has tended to predetermine the future direction of a person's life based on that person's sex.[5] (emphasis added)

Women are seen to be particularly disadvantaged by their gender socialization for, as Ros Kelly, Labor member for Canberra, argued:

> Values in society determine a stereotyped role for women, that is, that women's participation in the workforce is peripheral and secondary to their roles as homemakers and childbearers.[6]

This, it was suggested, was why women tended to be poorer and less educated than men, with fewer prospects of achievement in the public sphere. A review of inappropriate and old-fashioned sex roles was then deemed necessary for women to attain equality with men.

The degendering discourse posited 'gender' as the *arbitrary* assignment of social characteristics and roles to each sex. While a person's 'sex' was regarded as biological and therefore fixed, their 'gender' was seen to be 'social' and thus mutable. As women were socially disadvantaged by the gender roles and characteristics imputed to their sex, a 'degendering' of the public sphere was necessary. This, it was argued, would ensure that women could compete equally in the public sphere, enjoying the same rights and duties as male citizens.

The 'biological discourse', on the other hand, refused the sex/gender distinction and contended that the different social roles adopted by men and women reflected an immutable and biological division between the sexes. As one Liberal Senator argued:

> Not one Bill or even dozens of Bills are going to change the natural characteristics of men and women ... most ordinary, natural women are homely and caring ... they are not wildly ambitious ... they are not naturally dominating ... they are mostly inclined to avoid authority. They are, by nature, more cautious and more considerate. It strikes me that ... [this] Bill makes it an offence for those characteristics to be taken into account.
>
> Men by nature are more likely to be leaders, providers and protectors.[7]

In this view the 'natural' characteristics of men and women and, in particular, their different reproductive functions determined quite different social roles for each sex. Sex discrimination legislation was deemed 'unnecessary' for the different treatment accorded to each sex in the public sphere represented not 'sex discrimination' but an acknowledgement of fundamental sex disparities.[8] The biological discourse also saw anti-discrimination legislation as disruptive to the 'natural' order of society. Relations between men and women were, it was argued, based in complementarity rather than equality and found their fullest expression in the traditional, patriarchal family.[9] The existing sexual division of labour and the key role which women played in the maintenance of the private sphere was, therefore, both recognized and vigorously defended as the basis of all order in the public sphere. As one Liberal senator argued in his attack on the Bill:

> The real intention and purpose of this legislation ... is to redefine and to restructure the role of women, more particularly the family unit within the society. It is a not too subtle attempt to destroy the structure, the fabric, the values and the intrinsic role of the family unit which, for centuries, has been the foundation of our orderly and disciplined society.[10]

The biological discourse saw the traditional, patriarchal family and the privatization of women therein as the only foundation of a stable and healthy society – that is, one with a foundation in nature. This clearly cut across the sense in which women were free and equal individuals or citizens with the same rights and duties as men.

Proponents of the degendering discourse on the other hand tended to view the family as a flexible and resilient social institution amenable to rational social change.[11] One senator argued that certain 'less palatable' aspects of the family – which, in her words, included its nuclear structure and patriarchal dominance – were 'already in the process of modification'.[12] Another senator suggested that, by extending the rights of all individuals, sex discrimination legislation would 'improve family relations, not undermine them'.[13] Similarly, senator Olive Zalcharov contended that the Bill stood to strengthen the family unit because 'improved access to education should produce mothers better able to assist their child's development.'[14] In general then, supporters of the degendering discourse were optimistic about the future of the family. They sought to preserve the existing separation of public and private spheres but argued against the fixed allocation of men and women therein. Both sexes were to have equality of opportunity and to be free to move between both spheres.[15] Indeed, the achievement of equitable relations between the sexes in both public and private spheres was seen to be the only secure foundation of social harmony and order.[16]

While this position on the family was widely adopted by supporters of the degendering discourse in parliament there are also some indications of a deep unease about the effects of 'sex equality' on the family unit. A variety of conceptual and rhetorical strategies were deployed by the degendering discourse to permit a defence of the traditional patriarchal family. Sex discrimination was seen to be an issue of relevance to the public sphere alone with the 'private' aspects of family left essentially separate and unconnected. Thus, the biological and degendering discourses converged in their need, or desire for, the preservation of an existing sexual division of labour in society.

Sex Equality and Sex Discrimination

On presenting the Sex Discrimination Bill to Parliament, Senator Susan Ryan cited statistical evidence of 'deeply embedded structural inequalities in our society'. Her figures demonstrated significant sex disparities in such areas as average weekly earnings, unemployment rates and the numbers of each sex engaged in vocational training programs or apprenticeships. The Bill was presented as 'an opportunity to combat some of these inequalities' by legislating to outlaw sex discrimination.[17] This suggested that discrimination in the public sphere was wholly and directly responsible for the aggregation of women in unskilled and poorly paid occupations and for their lack of representation in the public institutions of political decision-making.

This approach was rejected by supporters of the biological discourse who, like the member for Braddon, argued:

> The legislation seeks to eliminate some forms of discrimination. It is interesting to consider for a moment the word 'discrimination'. According to the Oxford Dictionary it means ... 'to distinguish between' or 'give due weight to differences'. Should we not give due recognition to differences which exist? The philosophy from which this Bill springs does not recognize any innate differences between male and female.[20]

For supporters of the biological discourse the Sex Discrimination Bill was attempting to eliminate innate differences and encourage an unnatural 'sameness' between the sexes. The concept of sex equality was connected to the perceived aims of an androgynous unisex society.[21]

Supporters of degendering were specific in their rejection of this view of 'sex equality'.[22] They argued that 'men and women just cannot be made into so-called unisex persons'.[23] As Senator Giles put it:

> 'Different' does not mean better or worse; it simply means different. We are all a mixture of masculine and feminine characteristics which have little to do with our intrinsic worth.[24]

The idea that individuals are 'a mixture' of masculine and feminine (gender) characteristics supports the more general thrust of the degendering discourse that, while there are two sexes, the most significant differences between men and women can be conceptualized in terms of gender roles that are both relatively superficial and eminently flexible. Thus there are no essential or non-negotiable differences which require unequal treatment in the public sphere.

For proponents of degendering the Sex Discrimination Bill was seen variously as 'a positive step to promote the equality of men and women'[25] or as 'a precondition' for the establishment of 'some sort of equality' between the sexes.[26] While one Labor senator suggested that the goal of women achieving 'equality with men' was 'subhuman' because 'we are ourselves stereotypes',[27] Senator Hill pointed out that the Bill was concerned only to establish 'equal treatment' for both sexes in the public sphere.[28] This meant that, in employment, women and men should compete with each other 'on the basis of merit and without regard to sex'.[29] The concept of 'sex equality' was, for supporters of degendering, intimately connected with the notion of 'social justice'[30] and with the Australian tradition of 'giving a person a fair go'.[31]

In what areas then did the degendering discourse and the Sex Discrimination Bill fail to give women 'a fair go' or contravene distinctions

of merit made 'without regard to sex'? Several exemptions from the Bill
are particularly important here. In response to heavy lobbying from
religious groups, the government agreed to exempt church schools from
certain provisions of the legislation. At first this permitted church schools
to discriminate on the grounds of sex, marital status or pregnancy where
it could be represented that such discrimination was in accordance with
the doctrine or creed of a specific church. Later, the exemption was
strengthened so that any discrimination committed 'in good faith' and
'in order to avoid injury to the religious susceptibilities of the adherent
of a particular religion' was lawful. Thus where the demands of 'sex
equality' conflicted with the moral, and often patriarchal, requirements
of a church school the concept of merit was deemed inoperable. Social
justice for women was treated as secondary to notions of religious and
institutional freedom.

Similarly, the exemption of the Social Security Act from the ambit of
the Sex Discrimination Act permits a continuation of the situation in
which social welfare is administered in a discriminatory manner.[32] Under
the Social Security Act a woman who begins living in a de facto
relationship is no longer eligible for welfare benefits, the assumption
being that the man will automatically assume financial responsibility for
that woman and her children. While this specific exemption was justified
in terms of fiscal constraints and the demands of the social welfare
budget it is clear that it is founded upon patriarchal assumptions about
the role of women, forcing them into (often fragile) relations of
economic dependence upon individual men.

The armed forces exemption allowed the military to discriminate
against women, on the grounds of their sex alone, in positions involving
combat or combat-related duties. Unlike the Social Security exemption
(which was justified by reference to general budgetary considerations) or
the exemption of church schools (justified by the need to guarantee
religious freedom), the armed forces exemption was defended only in
terms of 'customary practice' and the need to protect women from the
rigours of 'combat preparedness'.[33] While the employment ramifications
of this exemption are significant in a period of high unemployment the
mandatory exclusion of women from combat and combat-related duties
has broader implications. The armed forces exemption perpetuates the
notion of a sexually differentiated set of rights and duties for, historically, the most important duty of a citizen – indeed often a qualification
for full citizenship – was the readiness to bear arms in defence of one's
country. If women are specifically excluded from this important duty of
citizenship, on what ground can they claim to be citizens on an equal
basis with men?

Some recent feminist work has explored the traditional connections between masculinity, citizenship and the bearing of arms. Lloyd, for example, has argued that citizenship in western cultures has been a male preserve predominantly because of its connection to arms-bearing and the masculinity of war.[34] The exclusion of women from combat duties is, then a defence of what one former commander of the US marines has called 'the manliness of war'.[35]

Similarly, Pateman has suggested that combat units are 'fraternities in action'. It is in bearing arms and by engaging in warfare (real or otherwise) that men forge effective fraternal bonds, although, clearly, there are other sites in the social formation where this also occurs (for example in all-male schools, churches, sporting clubs, and so on). As Pateman argues, these fraternal bonds are formed in opposition to the 'female' aspects of culture and all that women's bodies symbolically represent. They permit men to share a common interest in upholding a 'fraternal social contract' which both 'establishes their right as men and allows them to gain material and psychological benefits from women's subjection'. By this argument, fraternal bonding is the means by which a specifically modern form of patriarchy is maintained.[36]

It can be suggested, then, that the armed forces exemption represents a successful defence of one particularly privileged site of fraternal bonding. For supporters of the degendering discourse, the armed forces exemption – as well as the other exemption discussed above – represented a strategic retreat from the concept of a fully degendered public sphere and a thorough-going equality between the sexes. While this was rationalized in terms of political expediency, the limitations of the political system can be said to reflect (and perhaps reconstruct) a set of significant cultural prohibitions and constraints upon the activities of women.

The Family and Equality of Opportunity

The preamble to the United Nations Convention on the Elimination of All Forms of Discrimination Against Women observed:

> a change in the traditional role of men as well as the role of women in society and in the family is needed to achieve full equality between men and women.

The degendering implicit in this call for a review of (gender) roles within the family, was clearly anathema to the biological discourse. Senator Flo Bjelke-Petersen described it as 'nothing short of social engineering' and argued that traditional sex roles were 'the means by which families have been nurtured for generations'.[37] Similarly, one Liberal party senator contended that it was 'grossly impertinent' to suggest that the sexes could only be equal if there was a change in the traditional family roles of men and women. Married women, he said, who remain at home 'have chosen the role which they have undertaken and are perfectly happy and perfectly equal'.[38]

For the degendering discourse too, there were some significant tensions associated with the anticipated effects of sex equality legislation on the family unit. As one member of the government argued:

> the family is the cornerstone of our democratic society. History has shown us that to ignore the importance of the family unit is to bring about society's downfall.[39]   .

For this speaker at least the family was a more vulnerable and less resilient institution than the degendering discourse as a whole might suggest. Indeed, simply by ignoring it, society's downfall could be brought about. While this position was not widely adopted by supporters of the Bill, many were careful to distance themselves from the charge that anti-discrimination legislation would alter the existing relations prevailing within families and in the private sphere. As one senator suggested, 'The Bill does nothing to undermine the traditional role of women as child-bearers and homecarers'.[40] Similarly, the opposition spokesman on women's affairs and a leading supporter of the Bill, told the House that:

> If families or children were to suffer because of anti-discrimination legislation, no member or Senator of this Parliament would even contemplate initiating let alone supporting such a measure.[41]

In other words, if anti-discrimination legislation was going to disrupt the orderly arrangements of the private sphere, women should continue to suffer discrimination in the public sphere. This reveals a traditional belief in a different hierarchy of rights and duties for women and men because, while men could operate in the public sphere without a detailed concern for 'families and children', women could not.

The biological and degendering discourses converge in their need or desire for the preservation of the traditional, patriarchal family. Unless women do indeed have 'natural' characteristics and roles in regard to 'families and children', it is clear that a defence of existing arrangements in the private sphere will cut across and significantly undermine the rights which women might hold in regard to citizenship and the public sphere.

The convergence of both discourses in a defence of the patriarchal family represents a specific recognition that the existing arrangements of the public sphere are dependent upon a sexual division of labour in the private sphere. While for the biological discourse this is both 'natural' and unproblematic, the same cannot be said for a liberal degendering discourse seeking to include women in the social and political order on an equal basis with men.

In order to address this problem the degendering discourse resorted to a very successful conceptual and rhetorical strategy. The concept of 'equality of opportunity' was mobilized to justify a defence of traditional family life while at the same time addressing issues of 'inequality' in the public sphere. Analysis of the debates reveals that the concept of 'equality of opportunity' was deployed in a specific manner to relations between the sexes. A different set of opportunities were seen to be available to men and women. One government senator, for example, argued that:

> this Bill is designed to create a situation whereby women in Australia can make a choice to find human fulfilment either within the mutual care and affection of a full-time family role within the household or within employment or some educational opportunity.[42]

Hence, for women (but not men) equality of opportunity involved, in the first instance, a choice between public and private spheres. Conceptualized in this way, claims to a substantive sex equality in the public sphere can be undermined by reference to equal opportunity and the 'choice', by women, of a privatized existence in the family. This has been a traditional strategy for both explaining and justifying the secondary status of women, as reference to the 'choices' which women make is seen as evidence of their 'consent' to the status quo.

In emphasizing the freedom to choose between various social opportunities 'equality of opportunity' does not require equal material rewards for equivalent work. The focus on equality of opportunity clearly circumscribed the egalitarian potential of the legislation and signalled a strategic retreat from a fully degendered concept of sex equality. While this retreat was politically expedient it stood to preserve and defend many of the privileges which male individuals enjoyed in the public sphere and an existing sexual division of labour in the private sphere on which the maintenance of such privileges depended.

The Strategy of Degendering

The conceptual effects of adopting a degendering strategy have not been widely addressed by feminists seeking to 'play the state'. It has long been assumed that the correct feminist objective is a sexually egalitarian society in which 'virtually no public recognition is given to the fact that there is a physiological sex difference between persons'.[43] Thus sex equality requires 'the destruction of gender'.[44]

Gatens, on the other hand, has argued that degendering proposals are fundamentally flawed in their assumption of a sex/gender distinction. Attempting to force a 'split' between the biological sex and the socially acquired gender identity of individuals is, she suggests, a misguided tactic that relies on a theory of mind and body in which both are posited as the neutral and passive mediators of social 'lessons'. As degendering is an implicitly rationalist strategy the determination of individual identity is seen to occur at the level of ideas or 'the mind' and the body is set aside as indifferent or irrelevant. This involves a specific misrepresentation of the significance of gender and its 'intimate relation to biology-as-lived in a social and historical context'.[45]

Degendering strategies generally posit a programme of re-education and re-socialization as the 'solution' to the oppression of women. The 1983 Discrimination Bill clearly aims at both of these as well as at providing a set of sanctions against individual recalcitrants. Such proposals involve a specific disavowal of mind/body connections *and* fail to take into account what Gatens calls 'the extreme resilience of expressions of sexual difference and the network of language and other systems of signification that both constitute and perpetuate this difference'.[46]

Degendering proposals ignore the psychical construction of sexed bodies. As distinct male and female subjectivities are embedded substantively in each individual's unconscious well before adulthood[47] degendering proposals cannot begin to address the unconscious bases for the apparently irrational adherence to sex-specific identities, behaviours and practices – especially those constitutive of 'Sex discrimination'. By allowing only a rationalist/behaviourist account of women's oppression, which is to say, admitting address only of what women subjects 'remember', what can be consciously known or demonstrated, they are doomed to repudiate, in varying degrees, the significance of the female body.

Degendering proposals may be not only ineffective but detrimental if the imposition of a rationalist framework requires the denial of the lived experience of a female body. The debates around the Sex Discrimination Bill provide some evidence for this proposition. In supporting the legislation, Senator Janine Haines argued:

> the Bill acknowledges that women are born with both a brain and a womb ... our brains ... remain productive and creative for a darn sight longer than our wombs do.[48]

In order to stress her essential sameness with men – a connection that is forged via the brain or mind – it is necessary for this speaker to deny her 'womb' or any connection between her mind and the lived experience of her body (including her 'womb').

In a similar vein, Helen Mayer suggested to the House of Representatives that:

> Either one accepts that pregnancy and childbirth are normal physical functions, impairing skills and expertise not at all, or one is faced with the proposition that there is something not quite right about these functions.[49]

As several opponents of the legislation pointed out, however, even a normal pregnancy may 'impair' some of the functions and skills which are privileged in the public sphere. While this is *not* the same as arguing that there is something 'not quite right' about women's reproductive capacities, it has traditionally been on these grounds that women's exclusion from the public sphere has been justified. It is understandable then that Ms Mayer should wish to deny that a pregnant body is likely to cause any 'inconvenience' in the public sphere.

It is women and not men who are forced to deny their sexual specificity in the public sphere. This calls into question the characterization within liberal philosophy of the public sphere as a realm without gender, or abstract individualism and universal values. It confirms Pateman's view that the 'civil body politic ... is fashioned after only one of the two bodies of mankind'.[50] The individual in civil society may be characterized as a masculine individual[51] with the public sphere being structured around 'ideal conceptions of manliness and traditional assumptions about the roles of men'.[52] The perceived autonomy of individuals in the public sphere and their freedom to choose between a variety of social 'opportunities' is premised on an essential independence from domestic concerns such as childminding. Within the traditional sexual division of labour it is women who are responsible for 'children and families', a practice which effectively excludes them from choosing between opportunities in the public sphere, on an equal basis with men.

One further indication of the 'masculinity' of the public sphere is provided by the analysis of official attitudes towards paid maternity leave. While the Sex Discrimination Bill outlawed discrimination on the grounds of pregnancy in the workplace, it did not establish any mandatory maternity leave provisions. In presenting the legislation to Parliament, the government specifically excluded this possibility. When it ratified the United Nations Convention on the Elimination of All Forms of Discrimination Against Women, the attached schedule of the Bill, it did so with two provisos, one of which negated the maternity leave provisions of this Convention in its Australian context. (The other proviso related to the participation of women in combat and combat-related duties.)

This means that most workers who become pregnant will be forced into relations of economic dependence, on their spouse or on the state, until they are able to return to their jobs. The organization of work in our society appears unable to accommodate one of the most common life experiences of adult females. The 'universality' of the public sphere is maintained only by displacing disruptive factors – such as women when they are pregnant and visibly not the same as men – out of the public sphere and into the private sphere. The 'efficiency of the public sphere is premised upon the ownership of an 'unproblematic' male body.

This conclusion is reinforced by a consideration of the attitudes towards abortion raised by debate around the Sex Discrimination Bill. Whilst in the Senate, the Bill came under heavy attack from 'Right to Life' groups which argued that the legislation could be used to guarantee 'abortion on demand'. The government agreed to insert an additional clause which specified that the legislation would have no application to the provision of services which, by their nature, 'can only be provided to members of one sex'.[53] Thus, although abortion is available throughout Australia – subject to a variety of different state laws, judicial decisions and administrative ambiguities – the consideration of 'sex discrimination' is set apart from the 'private' needs of women to control their fertility. It is clear that in the case of abortion and maternity leave, 'sex equality' implies that women would have only the same rights as men regardless of some major differences in needs and concerns.

Degendering proposals tend to impose a norm of male life experiences on female subjects. This process occurs within the context of a society in which 'masculinity' is already deeply embedded, indeed valorized, within the existing structures and values of the public sphere. As long as these issues remain both unacknowledged and uncontested, the application of degendering proposals is unlikely to significantly alter the conditions of women's lives and may actually reinforce their marginal position in the body politic.

Conclusion

The analysis of debates around the 1983 Sex Discrimination Bill reveals two major areas of concern for feminists. The 'sex equality' granted to Australian women by the promulgation of this legislation in 1984 is shot through with a range of cultural prohibitions and constraints. While some of these issues (for example, a limited extension of paid maternity leave) have been addressed in subsequent federal legislation for 'Affirmative Action', it is clear that there is, as yet, no 'sex equality' in the Australian body politic.

As a political strategy for feminism, the degendering framework has serious limitations. Nevertheless, anti-discrimination laws do provide an avenue of (limited) redress for individual complainants, and may assume an important normative function on society at large by specifying the unacceptability of certain acts and forms of behaviour.[54] The public discussion of issues arising from complaints of sex discrimination can have significant flow-on benefits for women other than individual complainants. For example, the concept of 'sexual harassment' has entered popular discourse in Australia over the last five years as a direct result of the intense media attention on several controversial cases in New South Wales and Queensland. Such publicity, while often sensational, may have had significant disciplinary effects on what is often regarded as 'normal' masculine behaviour in the workplace.

It is no accident that the demand for sex equality in the public sphere (rather than some of the other issues raised by feminists such as rape, pornography, sexist advertising, and abortion) has been taken up by political parties in Australia, North America and Europe. Degendering proposals engage with the existing categories and assumption of liberal discourse by positing an uncomplicated extension of the rights which male individuals enjoy in the public sphere to female individuals.

In attempting to make women 'equal' in the public sphere, liberal discourse is brought into direct confrontation with an existing sex-based hierarchy of rights and duties. In Australia feminists have been able to take advantage of this confrontation by making explicit the conditions necessary for women's equality in the public sphere.[55] By emphasizing the connections and interdependence of public and private life a range of other issues and demands, such as the need for child care, paid maternity and paternity leave, may be brought into focus.

If, as a feminist strategy, degendering tends to assume power and authority by its engagement with the premises of liberal discourse it is disadvantaged by the adoption of a liberal/rationalist framework. Sex discrimination legislation tends to impose a norm of male life experiences on all participants in the public sphere so that, in their public lives, women have to deny the lived experience of a female body. Sex equality legislation can, therefore, represent only one part of a broader political struggle to improve the circumstances of women's lives.

Notes

I would like to thank Don Fletcher, Judith Allen, Chilla Bulbeck, Rosemary Pringle, Sophie Watson and Mark and Maureen Finnane for their comments and encouragement during the writing of this chapter.
1. See for example Senator Susan Ryan, *Australian Senate Debates*, vol. 98, pp. 1184–5.
2. Lena Bruselid 'Women, Class and State: Evaluating Social Policy and Political Demand' in P. Boreham and G. Dow (eds), *Work and Inequality* vol. I, Macmillan, South Melbourne, 1980, pp. 107–26; Ann Game and Rosemary Pringle, 'From Here to Fraternity – Women and the Hawke Government', *Scarlet Woman* 17, Spring 1983, pp. 5–11; Ann Game, 'Affirmative Action: Liberal Rationality or Challenge to Patriarchy?', *Legal Service Bulletin* 9(6), 1984, pp. 253–57.
3. Karen O'Connor and Nancy E. McGlen, 'The Effects of Government Organization on Women's Rights: An Analysis of the Status of Women in Canada, Great Britain, and the United States', *International Journal of Women's Studies*, vol. 1, no. 6, pp. 588–601.
4. Section 43, Sex Discrimination Bill 1983.
5. Gear, *Australian House of Representatives Debates*, vol. 135, p. 371.
6. Kelly, Ibid, p. 326.
7. Archer, *Senate Debates*, vol. 100, p. 2297.
8. See for example Walters, *Senate Debates*, vol. 101, p. 2949.
9. Braddon, *House of Representatives Debates*, vol. 135, p. 368.
10. Crichton-Browne, *Senate Debates*, vol. 135, p. 2310.
11. Ibid, p. 2310.
12. Ibid, p. 2313.
13. Ibid, p. 2310.
14. Ibid, p. 1936.
15. Ibid, p. 2310.
16. Ibid, p. 1936.
17. *Senate Debates*, vol. 98, pp. 1184-5.
18. *House of Representatives Debates*, vol. 135, p. 370.
19. *Senate Debates*, vol. 101, p. 2949.
20. *House of Representatives Debates*, vol. 135, p. 370.
21. *Senate Debates*, vol. 101, p. 2963.
22. For example, *Senate Debates*, vol. 98, p. 403 and 404; vol. 100, p. 1927.
23. *Senate Debates*, vol. 101, p. 2955.
24. *Senate Debates*, vol. 98, p. 403.
25. *Senate Debates*, vol. 100, p. 2918.
26. *Senate Debates*, vol. 101, p. 2293.
27. *Senate Debates*, vol. 100, p. 1923.
28. Ibid, p. 2687; *Senate Debates*, vol. 100, p. 1934.
29. *Senate Debates*, vol. 101, pp. 3687, 3688.
30. Ibid, p. 3687; *Senate Debates*, vol. 100, p. 1934.
31. *Senate Debates*, vol. 101, pp. 3687, 3688.
32. Chris Ronalds, *Affirmative Action and Sex Discrimination: A Handbook on Legal Rights for Women*, Pluto, Sydney, 1987, p. 159.
33. Tate, *Senate Debates*, vol. 100, p. 1923 and Teague, *Senate*, vol. 101, p. 2958.
34. Genevieve Lloyd, 'Selfhood, War and Masculinity' in C. Pateman and E. Gross (eds), *Feminist Challenges*, Allen and Unwin, Sydney, 1986, pp. 63–76.
35. Ibid, p. 64.
36. Carole Pateman, 'The Fraternal Social Contract: Some Observations on Patriarchal Civil Society', Unpublished Paper presented to the Australian Women's Philosophy Conference, Adelaide, August 1983.
37. *Senate Debates*, vol. 101, p. 3336.
38. Crichton-Browne, ibid, p. 3627.

39. Mountford, *House of Representatives Debates*, vol. 135, p. 470.

40. Giles, *Senate Debates*, vol. 100, p. 2310.

41. MacPhee, *House of Representatives Debates*, vol. 100, p. 2310.

42. Tate, *Senate Debates*, vol. 100, p. 2310.

43. Alison Jagger, 'On Sexual Equality', *Ethics*, 84, 1974, p. 276.

44. Zillah Eisenstein, *Feminism and Sexual Equality: Crisis in Liberal America*, New York Monthly Review Press, 1984, pp. 240–43.

45. Moira Gatens, 'A Critique of the Sex/Gender Distinction', in J. Allen and P. Patton (eds), *Beyond Marxism? Interventions After Marx*, Intervention Publications, Sydney, 1983, pp. 143–60.

46. Ibid, p. 150.

47. This approach has been adopted by several theorists, for example: Nancy Chodorow, *The Reproduction of Mothering: Psychoanalysis and the Sociology of Gender*, University of California Press, Berkeley, 1978; Elizabeth Gross, 'Philosophy, subjectivity and the body: Kristeva and Irigaray', in Pateman, and Gross, *Feminist Challenges*, pp. 125–43; E. Fox-Keller, *Reflections on Feminism and Science*, Yale University Press, New Haven, 1985; Tony Eardley, 'Violence and Sexuality', in A. Metcalfe and M. Humphreys (eds), *The Sexuality of Men*, Pluto, London, pp. 32–47.

48. *Senate Debates*, vol. 100, p. 1927.

49. *House of Representatives*, vol. 135, p. 344.

50. Carole Pateman, 'The Fraternal Social Contract', p. 2.

51. Anna Yeatman, 'Despotism and Civil Society: The Limits of Patriarchal Citizenship', in J. Stiehm (ed.), *Women's Views of the Political World of Men*, Transnational, New York, 1984, pp. 153–76.

52. Marion Tapper, 'Can A Feminist Be A Liberal?', *Australian Journal of Philosophy*, Supplement to vol. 64, 1986, p. 43.

53. As reported by Tate, *Senate Debates*, vol. 100, p. 1924.

54. See Ronalds, chapter 8.

55. Hester Eisenstein, 'The Gender of Bureaucracy: Reflections on Feminism and the State', in J. Goodnow and C. Pateman (eds), *Women, Social Science and Public Policy*, Allen and Unwin, Sydney 1985, pp. 104–15.

13

Interpretation of a Frontline State: Australian Women's Refuges and the State

Ludo McFerren

In June 1975 the Labor government of Australia funded a national women's refuge programme. Twelve refuges across the states of Australia were rushed funding cheques in the last days of the financial year. The event which prompted this level of national commitment to the struggle against domestic violence and homelessness was squatting by Sydney feminists of 'Elsie', Australia's first women's refuge in Sydney, in March 1974. The progressive Labor government quickly promised to support the development of women's refuges, as part of their major objective to resource local community health and welfare initiatives, which had hitherto been a state prerogative. During their administration the non-government welfare sector blossomed.

Although feminists debated the contradictions of seeking funding from the state, which represented for them a pillar in the structural oppression of women, state resources were essentially accepted for very pragmatic reasons. The needs of Elsie quickly outstripped the resources of voluntary woman hours, donated food and furniture. Pandora's box was open, and the reality of the scale of domestic violence and women's homelessness shocked even feminists who had been theoretically prepared. Australian feminists did, however, accept that by accepting state funding they took a calculated political risk. They understand there to be an element of mutual compromise, for if the refuges could retain their political autonomy and agendas, the transfer of resources to overtly feminist services could compromise the state perhaps more.

Turning the state back on itself was to be an artful game, in which the relationship between the feminist on the refuge frontline and the state's intermediaries, increasingly feminist bureaucrats, was to be crucial. The elevation of feminists to influential and well-paid jobs advising the federal government on women's issues caused general consternation throughout the Australian Women's Liberation Movement. Where did this leave the relationship between feminism and the state? As employees of the state, but with political allegiance to feminism, who did these women really represent? Should individuals personally benefit from the push of a movement of women on behalf of all women? Could a young movement, based on a system of consensus and allergic to notions of leadership deal with such tall poppies so soon? These were questions refuge activists soon found themselves asking.

The Federal government set up an International Women's Year (IWY) Secretariat in 1975 staffed by feminists. One of its jobs was to distribute on–off grants to women's groups throughout the year. Refuges, which had been operating on donated energy and resources, rushed submissions into the secretariat. There seemed to be no better or more urgently needed women's activity than theirs. But the Secretariat also had the job of initiating changes to policies affecting women in government departments, and pulling those dragging their feet into line. The Commonwealth was searching for a suitable departmental candidate to permanently administer refuge funding. The most likely funding agency, the Commonwealth Department of Social Security (DSS), was exhibiting hostility to the prospect, and showing anti-feminist tendencies which the Secretariat could not ignore. By funding refuges in 1975 with IWY money, the Secretariat believed it would be letting the DSS off the hook. These were niceties of power broking which activists found hard to appreciate from the squalid and overcrowded circumstances of the refuges, and there were some angry meetings between IWY representatives and frontline feminists.

The Secretariat was able to redeem itself to some degree by playing a role in the resolution of this deadlock. By mid 1975 the Labor government was under great electoral pressure and faced a critical by-election. The 'women's vote' was seen as a deciding factor (women had been steadily drifting towards Labor), and a Secretariat member was sent on a whirlwind tour of the country to find out what the women of Australia wanted. She found overwhelming agreement across the political spectrum that women's refuges were considered the highest priority of need. On the advice of the Secretariat, the Prime Minister Gough Whitlam ordered the immediate establishment of a national refuge programme, fully funded by the Commonwealth. He by-passed the reluctant Department of Social Security and gave the programme to the more willing Health Commission.

The popularity of refuges was extraordinary, coming barely a year after the squatting of the first refuge in a classic exercise of feminist direct action. It was, however, significant that Australian women had not been similarly excited by the funding of rape crisis and women's health centres in the same period. It was an indication that the victims of domestic violence were perceived as less blameworthy than rape victims. Rape failed to take off as a major community concern for Australians as it had done in countries like the US, despite, or perhaps because of Australia having the highest incidence of recorded gang rape in the world. Only a handful of community-based rape crisis centres were eventually funded. More extensive rape services were incorporated into the public hospital system. This left rape as a politically marginalized issue. Less surprising was that the preventative benefits of women's health centres had not the same impact on the minds of women as refuges. Yet it would be a mistake to see this positive response as a wholehearted endorsement of the radically feminist demands made by Elsie women's refuge. It was rather an emotive reaction to the image of the refuge resident projected by the media – that of the faultless working-class wife and mother, trying to protect herself and her brood from the psychotic and inebriated batterer – later to be known as the 'beast of suburbia' syndrome.

It was an image which refuges exploited when seeking community support, and one that would come back to haunt them, because it limited the sort of refuge programme they projected into the Australian community. As Melbourne's refuge, Women's Liberation Halfway House reflected in 1975:

> One is left to wonder how much of this image is true (since it is so acceptable) and how relevant it is to what we are actually doing. Is it helping to increase public awareness of the oppression of women as we hoped it would, or just serving to label oppression in a way that most women can avoid relating personally to, and seem to deal with it so that problems appear to be being solved?[1]

When preparing guidelines for the refuge programme, Commonwealth health and women's bureaucrats stayed loyal to the original feminist image. They drew heavily on the feminist models which had been developed primarily at Elsie and Halfway House. These had travelled beyond the provision of mere shelter, beyond the traditional hostel models which had existed before, to a non-institutionalized and self-help environment, run by consumers and supporters of the refuge in a collective and consensual system. The model also called on refuges to use the experience of the women and children residents to research and develop community awareness of domestic violence and homelessness, to uncover the root causes, which lay in women's oppression, and to demand an end to it. By doing so, the need for refuges would disappear thereby guaranteeing their own obsolescence.

But the days of exclusive Commonwealth funding of refuges were numbered. In November 1975 the centralist Labor government was overthrown, and a federalist, right-wing government elected, which targetted welfare spending as a major source of heavy tax burdens. Nevertheless, the electoral popularity of women's refuges was recognized by the conservatives. In fact the principles of self-help and reliance appealed to the Liberal Party philosophy, and in its second budget of 1977 the Fraser government pumped one million dollars into new refuges.

Over the next two years there was an astonishing expansion of the programme, from nineteen Australian refuges to ninety-nine. Funding for women's refuges was one of the few growth areas of Commonwealth spending during the period. There was a steady drift towards privatization of welfare, towards the unregulated and largely voluntary non-government welfare sector. The expansion of the refuge programme was also dependent on the co-operation of the state governments. The Commonwealth called on them to contribute an increasing proportion of funds to the programme.[2] The result was that new refuges were set up with ridiculously poor funding and funding for existing refuges stagnated.

Aware of the danger that the administration of the refuges could be passed on to the states, feminists in the Canberra bureaucracy in 1975 had advised refuges to form themselves into a national confederation for the purpose of maintaining a voice in the nation's capital. They agreed with the argument developed by refuges on the need for a national programme. Even after the fall of the Whitlam government, refuge activists saw more potential in lobbying one central government than the administrations of six states and two territories, the majority of which were run by conservative governments. They could not accept an uneven development of refuges in the separate states, and were pessimistic that development would occur in the most conservative of these. They also recognized that if they were to campaign effectively on federal issues such as welfare benefits, family law and public housing, they had to campaign nationally.

But the refuge movement rejected a formal national organization in favour of a loose confederation, preferring to operate on a 'low key, grassroots level' instead of 'imposing a grandiose structure'. The most vocal refuges from Sydney and Melbourne had interpreted the Canberra proposal as a bureaucratic attempt to railroad them into the type of peak organization much loved by bureaucracies craving a formal and stable group for consultations. As feminists, they also foresaw being outvoted in this confederation by the wave of conservative groups opening refuges. The debate was to continue for several years, with 'autonomy' being the key word. Refuges in the more isolated states were happy to sacrifice some of their autonomy for more contact with each other.

For Sara Dowse, senior adviser on Women's Affairs' the rejection was a serious one, signifying that the refuges had failed to understand that the state was not a monolith, but had its parts which were friends of the refuge programme:

> the plan was defeated, largely through the refuges' suspicion of the bureau-cracy and the inability of many of them to look beyond the immediate needs of their individual collectives.[3]

To a large extent the rejection was an effect of the isolation of Canberra from the rest of Australia, and the problems in such a vast country of forging and maintaining a national politics. Feminists suffered from this effect as badly as many other political movements. Because the refuge programme was rushed into existence at the end of June 1975, refuges were given literally a few hours to agree to the concept of a national confederation. They were being prompted by people in Canberra they barely knew, and generally misunderstood the source and the motives behind the proposal. Their alternative, the loose confederation, survived a number of years, but the national refuge movement was then reduced to meeting at occasional conferences, where representatives almost seemed to speak different languages. Refuge activists were forced to look to their local state, their state government, for a more productive relationship.

Two States

The Commonwealth continued to provide the bulk of government funding to refuges across Australia, but from 1976 handed over the administration to the states. Refuges were no longer funded directly from Canberra. Their funding was earmarked in the federal block grants to the states, but whether or not this was passed on, and to what sort of refuges, became the sole concern of the local administration. The Commonwealth washed its hands of the quality of the programme.

As state governments took over the administration of the refuges during 1976 and 1977, the expected backlash came in the then most conservative states of Queensland and Western Australia. Feminist refuges had funding withheld, and these state governments refused to make up the twenty-five per cent gap in refuge funding left by the Commonwealth. They insisted that the ability of refuges to raise this gap themselves would demonstrate the level of community support for their work. In New South Wales, the recently elected government not only filled the gap in funding but supported new refuges on state funding alone. As on the federal level, a supportive state government with women's advisers was now to be critical of the ability of a refuge programme to achieve its aims. This is thrown into relief by comparing the experiences of the refuge programmes in two very different Australian states, Western Australia and New South Wales.

Support for women's refuges was part of the election promise of New South Wales's Labor Party package in opposition. Once elected in 1976, one of its first acts was to set up a Women's Co-ordination Unit (WCU) as policy adviser on women's issues to the Premier. The unit was involved in ensuring that the state fully filled the gap in funding for refuges. This was not an insignificant financial commitment, as funded refuges in New South Wales were to increase to twenty-one by 1977. The unit was also involved with the New South Wales funding depart-ment, Youth and Community Services (YACS) in drawing up early refuge guidelines which were feminist because, like their Common-wealth predecessors, they incorporated the aims and philosophy deve-loped at Elsie women's refuge. Comprehensive feminist guidelines were later developed in a joint exercise by the refuges and YACS.

The policy of the refuge liason officer in YACS was that women's groups should set up women's refuges. When the boom in women's refuge funding attracted the attention of the religious charities, she was supported by her minister in opposing the funding of church-run refuges, because they were considered incompatable with the model of existing refuges. Church refuges would not 'broaden the service they were providing and involve the women using the refuge in the manage-ment of the refuges', according to a Cabinet memo by the minister in December 1977. To his annoyance, this policy was overidden by the Premier for reasons of political expediency. The Catholic organizations had been able to exert telling political pressure on the right-wing Catholic Labor Party of New South Wales, but it was not just a question of votes; it came back to image.

This was well understood by the head of the WCU, who saw her role as interpreting to the overwhelmingly male bureaucracy and govern-ment, in language they could understand, the issues and demands coming from the feminist frontline, and vice versa. She recognized that support for refuges was often based on a misreading of their role as defined by feminists, and that many of the Catholic Labor men who made up the backbone of the administration would see refuges not as an exposure of the structural inequality of women, but as temporary safe places for working-class women and children to stay in while the husband sobered up after a drinking bout. From this angle, the inclusion in the programme of a number of sensible well-run hostels offering religious solace could only be positive.

Other politicians were better informed, particularly the Premier. But for Wran, a consummate politician known throughout Australia as Nifty Nev, it was a question of votes. The catholic organizations in New South Wales were too powerful to ignore. Nevertheless, the opposition did limit the number of funded religious refuges there, and feminists in the bureaucracy remained confident that those in the frontline could politicize their conservative sisters, joining them in the refuge programme.

In Western Australia, the right-wing government of Sir Charles Court, which saw no need for women's advisers, did not welcome the funding of women's refuges. Rather, they were appalled that the Commonwealth had unilaterally set the ball rolling and was now foisting this relatively expensive programme onto the state. The relative popularity of the programme meant the government there could not refuse to take it on, but they had their own ideas about the quality of refuge funded. Nardine, the first feminist refuge in Western Australia, represented all that was objectionable to a reactionary state government. Their challenge to the structural oppression of women in marriage was in marked contrast to the Premier's own analysis; in a 1977 radio interview, his recipe for a successful marriage had been a tolerant and patient wife.

A delegation of Liberal women went to the Western Australia health minister to ask why the government was funding an anti-Liberal refuge. The minister considered legislation to bring the refuges under the control of the state, until, it seems he was persuaded of the economy of having the service provided from the non-government sector. He did, however, see installed a system of scrutiny of Nardine and other refuges, which included quizzing refuge children in their schools, and obtaining detailed reports on conditions in the refuges from visiting health nurses.

The funding policy developed by the Western Australia funding department, the Public Health Department (PHD), was to fund those organizations which could guarantee a substantial proportion of their own funding. The PHD believed that the ability to do this demonstrated community support for the refuge in question. They also believed that under these conditions only well established and respectable organizations would be successful applicants. It was a policy which clearly excluded impoverished women's groups, and by late 1977 the nine Western Australian refuges were characterized by their association with local councils and religious charities. Nardine was ominously isolated. In the following years the PHD forced strict guidelines and a system of data collection onto the refuges, which was cynically limited to a cost-effectiveness exercise, comparing the number of 'bums on beds' with the funding received. The PHD was actually relieved to find that Nardine, with an occupancy rate of 101 per cent, was extremely cost effective.

At meetings of interstate and federal bureaucrats held to discuss funding and administrative policies for refuges, representatives from the Western Australian PHD, invariably men, were astonished by their encounters with bureaucrats responsible for refuges from other states. They thought them weak-kneed in the face of feminist demands, and believed that the Easterners could learn something from the tough line adopted in the West. In fact from 1978 a number of eastern states did crack down on feminist refuges. For several years there appeared to be an orchestrated attack spearheaded by the right-wing 'Women's Action Alliance'. Conservatives asked parliamentary questions about the right of refuges to specify a belief in feminism as a job criterion in advertisements. The Tasmanian Welfare Minister was censured in state Parliament for exercising inadequate control over his state's refuges. In Victoria there was a storm over the refusal of refuges to provide Commonwealth or state administrations with their addresses. Refuges cited security as a reason. The Commonwealth demanded accountability.

This last dispute was blamed for the eventual dumping of any responsibility for refuge funding by the Liberal-Country Party government in Canberra in 1981. The states were told that after the budget that year it was entirely their concern whether or not refuges continued to be funded. The decision was taken in a general atmosphere of sweeping cutbacks to health and welfare as the bottom fell out of the Australian economy. It was a disaster for refuges in the conservative states. Feminists in the enfeebled and cowed Office of Women's Affairs in Canberra had been powerless to stop the rot, but they had also failed to see the Victorian dispute as a thinly veiled campaign against the best organized refuge movement, which bore little connection to the issues of accountability once the Victoria refuges had come to an agreement with their state administration. Once again feminists in Canberra found themselves isolated from the real debate, and along with federal politicians and bureaucrats, bore the brunt of some of the frustration and anger felt that year by refuge residents and workers, which spilled over into violent demonstrations in the corridors of Federal Parliament.

In New South Wales the state had steadily increased its proportion of funding since 1977. It had made special capital grants to the refuges, and was supporting six refuges without Commonwealth assistance before 1981. By the financial year 1981–82 the state was matching Commonwealth funding almost dollar for dollar. The state then tried to dampen demands for new funding, but the programme received consistent support from feminists in the bureaucracy during several drought years. A case in point was the issue of staffing levels.

Since the dark year of 1981 workers had been steadily joining their union, and campaigning for award coverage.[4] The state government had been prepared to bail out many refuges in 1982, but it had become clear to refuge activists that the payment of decent wages and the provision of regular conditions was the key to sufficient funding. Beyond this lay the need to have enough salaries funded, to stop the widespread practice of wage splitting, dividing the available salaries between a greater number of workers. After an exhausting debate, refuges rejected a deeply entrenched tendency to volunteerism amongst conservatives and masochism amongst feminists by agreeing to a minimum staffing formula. YACS backed away from the issue, but the WCU took it up with enthusiasm, ensuring that the New South Wales Government had a progressive position on the need for adequate staffing. When the Labor party was elected again in Canberra in March 1983 and boosted the national refuge programme with a desperately needed four million dollars, increased staffing was seen as a state priority by the New South Wales government.

In contrast, Western Australia seemed to have adopted a policy of attrition. The Commonwealth may have been reducing its proportion of refuge funding since 1976, but in 1980 the Commonwealth was still contributing $470,000 to the Western Australian refuges compared with a paltry $57,000 from the state government. The refuge workers paid the cost. Western Australia had probably the lowest refuge wages in the country, and they were to drop even further. In 1981 salaries were reduced to $7,000 per annum, though real wages were less as women had to split salaries to cover the rosters.

Incredibly, the women's refuges in Western Australia had managed to maintain a political organization during the late seventies, despite repeated attempts by the PHD to discredit this, and to tap away steadily at the social conscience of their state. They took their case to the media, where comparisons with the support given by other state governments to their refuges became particularly damaging by 1981. Ironically the state budget that year boosted refuge funding by 20 per cent, an increase which was matched in 1982. But it was all too little too late. The years of chronic underfunding now required increases of a much greater magnitude to put Western Australia's refuges on a par with other states, and the conservatives were still left looking like an uncaring government. Cheapskate policies finally rebounded badly on the Liberal-Country Party government, who lost the state election in 1983 to the Labor party. The mud had stuck.

A Less Simplistic Picture

So far I have painted a fairly simplistic picture of the obvious benefits a
supportive government can bestow on a programme like women's
refuges, and of the successful liason which can occur between feminists
in the state apparatus and grassroots activists. I have concentrated on
funding of the programme, and a comparison of two very different states
of Australia. Naturally, the picture is in reality more complicated.
Western Australia is geographically an isolated state, dominated by a
spirit of fast money and last frontiers. Vast areas are owned by mining
companies and pastoral companies. It is not a state where women, aboriginals, or welfare rights have ever been high on the agenda. The mere
election of a Labor state government does not necessarily alter this. The
one elected in 1983 has proved to be conservative in its attitude to
women's refuges, even with a welfare minister who was active in setting
one up.

New South Wales, on the other hand, has relentlessly expanded the
refuge programme to forty-nine in 1988,[5] often against the advice of its
welfare ministers. Much of that expansion has been in country areas,
because, as a Labor government, it has been driven by electoral necessity to spread its appeal beyond its traditionally urban areas. The New
South Wales government can rightly claim that it is the largest state
contributor to women's refuges in Australia, yet the state also has the
largest population. Despite the expansion, the number of New South
Wales women's refuges per head of female population ranked New
South Wales seventh out of the eight states in 1983, with only one
funded refuge for every 47,545 of female population. The policy of
expansion also neglected the need to consolidate existing refuges, which
were often left understaffed and underfunded. The Labor government,
while officially having to support the pursuit of award wages for welfare
workers, has directly intervened to obstruct and delay the achievement
of these awards. On one occasion, the government introduced overnight
legislation to incorporate a substantial non-government welfare
programme into the public sector, shifting management away from the
local committees who had been prepared to sign a consent award with
the ASWU

The scope for simplistic state comparisons was reduced when the
focus shifted back again to the Commonwealth in 1983. The election
that year of a federal Labor government committed to a national
women's refuge programme promised an end to the uneven development. In January 1985, under the collective title of Women's Emergency Services Programme (WESP), women's refuges entered a new
super-programme, unfortunately named the Supported Accommodation

Assistance Programme (SAAP), with youth refuges and hostels for homeless people and other women's services. While women's refuges complained that they did not want to be labelled as 'accommodation' services, and would prefer a national 'women's services programme' under a 'women's ministry', there were real incentives to join SAAP. It provided five-year funding agreements and improved wages and conditions for women's refuges, financed by an injection of Commonwealth money, though this was to be conditional on the states matching it dollar for dollar.

The debate raged throughout 1984, but the refuges were at a disadvantage from the beginning because of their lack of national organization. Their communication channels could not keep up with developments, and they could not overcome fairly entrenched state interests in time to formulate a well-conceived and strongly supported alternative to SAAP. Canberra sent women bureaucrats into the fray to argue the case for SAAP. These women's inexperience in dealing with the people beyond the policy papers, and their tendency to play one state off against another, turned the consultation process into a conflict, confirming in the minds of some new ministers that women's refuges were 'difficult'. The Commonwealth behaviour played right into the hands of the states, who got on with what was for them the real job of negotiating funding discounts through separate state funding agreements with the Commonwealth. For most states these agreements reduced their contribution to less than the fifty per cent initially demanded by the Commonwealth.

Bureaucracies and refuge workers then found themselves tied into the consultative processes which criss-cross SAAP. Bureaucratic intervention and refuge lobbying in funding rounds became theoretically less crucial as the annual scramble for bitterly contested money was replaced by some of the certainties of the five-year funding agreement. While it is true that since SAAP refuges have no longer to fear the nail-biting moments around budget time, and have experienced sustained growth, one result has been their invisibility. The annual rounds at least forced refuges to take their funding inadequacies to the community, and the need for funding threw up questions about why refuges were still needed, and why domestic violence and homelessness wouldn't go away. It kept the refuges and the issues in the public eye. Lobbying for funding still occurs in SAAP, but it is closeted in the backrooms and committees where priorities and distribution of finance are decided. In many ways, this rationalization has taken the edge off a debate which was forced to be feminist, and has turned refuges into part of the welfare furniture.

A feeling of invisibility has also been produced in the area of social action. The first feminist aims of refuges committed them to campaigning for social change which would wipe out domestic violence and homelessness at the roots. But it was this analysis which risked their being wiped out, as feminist refuges became just 'one of the crowd' amongst non-feminist groups funded from 1977 to run refuges. Feminists in New South Wales were very successful at organizing many of these politically inexperienced groups into a powerful and political refuge movement, a process in which they were assisted by sympathetic liason officers in YACS. They concentrated from 1978 on the key issue of housing and legal reform. Their demands were often radical as well as reformist, and were pursued with determination and great flair, using all the right channels as well as direct action. In many ways the state in New South Wales was responsive, but it absorbed the surface of the demands and in doing so bleached out much of their energy.

In the area of housing the refuge movement demanded that the state housing authority become publicly accountable for its housing policies and allocations, but won only the dubious achievement of becoming a case for special treatment, speeding up the allocation of housing for refuge residents. This produced bottle-necks in the refuges of homeless women waiting for applications to be approved; women who were often referred to the refuge by the housing authority itself. As public housing waiting lists spiralled and supporting mothers paid up to eighty per cent of their pensions on private rents, the refuges demanded rent control or rent subsidy in the private sector. Instead they gained a four-million-dollar women's housing programme for just over one hundred women and an advisory committee to the minister on women's housing.

Refuges demanded proper protection by the forces of law and order for women assaulted in their homes by their partners, and an ideological shift in the state from tacit acceptance of domestic violence to unequivocal opposition. They took examples of police inaction and magisterial indifference to the Women's Co-ordination Unit, who advised the Premier to set up a task force into domestic violence. In a good example of feminist co-operation between the frontline and the bureaucracy, the 1981 Report of the New South Wales Task Force on Domestic Violence produced a series of wide-ranging recommendations. The state government then concentrated only on the affordable area of legal reform, essentially extending and defining police powers, a contradiction for many feminist refuge workers. But the spirit of the legislation came up against the New South Wales police and magistrates, who would not use their new powers. For them domestic violence remained a private affair.

The consolation for feminists was that they could witness senior police officers dressing down members of their force for failing to carry out the letter of the law, and that the debate this generated, which became so quickly ideological, continues within previously impenetrable male institutions. But this has to be kept in perspective. Labor parliamentarians, apparently well briefed by feminist bureaucrats, thundered their disapproval of domestic violence. The community education campaigns were launched with the themes 'You don't have to put up with it', and for the non-English-speaking communities 'It's a crime'. But these were so poorly resourced that they were hardly discernible when compared with the mega-media blitz by the state on drunken driving.

The product of ten years' campaigning by refuges has been that many of the initiatives started by their exhausting campaigns have been claimed by the state government. The director of the Women's Co-ordination Unit, who was the only Australian representative at a UN 'expert group meeting' on domestic violence, felt able to claim in a case study on New South Wales:

> The government took up the concern of the women's movement in implementing a multi-faceted programme through which it has reformed laws, provided crisis and long term accommodation and support for battered women and their children and conducted community education programmes (including multi-lingual) on wife bashing.[6]

Much of the ongoing work in social reform is carried out by committees run by parts of the feminist bureaucracy, and on which refuges have a lone representation. Issues which would have been taken into the community are now filtered through the committee systems, rarely reaching the minister, never mind the six o'clock news. Times have changed. As the state took up women's issues and achievements occurred in fields such as the growth of women's services, legal reform and equal opportunity, the feminist bureaucracy in New South Wales appeared as less of an interpreter for the grassroots and more of a publicist for the Labor government – a government which was running out of steam after twelve years in power.

It can be argued that the achievement of assured funding, and the pursuit of reformist measures by the state government should free refuges to concentrate on new issues, harder demands, building a national organization and refining their services. Certainly the most productive work in refuges recently has been to improve the services for aboriginal and immigrant women. This has mainly been achieved by increasing the numbers of women from these communities employed as refuge workers. But refuges in many other ways have failed to adapt to the new circumstances. Despite the creation of a national programme, they still have no national organization and carry out no effective national campaign work. Despite the commitment to aboriginal rights, and a proportion of aboriginal residents much higher than the proportion in the Australian population, refuges have not been in the forefront of debate in 1988 about what the celebration of white Australia has meant for aboriginal people.

Part of the failure to adapt has been an ongoing tendency to see the state as a fixed monolith. Refuge workers have remained unclear about the role of feminists in the state apparatus, and their relationship with these 'femocrats'. When confronted with a problem with the state, the refuges will concentrate their attacks on the bureaucrats. It has often left refuges beating their heads against the wrong brick wall. Ironically, for a movement without models or frontiers, this failure seems to have stemmed from a desire for tradition. Early radical statements about the co-optive role of the state, the need for refuge autonomy, the contradictions of feminists in the system have become fixed in a type of refuge mythology. They are often repeated religiously without criticism or further examination, as are references to grand old struggles and epic debates. Any researched look at a history of the refuge programme, at least in New South Wales, shows the value of the relationship between the frontline and the feminist bureaucracy, and provides a perspective for understanding what might otherwise appear as cynical tendencies on the part of the state and its servants.

The need to keep up with the times is pressing. Australia, like Britain and the US before it, faces a swing to the right following a disillusionment with social democracy. This has already occurred in New South Wales. The Labor government was defeated in the state election of March 1988 by a landslide vote. There were many reasons given. One of the most popular was that the state Labor Party had lost touch with its traditional base. Lifelong Labor supporters were alienated by the arrogance and bullying tactics of the right-wing Labor machine and the absence of bread-and-butter Labor policies. Certainly the Labor government seemed accident prone, worn out and in a state of panic by the March election.

The greatest damage to the Labor vote was done in the rural areas reacting to conservation policies and anti-gun laws; in industrial towns resentful of the massive resources poured into Sydney for the 1988 celebrations; and in the sprawling Western suburbs, where home owners, living out the great Australian dream of home ownership, have been squeezed by high interest rates and spiralling home costs. While a full scale analysis is needed of what was a most extraordinary election, the efforts of the Labor government in terms of women's policies seemed to have affected the 'women's vote' less than the general bread-and-butter issues. The results of the election, however, put these policies in jeopardy.

The election was Labor's loss rather than the opposition's victory. The Liberal and National Party coalition offered little that was new: the Labor government had provided effective conservative financial management of the state for many years, but they had promised a new boom. As a government they immediately moved to repeal aboriginal land rights legislation and abolish aboriginal Land Councils. They gave the green light again for wood-chipping of disappearing forests. They also moved on the Women's Co-ordination Unit, attempting to demote it from its place in the Premier's Department to a junior ministry. The work of monitoring and developing many of the campaigns and laws introduced by the previous government is subsequently downgraded.

The message of the election was that fundamental issues cannot be ignored. While refuges have to force new and deeper issues into the public eye and onto the state's agenda, they also have to continue plugging away at the more fundamental and largely unchanged issues which underlie domestic violence, such as poverty. Australian women raising children on their own who depend on government pensions are still living below the official poverty line, and still face public intolerance. In a survey of groups deserving government aid, single mothers polled last in a line-up which included farmers, small businessmen, and first-home buyers.[7] There is no room for complacency in our 'lucky' country.

Notes

1. 'Half way Where', *Scarlet Woman*, September 1975.
2. 25 per cent of operating funding (including wages) and 50 per cent of capital.
3. Sara Dowse, 'The Bureaucrat as Usurer', Paper for the Social Justice for Women in Australia Conference, ANU, August 1983.
4. Ninety per cent of the minimum industrial wages and conditions in Australia are determined by awards negotiated between the unions and employers in the federal and state industrial commissions. Non-government welfare is one of the last award-free areas.
5. With another thirteen Women's Emergency Services Programme (WESP) services, New South Wales WESP in 1987–88 had a budget of $10.22 million.
6. Helen L'Orange, Chairperson New South Wales Government Domestic Violence Committee, 'Case Study on Forms of Crisis Intervention and Types of Immediate and Structural Measures to Render Assistance to Women Assaulted in the Family: New South Wales'.
7. 'Self-interest Takes Top Billing', *Sydney Morning Herald*, 14 April 1986.

14

Encounters with the State: Co-option and Reform, a Case Study from Women's Health

Jocelyn Auer

The women's movement of the 1970s defined the need for women to reclaim their bodies and take control of their health as an essential step in overcoming oppression and achieving liberation. The establishment of women's health programmes was seen as one step towards achieving this goal. These took a variety of forms, including self-help groups, information centres and women's health services. The choice of programmes was shaped by the funding options available to women. Thus in the US the essentially private enterprise nature of the health and medical system contributed to that country's focus on lay health workers and self-help groups which were free to explore new perspectives on women's health care and sexuality.[1] In Australia a number of groups of women chose a different path. They sought public sector funding to establish their centres; and this direct engagement with the state has significantly affected some of the outcomes. It is with this relationship between feminism, women's health centres and the state that this chapter is concerned. It looks at the formation and development of government-funded women's health centres in South Australia and examines the constraints, difficulties and dilemmas which arose out of the contradictions between the attempt to create an organization and service based on feminist principles, within the confines of a government-funded, bureaucratically administered community health programme.

The acceptance of government funding entailed specific limitations and constraints on feminist goals and practices. On the other hand, the inclusion of women's health centres within the health system has given them some status and ability to seek reform there. This rests on women's ability to threaten the male power structure and patriarchal relations within the State[2] and to challenge the legitimacy and 'embeddedness' of male power.[3] It is not an easy task and is only made possible because of the contradictions that exist within the state arising from its protection of capitalism and patriarchy on the one hand, and its need for acceptance as a legitimate, just and democratic government, on the other.[4] In practical terms it is possible to exploit these contradictions in the health bureaucracy and to achieve some measure of reform. This is what the women involved in women's health centres have sought to do.

The early to mid 1970s was a period of rapid change and planning for change. In the health arena this desire for change was stimulated by rising costs, fragmentation of services and a questioning of the dominance of the bio-medical, curative model of care. It was reflected in the moves to shift resources into the public sector to improve co-ordination of services and equity of access. A universal health insurance scheme was introduced.[5] The community health programme, initiated in 1973, was part of this package. Its aims were to provide co-ordinated health and related welfare services based in the community and particularly for those with unmet needs. Prevention was to be emphasized, a multi-disciplinary approach was to be used and the community was to be involved in decision-making processes affecting health care. Federal government funding was available without any requirement for a state financial contribution.

The 1970s was also a time of vigorous social movements, of which the women's movement was a vital part. For women, health was one important aspect of a wider agenda which also covered education, jobs, wages, child care, marriage, sexuality and sexual exploitation. Women wanted information about their bodies, the right to a safe abortion, access to contraception. They wanted to be treated as 'normal' individuals by a medical system which defined 'normal' as male and saw female functions as pathological. In response to these ideas and demands groups of women in all states began organizing and asking for government funds to run new programmes specifically for women. They looked to the federal government which was publicizing its support for International Women's Year and its community health initiatives.

By 1973–74 Leichhardt Women's Health Centre in Sydney was operating successfully on a grant obtained under the Community Health Programme. In 1974–75 further Commonwealth grants were made to women's health centres in Darwin, Melbourne, Sydney and Perth. Women's shelters were also established under this programme. It was in this climate that Adelaide Women's Liberation organized a meeting and a decision was made to apply to the Commonwealth for funding of a women's health centre. The early involvement of two medical women, one of whom was particularly well known and highly regarded, bestowed a helpful degree of respectability on the project.[6] An association was formed from the interested women and the first grant was received in 1974–5. These funds, to cover capital as well as operating costs, were lodged with the South Australian Hospital's Department, to be made available to the women establishing the programme.

These women saw the health centre as being for women who were tired of having to go to unsympathetic, or even hostile male doctors and who wanted a different sort of medical and health service. They believed they had a right to such a service and that there were many other women who felt the same way but had not yet recognized the possibility of a better service. The centre was to serve women both in the community locally and more widely. It opened in temporary premises at Women's Liberation House in the city centre, then moved to the home of the doctor. However, the intention was to operate at Hindmarsh, a low-income, inner suburb in the west of Adelaide with a large migrant population and few services. The Hindmarsh premises were selected because the women believed that the old and unpretentious building would make it more approachable to women in the area. In contrast the South Australian Hospitals Department representative saw the premises as unsavoury and in need of too much repair. In this latter respect the Department proved correct. The funds secured for capital works to establish the centre were completely inadequate and enormous amounts of time and energy were expended by a large group of women to make the place habitable.

The Hindmarsh centre was opened officially in February 1976. The feminist principles of the founding members informed the style and range of services and activities undertaken. It led to an emphasis on providing a service for individual women which incorporated treatment with education and information about how our bodies work, how conditions develop and how they may be prevented. Attention was given to the social and environmental circumstances which could be relevant to treatment and prevention. The centre took a 'holistic' approach which attempted to address the needs of the whole person rather than just symptoms or specific parts of the body. Self-help and discussion groups 'in which women learn and share information about their health with other women', were recognized as important ways of building confidence. Their approach also involved an understanding of the importance of taking action in and with the community to make the health system more responsive to the demands of women and ensure that other aspects of the social environment which had an impact on women's health could be addressed.

For the women who established it, Hindmarsh was seen as the first in a network of women's health services, which were to be small and locally based so that they would be accessible at the local level and would maximize community involvement. The centre began with just a few workers, including a doctor. By 1979 it had eleven workers in the equivalent of just over six full-time positions. There were three part-time doctors, two nurses, an information/research worker, an Italian and a Greek worker, two very part-time group workers and an administrator. Submissions and funding arrangements required the specific identification of workers in their professional or other work roles. From the beginning these were defined in traditional categories – doctor, nurse, social worker, adminis-trator. Usually workers contributed to the service on the basis of their skills and training in these or other relevant areas. A small library was quickly developed and a range of pamphlets written and published to provide information on matters such as cystitis, vaginal thrush, forms of contraception, and menstruation. Some of these were printed also in Greek, Italian, and Serbo-Croatian.

In the early years the main users of the centre were associated with the women's movement or were Greek and Italian women drawn in by workers who spoke these languages and had community contacts. Later the centre attracted women from all over Adelaide, including larger numbers of migrant women. By 1978, 22 per cent of the total number of clients were migrant women who accounted for 40 per cent of medical and counselling work. In June that year a decision was made to en-courage native English-speaking women to seek services elsewhere to ensure that non-native, non-English-speaking women would have better access to the service.

Many of the migrant women were referred by other government and non-government agencies. They often came to the centre with a long history of receiving poor or inappropriate treatment. It would have been relatively easy for the role of the women's health centre to have been defined by this and similar demands. It would have filled a gap by providing services for women who were seen as too difficult or having too many problems. If the centre had allowed this to happen workers would quickly have been swamped under the weight of individual case work. However, it kept its broader vision and continued to see its role in changing the position of women and in gaining them a voice. The centre was for the well women who were major users of health and medical care systems by virtue of their normal reproductive functioning, as much as it was for ill women.

The association established the health centre and was legally respon-sible for it. It included a wide membership of interested women some of whom were employed as health centre workers. It sought to operate as a collective and to equalize decision-making power amongst members. This broadly-based collective was responsible for policy direction, with a smaller group of association members, including staff, holding delegated powers for ongoing health centre decision-making. In practice the distinctions were not clear and the smaller group made many policy decisions. Confusion and eventually conflict arose from this situation with both workers and the health bureaucracy questioning the authority of the association.

The process of joint decision-making was unfamiliar and brought both internal and external tensions. For example, the doctors employed by the centre were part of the collective and subject to its decisions, but their training and medical status gave them a central position and an inherent degree of power. Personal power differences were also evident. The health bureaucracy, used to its hierarchical structures, found the referring of questions for decision to the collective enormously frustrating and several bureaucrats described the process as 'impossible'.

Other aspects of collectivity were job sharing and skill sharing. These were conscious attempts to address the power imbalances that existed between workers with different skills and training, and between workers and women using the centre. Efforts were made to enable workers to learn new information and skills from each other and to give women information and skills to understand and take better care of their own health and make more informed choices about their health care. These efforts were significant also because they challenged current medical practices, powers and popular images. They frequently drew scathing comment from members of the medical establishment. In practice the steps taken were relatively small and careful.

There was a clear basis for defining the extent of medical skills which could be shared and this was derived from the principle that women should, where possible, control their own health. The concern was to make more visible the power that the, mostly male, medical profession had come to have over women by defining concerns relating to their normal bodily functioning as illnesses requiring medical care and hospitalization, and by demystifying simple procedures. Workers were encouraged to learn to carry out smear tests, pregnancy tests, to undertake contraceptive counselling, paint warts and insert diaphragms. Women who wanted to know were taught how to use speculums for self-examination. The importance of equal pay in achieving equality between workers was acknowledged, but was seen as too difficult to implement because salaries were paid directly to workers by the Hospitals' Department on the basis of their job classification.

The grant for the initial six months in 1974–5 was $52,000. For the full year 1975–6 it was $118,600. The Commonwealth Community Health Programme provided 100 per cent of funding in 1973–4 and then up to 75 per cent of capital costs and up to 90 per cent of operating costs until 1978–9 when these arrangements changed to 50 per cent

Commonwealth and 50 per cent state. Regardless of who paid, it was the State Department which administered the funding and the arrangements were based on strict, regulatory notions of accountability which were quite at odds with the health centre's view of what was appropriate. The centre believed that accountability meant spending the money carefully to provide the best possible service to women along the lines drawn in their submission. The department believed that the money should be spent on the items and salaries it traditionally defined as necessary for health services. It was acceptable to spend large amounts of money on medical equipment, medical consulting rooms, and doctors' salaries but not acceptable to spend infinitely smaller amounts on transport for poor, migrant women to get to the centre. There was little room for discretionary spending. Financially the centre was closely regulated and all pay cheques were made directly from the department to workers. Furnishings, equipment and supplies were ordered from the centre on government order forms and accounts were paid by the department. The centre was eventually allowed small petty cash and stamp floats. Financial accountability was ensured through the provision of audited financial statements and an annual report. The auditor was elected at the Annual General Meeting. Monthly financial statements were required by the Hospitals Department.

Almost immediately after the centre opened it was faced with a high and continuing demand for individual or one-to-one work. This led to passionate discussion about what to do in relation to other areas of work – how much talking to groups outside the centre should there be? Was job sharing working? Was it inefficient? What about the planned emphasis on prevention? Was it being lost? There were personal stresses and anxieties about how efficiently individual staff members were working. And there was the ever-present pressure from what has been described as the women's enthusiasm and naivety in taking on too much.

Outside, the centre was criticized for not seeking department approval before taking action to secure their chosen premises, or purchase equipment. It also faced persistent and angry disapproval from the medical profession. Neither the workers nor the premises were thought to be sufficiently respectable. Altogether it was too difficult to deal with. The state health bureaucracy appears to have had an unfavourable view of the women's health centre from the start. The first doctor at the centre said that some years later she had been told by the doctor responsible for the community health programme in South Australia that he had deliberately made things difficult for them because he thought they couldn't possibly succeed and he didn't want to waste the money. That this sort of attitude existed has been confirmed by discussions with other department officers.

Whilst some of the criticisms levelled at the centre may have been valid they do not adequately explain the degree of opposition. It is possible that the very presence of such centres constituted a challenge to bureaucratic and medical male dominance and authority. Subsequent women's health centres have fared little better, and there continues to be a strong element of opposition in traditional medical and health bureaucracies. However, this opposition isn't universal. There are now pockets of support which make things easier, if still complicated. At times it has been necessary to engage in considerable contortions to find ways of working through the people who are co-operative.

At another level one of the problems faced by the Hindmarsh health centre related to the apparent conflict between the policy directions of the Commonwealth government, and the state government's administrative responsibility for services established under these directions. This was evident in the contrast between the Commonwealth grant conditions which offered flexibility and considerable autonomy to new units in order to encourage a different model of service, and the state health administration structure. While on paper the latter had, by 1975, been brought into line with these new directions in services, this was not evident in practice. Implementation was slow and most of the staff unchanged, bringing their old mentality with them.

The women at the centre worked from the Commonwealth policy and believed they had a mandate to provide a 'different sort of service'. Thus they were in constant friction with the state bureaucracy. In the midst of this period of reform the federal Labor government was dismissed in 1975 and shortly after the national health insurance scheme, Medibank, began to be progressively dismantled. In South Australia the Labor Party lost the 1979 election and the Liberal Party appointed a woman as the Minister of Health. The old Hospitals Department was replaced by the South Australian Health Commission (SAHC).

The changing climate and the growing pressures, fears and antagonisms were aggravated by the public release of a new draft constitution which sought to protect the founding principles of the centre by inserting a clause which restricted association membership to women who supported socialism and feminism. The Liberal government reacted promptly and the SAHC was directed to intervene. It did so by sending in its own manager in mid December 1979 and informing the workers that it was the employer, not the association. Many of the services were curtailed, and health centre pamphlets were withdrawn.

During these months a clear division occurred between women on the staff and in the association who believed it was imperative to unite to fight for the centre and its original goals and those who thought the real choice was to concede or to lose all. The majority of the workers fell on the latter side as did the Women's Adviser to the Premier. These women sought to negotiate and to meet with the Minister of Health. The Commission stalled, but the meeting was finally arranged. The issues with the Commission are clearly spelt out in a letter from the Women's Adviser to the Minister of Health[7] which reflected her concern with the future of the centre and its staff and reaffirmed the need for a women's health centre of the type that had been operating at Hindmarsh. She warned that it was important that the centre was not transformed into something like a traditional outpatients' clinic of a women's hospital, and that if that happened the centre would lose much of its justification for existing.

Finally concessions were made by both the Commission and the negotiating women with the Minister of Health, who by then was in support of the idea of a cleaned-up and more controlled version of a women's health centre. The indications are that agreements could have been reached much less painfully and with much less trauma to the women's movement in Adelaide if the women from the collective had been able to meet with the new Minister of Health soon after the Liberal government came to power. Any problems and concerns could then have been addressed in a far less tense atmosphere than that engendered by SAHC actions and its imposition of manager. Nevertheless, the outcome would probably have been similar. Neither the government nor the Commission were satisfied with the accountability arrangements for the centre. The government could not allow funding to go to an organization which seemed bent on declaring publicly its commitment to socialism and to feminism, and the Commission could not contain its frustration with dealing with a collective. All of these concerns were clearly addressed in the arrangements established for the management of the new women's health centre.

Funding for a women's health centre continued and the Adelaide Women's Community Health Centre (AWCHC) was established in new premises in North Adelaide. By May 1980 it was incorporated under the SAHC Act. The women supporting the original centre at Hindmarsh established a new collective and continued to operate without government funding for the next five years. With the removal of the structural barriers to the operation of the collective and of the pressures of negotiating with a hostile bureaucracy it functioned more smoothly. But without resources its influence was limited. Its energies went mainly into survival and the provision of information and direct services.

There were a number of areas in which arrangements and services in the new centre differed from those at Hindmarsh. It had clearly structured levels of responsibility and a management committee, the majority of whom were appointed by the Minister of Health. It was accountable to her for the management and administration of the centre. A co-ordinator was appointed to undertake the delegated management and administrative responsibilities entailed in the day-to-day running of the centre. The decision-making structure was participative but the idea of collectivity was rejected. Workers were granted status as health commission employees, although the centre retained the right to employ its own staff. The centre was situated in an attractive, well-furnished building, in a non-residential area close to the city. Any direct relationship with a local community became impossible to sustain. Sharing of medical skills with non-medical staff was discontinued. The firm and visible commitment to feminist principles was tempered. The centre gained respectability and status. Within the system it was beginning to seek and find a new legitimacy and a voice.

The developments in women's health centres in South Australia since 1980 can be divided into three broad areas, namely, contact with women in the community, broadening the definition of women's health, and policy. Adelaide Women's Community Health Centre initially lost much in terms of its contact with women in the community. It had moved away from any direct contact with radical feminists and away from its local community to an area with quite different socio-demographic characteristics. However, it remained committed to community contact and, in time, took an important role in assisting in the establishment of women's health centres in three outlying metropolitan regions, ensuring the active involvement of local women in planning the centres and in managing them. This included making sure they were a key part of any negotiations with the Commission and supporting them in becoming separately incorporated units. Incorporation of the new centres legalized their management committee status and gave them a formal base from which to negotiate on behalf of local women. The actual physical location of these centres, out of the city centre and in working class areas, is important. They are situated in or near shopping and housing and have a strong commitment to being responsive to the concerns of local women – seeing and talking to them about their problems and experiences and using this information in planning services.

All of the centres have had a commitment to the greater involvement of women in health planning and policy-making at regional and state levels. They have worked for the development of more open and democratic decision-making within the health bureaucracy and have given their strong support to the development of consumer health and welfare forums in South Australia.

The women's health centres in the 1970s were almost entirely engaged in activities to do with reproductive and vaginal health or with women's mental wellbeing. In the 1980s there has been a broadening of interests to include other aspects of women's lives. One good example of this was the Repetition Strain Injury (RSI) project initiated by AWCHC and the Working Women's Centre. Both centres became interested in RSI and its dramatic impact on the lives of women and their families, from the work that had been undertaken at the Lidcombe Workers' Health Centre in Sydney and because more and more women were coming to the Working Women's Centre with chronic arm and shoulder pain. One of the doctors began to accept referrals and eventually funding was obtained for an action research project. This enabled the centre to develop referral networks for treatment and worksite assessment and to provide more services itself. Groups were established which provided support and information to assist women with the major events and changes that were occurring in their lives because of court cases, insurance battles and disability. Many of these women joined the RSI campaign which involved people from unions, student activists and other interested individuals. The campaign was important not only because of what it achieved in raising awareness of the issue, but because it involved the health centre in working with a range of groups from outside the health care system in an effort to achieve change. One interesting feature of such an alliance is that it entailed contact with some groups who regard bureaucracies and state government services with some suspicion or even antagonism.

Policy making, on the other hand, is quite different. It is, by its very nature, a 'drawing-in' process. It takes those concerned right into the midst of bureaucratic modes and imperatives.

Representatives from the centres have been active in policy-making committees for a community health policy, a women's health policy, a primary health care policy and a health promotion policy amongst others. A considerable amount of time and energy has been involved. None of these policies has ever been finalized or implemented. Nevertheless, women's concerns have been heard and have gained some legitimacy. The position of Women's Adviser on Health, created in South Australia in 1983, and the first such position in Australia, may be seen as a consequence of this as well as contributing to it.

Women's health activity in South Australia has been influential in the establishment of centres in some other states and in the recent federal government initiative to develop a national women's health policy. Women's health centres have maintained a fair degree of integrity, an ability to exert pressure for reform and to present some challenge to the 'embeddedness' of masculine power. In the earlier years difficulties primarily took the form of direct constraint and opposition. Over time this has lessened, or become more covert. The centres have gained greater bureaucratic acceptance and this provides encouragement to pay greater attention to policy with its enticement of 'whole system' change. Here, with the logic of policy production 'based on bureaucratic rules, purposive action and consensus formation',[6] the primary danger is co-option.

There is a constant tension in seeking to maintain a commitment to feminist principles and goals whilst working within the state. In my view, there are two key strategies in sustaining this commitment. The first is in holding and developing the community base for women's health, to keep in touch with the reality of women's lives and to maintain an independent power base or constituency. The second is the continuing development of broad but sympathetic alliances thereby maintaining a strong power base.

Notes

Thanks and acknowledgement to Barbara Smith, Marg Merrilees, Andy Malone, Judith Dwyer, Chia Moan, Marg Madder, Jane Tassie and Jan Anderson for their ideas, encouragement and support.

1. The Federation of Feminist Women's Health Centres, *How to Stay Out of the Gynecologist's Office*, Peace Press, 1981.
2. Hester Eisenstein, 'The Gender of Bureaucracy', in Goodnow, J. and Pateman, C., eds, *Women, Social Science and Public Policy*, Allen and Unwin, Sydney, 1985, pp. 104–15.
3. Ann Game and Rosemary Pringle, *Gender at Work*, Allen and Unwin, Sydney, 1983.
4. See Suzanne Franzway, 'With Problems of Her Own: Femocrats and the Welfare State', *Australian Feminist Studies*, Summer 1986, pp. 45–57.
5. The Australian Constitution, in a special amendment passed in 1946, protects the medical and dental professions from any form of civil conscription by the federal government. This forms an important constraint on the introduction of any form of nationalized medicine.
6. The first South Australian Women's Adviser, to the State Premier, was not appointed until 1975; thus there could be no support from femocrats at this stage.
7. Minute to the Minister of Health from the Women's Adviser, Premier's Department, 11 January 1980.
8. Suzanne Franzway, p. 52.

15

Feminist Cultural Production: The Tampax Mafia, an Interview with Chris Westwood of the Belvoir Street Theatre

Sophie Watson

SW: *What are the origins of feminist theatre in Australia?*
CW:There were certainly feminists attached to the New Theatre in the 1930s. But of the recent feminist wave, there was a group in Melbourne attached to the Pram Factory in the 1970s. Between 1973 and 1982, there were a number of 'pro-am' feminist productions [women from professional theatre mixed with women with no professional experience], particularly in Adelaide. They were interesting because they used conventional popular forms such as melodrama or revue or cabaret. However, in the commercial theatre there was – to the best of my knowledge – no 'feminist' theatre and only a little 'women's theatre'.

In 1981 Jude Kuring and I were sitting around in the Nimrod Theatre. I was a project officer and she, an actor, was whingeing about lack of work for women. In every play there's six roles for men and one for women and that one is the heart-of-gold whore or the mother; those stereotypes. We decided to invite some other actors to see if we could do something about it. We wrote out a questionnaire with questions such as: 'Do you ever feel like punching your director in the face?' 'Are you fed up with earning less in an average year than a boy?' and asked them to come to a meeting.

We were sitting around in this theatre with about a hundred and fifty women and we decided to go to the Theatre Board of the Australia Council for a Limited Life Project grant. Jude and I did a lot of lobbying and conning, and filling in application forms (which I am quite good at) and we went up there and persuaded them into giving us $110,000 for a year to do a variety of projects, two sets of play readings, lots of workshop, two intensive big projects, of which was one on Women and Comedy and Music. The female stereotypes in music and comedy are obvious, but the women wanted to do things that were not stereotypical. There was another group including Kerry Dwyer, who did a much more stylized non-naturalist thriller-plus-dykes-in-overcoats. Many serious actors from the main stage houses didn't want to be involved in this, because that was like alternative theatre to them. So one group comprised the mainstream theatre and the other the alternative theatre. As well, an elected steering committee of nine distributed five grants of five to ten thousand dollars to different groups of women in theatre.

That year went by with a great deal of very hostile reaction from both the funding authorities and the press. Most of the mainstream actors wouldn't credit it in their biogs (I notice that they nearly all are now) so in some ways, it was a really horrible year. A lot of famous actresses were being told by their boyfriends, their colleagues and their agents not to have anything to do with it. 'You're off to a Mo Brigade Meeting now, are you?' was a common one. It was really awful.

A lot of Nimrod's problems were laid at the doorstep of the Women in Theatre Project. What happened was that Nimrod got so frightened of losing business from the 'feminists' that they sacked one of the women and practically all their women employees left too. Of course this was the bulk. Of any given theatre company, there is usually one male director, one male general manager and one male production manager and almost everything else in a theatre is done by women. So then, some of us who were working at Nimrod decided that the only way to follow through the Women in Theatre Project, keep the momentum up and widen it out, was to have a Women and Arts Festival. The idea was put to the Women's Advisory Council of the Premier's Department, who then joined with the Arts Grants area of the Premiers Department.

SW: *So it was actually a collaboration between you and the femocrats in a sense?*

CW: That almost always has been the case in the funding of women and arts – the collaboration of me 'outside' and a mate 'inside'. It is impossible for feminists to attack the arts funding bureaucracy from outside with no contacts inside, or for new ideas to develop, not just feminism. It means you have to go and lobby and curry favour and become friendly with the bureaucrat inside (who is invariably male). You have to make them think that you are so terrific that whatever you want to do, they will give you the money for it. I think it is true of all funding in Australia in the arts. In health or welfare, I reckon that there is a policy that can encourage applications and get a response. In the arts, there is no policy as to where we are going or why. It is quite good for people like me because I play it ad hoc and get what I want. It is the only way you can work because there is no policy which you can change to make funds available automatically to women. So we have had to do it project by project, like the Women and Theatre Project and the Women and Arts Festival.

SW: *What were the main objectives and outcomes of the festival?*

CW: We insisted there be a research committee to look into what was going on, because there had been no stats gathering, analysis or research into women in the arts (except some sporadic work by some women in film and some by women in visual arts). The committee included lots of interesting people – Hester Eisenstein, for example, who was working at the Department of Equal Opportunity and Public Employment; Andrea Hull, director of policy and planning at the Australia Council, provided the funding. I think she just put it into her programme and paid for it. I don't know that it was officially a grant. It is interesting to note that the feminist in a position of power simply throws the money quietly sideways when there is no policy and therefore no programme to fit in. Andrea helped the women writing the report to structure recommendations that could reach her officially, from which she could then create a policy to execute. It was called the Women and Arts Strategy. So there is this big glossy report followed by a set of recommendations to the Australia Council (which is the federal arts funding body) to follow up. One of the things the Australia Council had to do was create its own internal Women and Arts Advisory Committee to provide advice to all of the boards which fund arts, whatever art form (visual arts, literature, Aboriginal arts, music, theatre). This kind of strategy was created so that when funding arts, they actually took account of women.

The festival was in 1982. In 1983 the report was delivered to the Australia Council. In 1984, the Australia Council formed a committee which worked on all of these things – gender-based difference, the things that limit women from creative work and so on. It has less to do with feminist ideas than with industrial issues. Chris Ronalds constructed an affirmative action pilot programme for arts companies modelled on the one she did with corporations. It also undertook some 'educational' work like 'how to be a chair' workshops, which many women in the arts found difficult. Really basic work. The work that everybody else was doing in 1969, the arts are doing in the 1980s.

SW: *Was the report effective?*

CW: One of the things that came out of it was that now everybody who receives a federal government arts grant has to ensure equal employment opportunity for women. It is not mandatory, there are conditions of grant to which you have to agree and there are guidelines as well, and it is in the guidelines. Since the Women and Theatre Project, there have been other spin-offs, such as a Women Theatre Workers' Association which has formed and has nothing to do with the arts unions. There is a group in every state. They are not, on the whole, women who are big stars or big names. Attitudes remain really unaffected, I think. The other day Actors Equity issued a letter to all theatre companies in Australia saying 'you have got to employ equal numbers of men and women'. This good thing has come because of feminist pressure and the fact that there are now a lot of feminists in Actors Equity as union organizers. One well-known media personality refers to Equity as 'the tampax mafia'.

SW: *Have feminist organizers had much success in challenging traditional structures and shifting the discourses?*

CW: In theatre men work in technical areas, women in the service areas (box office, administration and whatever). Men are the creators; actors and actresses are the fodder for it. So there are two unions, Actors Equity and the technical union (ATAEA). In the ATAEA, because it is male dominated, covering technical workers, its focus is on fun parks and speedways. The theatre workers' representation is very small, and the ATAEA brings in very draconian things to protect the fun parks and speedway people rather than serving the interest of the theatre side. This has a very bad impact on the theatre in that women working in the technical areas won't go to the meetings. It is appalling as far as women go. It has no women organizers, hardly any women on its executive, either state or federal, it does nothing for women and couldn't care less. Whereas, Actors Equity has plenty of feminists who have come from other unions. Actors Equity has been quite good in terms of women for the last couple of years because of its feminist organizers.

SW: *To change track slightly, how did the Belvoir Theatre get set up?*

CW: It was set up by Sue Hill and I, who enthused 600 members of the industry to each put in one thousand dollars to buy it. So it is the only theatre that is owned by the industry, actors, directors and writers. A board of nine is elected to arrange the programme, so it is unlike any other theatre company in the western world. To determine the policy, we had a two-day open day which is also unique in theatre. Other theatres generally appoint a (male) artistic director and say, 'What's the policy going to be?' but we actually broke everybody into groups to report back their views. One group said, 'We think there ought to be more Aboriginal stuff, more kids' stuff, more ethnic stuff' and another group said, 'We should only do Shakespeare' and a feminist said, 'We want to see more feminism – no matter what it is – whether it's Shakespeare or kids or postmodern culture or alternative in its style and content'. The people who came to the meeting were a cross-section of the arts who, with a great deal of enthusiasm, elected the board (of which there are five women and four men this year). It is quite interesting that the industry has come round to the point where they are prepared to have their 'Artistic Director', as it were, be more female than male.

SW: *Do you also have government funding?*

CW: Yes. This year's grants were sixty thousand dollars from the state and one hundred and twenty thousand from the federal arts funding authorities, plus money from the Bicentennial Authority for Capricornia.

SW: *How is the programme decided?*

CW: Those nine people decide it. Or rather, what happens is that I might think, looking at the year's programme there's too much boys' stuff in it, so I ring up Robyn Archer and say, 'Quick, find me a few feminist plays that I can put before the board at the next meeting'. We're now at the stage when we're planning next year's programme so we are looking at the need to be more radical in the light of the overall conservative climate and the need to distance ourselves further away from the Sydney Theatre Company. We are becoming a bit too 'smart' in some ways.

Recently a journalist doing a story on Belvoir Street Theatre said to me, 'You're not radical any more'. I said, 'Look, this is January right? Upstairs we've got Asinimali from South Africa; downstairs we've got lesbians from New Zealand; in February, there's *Ghosts*, a classic with contextual reference to AIDS. Then *Capricornia*, a multi-cultural cast in a play about race relations in Australia, and then Robyn Archer's piece about black women. Tell me that's not radical.' We're still doing exactly the same sort of work we were doing a few years ago. So either the press have caught up with us or we're presenting it in a way that's not scary, not threatening.

SW: *In many ways this is similar to a fairly mainstream theatre, in terms of its physical structure, interior, management and plays performed. Is this intentional?*

CW: You can run 'mainstream' culture with 'alternative' culture and make both sides feel comfortable and hopefully cross them over. Also I've tried to broaden out the use of the theatre. I like to see the foyer of the theatre used for things which are natural to feminists and feminist academics (like launching books, or running public debates and campaigns, or women's events), so that they feel at home going to the theatre. So that when you say to them, 'Why don't you come and see *Ghosts* they don't say 'I never go to the theatre, or 'It'll be all about boys', they say, 'OK, I'll go'. And vice versa, it stops all the boys doing 'Ghosts' thinking that's all the theatre should be about.

SW: *So what you aim to encourage is a whole range of people to come to the theatre to see both radical and more traditional theatre?*

CW: This means that you have to work out how to make feminism marketable. The 'Pack of Women' in 1983 is the classic example. What we did was to try to put in well-known stars (who actually tried to get out of their contracts the week before it opened because they were so frightened of going on stage and saying feminist things and never working again!). One came from a television soap and one from the club circuit and one was well known in bourgeois theatre. So we hoped that they would draw three different audiences which could be hit with feminism. And the first night went through the roof. The audience just would not let the actors off the stage. It sold out, right round the country. It was the first time there had been a really slick, upmarket professional production saying things feminists wanted to hear and which didn't alienate the non-feminists who went along to see the stars.

SW: *How was it funded?*

CW: Privately. Five hundred dollars from people like you and me. I told everyone, 'If it works you can have it back and if it doesn't you've blown it'.

SW: *That's been your procedure for quite a few plays hasn't it?*

CW: Yes, because you can't get big male backers to put money into feminist theatre. The male producers, of course, appropriate feminism and create instead a 'women's market' through plays such as *Steel Magnolias.*

SW: *So you draw on the women's movement for finance, at least the wealthier sections of it?*

CW: Yes, the femocrats mainly. That's where state intervention comes in, you see. The state pays them a high wage, then they can afford to give me five hundred dollars. Then I can afford to do shows to push their ideas along a bit so they can earn their money, and it all comes around in a circle again. But there seems to be much less money around now. Things have tightened up. But nevertheless, lots of feminist enterprises in Australia have come out of femocrats and feminist academics opening their cheque books.

SW: *How do you extract funding from government agencies?*

CW: You have to say things to them like, 'Would you like it to be known to the press and other members of the industry that you're not the least bit interested in women?'

'Of course I wouldn't, it's just that we don't have any money.'

'I've got your annual report here and I notice that you've given quite a lot of money to this very esoteric Shakespeare project. Why is it that Shakespeare, in this day and age, in its traditional form, is worth a quarter of a million and women are worth nothing?'

'No it was another director, before me, who gave that money.'

'Oh really, it says here that it was in the period of your incumbency.'

'It must have been a mistake.'

SW: *So you embarrass them. What about private funding?*

CW: We don't have any success whatsoever in getting 'corporate sponsorship'. We are seen to be feminists and radicals and they do not want to have their company associated with that.

SW: *Turning now to the relationship between femocrats and cultural production, have there been any conflicts between the feminist performers and the feminist bureaucrats?*

CW: Oh yes, I can think of a fabulous one in 1975 on International Women's day in Adelaide where the state government provided lots of money to the Festival Centre to do a big International Women's Day event, and we organized Robyn Archer to do a concert. She put together a scratch band – and there, on International Women's Day is a male band on stage. Hundreds of mums, dads and ordinary people bought tickets for it and Robyn's singing feminist material. Feminists who'd all been out celebrating after the big march arrived and could only get seats in the second balcony because all the mums and dads had bought their tickets in advance. So there they are, up in the balcony and they take their riding boots and start banging them on the railing shouting 'Jocks off, Jocks off' and the whole concert had to be closed down because the house manager said, 'I'm not having this kind of behaviour in my theatre'. On the one hand, they were right. On the other, there weren't many professional women musicians prepared to do a concert such as this and an artist should have the right to choose whatever musicians he or she wants.

SW: *So at that point some of the feminist academics and femocrats were more strongly identified as feminist than many of the feminist performers were?*

CW: Certain of them were. Yes.

SW: *How effective have feminists in the arts bureaucracy been?*

CW: Well there's only been one or two until recently.

SW: *Can you tell me about feminist involvement with other areas of cultural production?*

CW: Well, the most important initial thing in radio was when the Australian Women's Broadcasting Co-operative set up the 'Coming-Out Show' in 1975.

SW: *Did they then move into the mainstream areas?*

CW: Yes. They had a policy of treating it as a training ground to get women producers and announcers up. They took women in from fringe radio stations or other areas of the ABC. The focal points of public literature (apart from publishing) were events such as Writers' Week. Since about 1973 or 1974 there have always been battles about Writers' Week at the Adelaide Festival not representing women, not having women panelists, not having a special section on women or whatever. Well, I was on the Writers' Week Committee from 1973–8 and helped change that. The Women's Adviser to the Premier came on, and when I left, it was in the hands of key women in the community, like a woman from the feminist bookshop. After that all the Writers' Weeks everywhere started doing more about women. The battle had been won to some extent.

SW: *What about film?*

CW: Film's very much like theatre. There's the mainstream feature film industry which doesn't even notice women in its ideas, in its intention or what it's trying to do. And then there's this huge group of women film makers doing interesting women's films, and they've been doing that since the early 1970s.

SW: *What's their relationship been with the bureaucracy and funding agencies?*

CW: The Australian Film Commission was forced by young feminist film makers to create a special Women's Film Fund in 1975, under Whitlam. They had money each year to give to women film makers but I think that's under a big cloud right now. And a lot of it's to do with a loss of energy of my generation. People who are now between thirty-seven and forty-three or so who were all the ones who set up funding and programmes in the mid 1970s have run out of energy to keep fighting. There doesn't seem to be a crowd coming through to take over. So, if they all walk out it'll probably all fold, I reckon, in terms of the structure, policy or money in all kinds of arts funding.

SW: *Where does the women's film money come from?*

CW: Initially all of the money that was given to women in any of those areas was provided by the Whitlam government to the normal funding programmes earmarked for women. The idea was that you gradually incorporate women's stuff into your annual budget. There are, however, women in positions of power, who even if they don't relate to feminism, keep saying at least, 'What about the women?'

SW: *What are the current debates preoccupying feminists in cultural production?*

CW: I think there's a big question in all areas as to what feminists think they're doing. The question is, 'Have we gone past the need for separatism'? In the past, if we pinpointed all the things that happened almost all of them were separatist. I know if I advertised a women's only performance now at Belvoir Street, feminists would complain because they want to bring their boyfriends. That's why we don't do it any more. It's not only that our own legislation works against us; I think we like having private parties with women, but I think if we have a public function, people get fed up if it's just women.

TV is still really out of the hands of women. There does not seem to be a feminist lobby inside commercial television. Indeed, there is not a feminist lobby inside any commercial (compared to subsidized) theatre, film, television, music or visual arts. There's a huge lack of communication. The training schools like NIDA which trains actors and designers was a participant in the Affirmative Action programme, but underneath the surface they're not really into it.

SW: *What is the nature of the relationships between Aboriginal, Migrant and Anglo performers? Do you find there are conflicts of interest?*

CW: Of the aboriginal women performers I don't know any feminists.

SW: *Is that because they don't like to identify with feminism?*

CW: Well they're trying to be famous actresses and I don't see that as being feminist really. I think they see feminists as wearing overalls, ugly and overweight and that myth still persists. Actors are a self-fulfilling myth! Their image is really important to their marketability in professional theatre. They're enormously grateful for people like me to help them but they really want to be up there looking beautiful and hearing rave reviews about what sexy, stunning, black actress today won an Oscar!

SW: *So there are no self-identified black feminist theatre groups?*

CW: I don't know of any.

SW: *What about migrant women?*

CW: A lot of actors in this county are of migrant origin. Anyone can walk in and be an actor if they've got some talent. Look at the cast of names for *Capricornia*. If you looked at the actors on the stage and just saw them singing and dancing – you'd say they were all WASP, but they have names like Jurisic, Vuletic. But there's no specifically migrant feminist theatre group that I know of.

SW: *How do you consider the future for feminists in cultural production?*

CW: I can think of probably five performers in the forefront of professional theatre who I'd consider to be feminists (out of about eight thousand registered actresses). There are several feminist companies such as Vital Statistix in Adelaide, who receive some government subsidy and would be considered to be fringe or alternative theatre.

SW: *So feminists still tend to be more in the policy areas, like you, or working around the side of theatre rather than as performers? And the future for feminist cultural production in theatre?*

CW: I suspect there isn't a separatist one. That's a bit depressing, isn't it? It's to do with the nature of the employment of actors. If somebody said, 'Get up on the stage and fuck this bear', many would do it because they're competing against three or four hundred actresses for the one job – being paid for six weeks in a year, they haven't got time to be political, and I think there are actors around who have gone mad trying to be a feminist and a performer. It's too hard. Directors won't work with a performer who says, 'I can't say this line – as a woman.' 'No, well we won't have you because you're too difficult to work with. Plenty more where you come from, love.'

SW: *Do you think people like you will continue to work on trying to introduce feminist ideas and practices into the theatre?*
CW: It's hard to get feminists to come and work here because many of the feminists who want to work here have no training and skills and think 'because we're feminists, it's good enough'. It isn't. You've got to have specific skills, you've got to be able to do scenic painting so you don't leave globs of paint on the set, you've got to be a trained carpenter to build sets, or you've got to be a trained clerical person to work in the box office. A lot of the feminists who come here think that just because it's theatre, anyone can do it. This is quite a healthy attitude on one level, but we can't employ them when they're working with professional actors who expect it to be done within five minutes, properly. People who do know how to do it all and are trained often come out of a conservative working-class background and accidentally happen to end up in this theatre and love it, but they aren't necessarily politicized as feminists. They learn it here.
SW: *What would you say were the greatest achievements of Australian women in cultural production?*
CW: One is the archeological stuff – digging up women's history and representing it on stage or in film. It's been quite a natural path hasn't it? Showing where we've come from. The radical stuff contributing to new ideas has often been English, rarely Australian. The other stuff that's happened is a step forward in the industrial area, like getting equal opportunity in training and employment. A lot of that is government. Like in literature, it's been through subsidized publishing. In fact, a lot of it is actually government when you look at it. The publishers who started publishing women's writing were not small feminist publishing houses but were existing publishers who got Literature Board, which is Australia Council, money, to subsidize them to take the risk on a woman's book. It all started under Whitlam. If they hadn't been funded by government a lot would have never happened.
SW: *How long have men been aware of a feminist presence in the theatre and how seriously do you think they take it?*
CW: Since 1975. They didn't take it at all seriously in the beginning and now the intelligent ones agree with Marcuse: that feminism is the most important philosophical development in the twentieth century. The bulk of them don't care. The bulk of them think we're still a bunch of ratbags. Also, now they've made it so unfashionable, some of the feminists are even disguising it a bit. This is really scary – the sense that feminism is passé and that increasingly conservative political and economic trends backlash against feminism, so we have to be prepared for attack.

16

Fathers, Brothers, Mates: The Fraternal State in Australia

Rosemary Pringle and Sophie Watson

It is no longer possible to theorize the state as a contradictory and complex beast which, in the long term, will act consistently to protect certain interests even if in the short term it may be fruitful for it to act otherwise. There are too many holes to the argument. More usefully, we can conceptualize the state, not as an institution but as a set of arenas; a by-product of political struggles whose coherence is as much established in discourse as in shifting and temporary connections. The current collection of practices which we refer to as 'the state' are a historical product, not structurally 'given'. This is not to say that there is no intentionality or purpose. But what intentionality there is comes from the success with which various groupings are able to impose themselves; it is always likely to be partial and temporary.

Marxists, liberals and feminists have shared a view of the state as, to a greater or lesser extent, a coherent unity. What they have also shared is the view of coherent interests which exist outside the state which can either influence the state or are represented by or embodied in it. Group interests do not pre-exist, fully formed, to be simply 'represented' in the state. Our concern is with how such 'interests' become defined and articulated. Arguably it is in the domain of the state that they are formally constituted.

This line of argument is taken a lot further by Alison Smith who suggests that interests are entirely constituted through discourse and have no independent existence.[1] While we do not wish to go that far, we concur with her argument that it is through discourse that interests are evoked and constructed. The idea that men or women, or specific classes, have a unitary interest is an illusion. Interests are not merely 'reflected'; in the political sphere, they have to be continuously

229

constructed and reproduced. It is through discursive strategies, that is, through creating a framework of meanings, that interests come to be constructed and represented in certain ways.

Just as women's interests are constructed rather than pre-given, so also are men's. It is in this context that the discourse of 'fraternity' which underpins ostensibly gender-neutral 'liberalism', is useful. For it presumes and evokes the notion that men alone are the political actors, that state and civil society have been established by men, who act on behalf of the population as a whole. In a day-to-day sense, it is obvious that men's interests diverge. But political differences tend to be constituted as differences between men, reinforcing at a more fundamental level the notion of the public, political domain as a masculine one. In a patriarchal society women, as a group, are constructed in relation to men, that is, in terms of the extent to which they are either similar to or different from men. Thus women's autonomous interests also get constituted in terms of differences between men. The maintenance debate, for example, is substantially about the interests of individual fathers in dodging liability versus the collective interests of the public purse. In many arenas, such as family law, the interests of men as husbands/ fathers have been subordinated to the construction of men's broader interests in the public arena.

This chapter addresses both the lack of coherence of the arenas that constitute the state and the discourses which construct it. Given the dominance of liberalism in the modern industrial state, we examine in particular the fraternalism that underpins it. We shall focus here on the erratic nature of the welfare state in relation to family and gender relations. If the state is to be perceived as an object of feminist strategy it requires an analysis which breaks with the various kinds of functionalism of the past. This will be one which examines the ebb and flow of power, its twists and turns, nodes and concentrations. It will not foreground the state but will instead situate it amongst the variety of strategies employed by men in constructing their interests. The state apparatuses here intersect with other levels and practices which have to be treated in their specificity rather than as a reproduction of pre-given structures.

In an illuminating book, Carole Pateman describes the explicitly 'fraternal' nature of social contract discourse which legitimates the modern state. She argues that while fraternity has evoked less attention than liberty and equality, its specific gender connotations largely denied or explained away, it 'does not appear by accident as one of the basic liberal and contractarian principle, and it means exactly what it says – brotherhood'.[2] In the seventeenth-century debate between patriarchalists and contract theorists, the sons overthrew the arbitrary rule of the father/king to establish 'civil society' with public rules which bind all equally. The parties to the contract are men acting not as fathers, for that would be contradictory, but as adult brothers. Women are excluded from the public world of justice, order and reason and, it can be argued, participate only at the price of being honorary men, that is, by being degendered. 'Liberal patriarchy' is a two-tiered system in which men continue to exercise power in the family as husbands and fathers, while in civil society they rule as a fraternity. Because the state is justified by an ideology of free, equal individuals the exclusion of women, as well as the continuance of 'naturally' unequal material and family relations, has always provoked contradictions and thus created possibilities for feminist intervention at both levels.

This century has seen a shift from a 'private' patriarchy in which men controlled individual women in the family towards a reliance on less direct and more 'public' forms including the state. While no one would deny the continued existence of domestic tyranny, the achievement of legal equality *has* seriously weakened men's authority as husbands and fathers. Power now more typically operates through representations, norms, forms of language, definitions of who we are and in what we should find pleasure. Though the discourses of liberalism assert that 'patriarchy' is archaic they create the space for a new form of male domination which is more subtle, and may be more stable and powerful than earlier forms. In response to conflict and resistance men have been able to consolidate, or at least defend, their power, and regroup as a fraternity, specifically through discourses which deny the relevance of gender.[3] This point is important, particularly in the light of the rather gung-ho approaches of some feminists to making the state 'work for women'. As the Canadian Lorna Weir has pointed out, the state is flexible in its responses to feminist demands and is able to reformulate them and shift the locus of meaning: 'Viewing the repertoires of official gender regulation as fixed and static – likely an inheritance from socialist functionalism – the capacity of the state for a limited reformulation of gender regulation catches us largely unprepared'.[4]

Carole Pateman's work marks an advance in feminist thinking about the state, and specifically in relation to Australia. Contract theory strikes particular chords here given the emphasis on corporatism and tripartite agreements between government, employers and unions. One of the first actions of the Hawke government after its election in 1983 was to set up a prices and incomes accord with the unions. Feminists have drawn attention to the way women were marginal to the accord and debated whether this is inherent or inevitable. Given it was an attempt by the Labor party, in opposition and then in government, to persuade the most powerful unions to exercise wage restraint, women's near-exclusion is no surprise. The accord was perceived as a pact between men – incidentally partly possible since the major protagonists on the government and union sides were old mates from Hawke's days as president of the ACTU. Following Castles's argument that the main strategies for maintaining living standards in Australia since the early part of the century have been through the protection of jobs through tariff barriers, the arbitration system and the family wage,[5] we could well argue a long history of a fraternal contract in welfare creating women's dependence. Meanwhile the Hawke government, in its search for legitimacy in this bicentennial year, has concerned itself with that other group which falls outside the social contract, aboriginals, and has been busily trying to draw up a treaty that will be acceptable to them.

While no one believes a social contract ever 'really' took place, such a notion is constitutive of capitalist and patriarchal relations as they have developed historically. It not only legitimates the contemporary state but actively constructs it. Under liberal patriarchy, detailed attention has been given to the operations of the state: to the constitution, to the relation between parliamentary, executive and judicial wings, the workings of government and bureaucracy, questions of ritual and protocol, parliamentary and voting procedures and so on. Power relations are actively constituted in and through these discourses: they do not simply reflect economic or sexual power. We do not mean by this that there is nothing outside discourse, or that there is no prior materiality which forms the interests constructed within the arenas of the state.

'Fraternity' also has a particular resonance in Australia. This is not only to do with the personal style of Prime Minister Hawke, or with corporatism. Australia has a long tradition of male 'mateship', and bases its national identity on the doings of these mates, the 'diggers', at Gallipoli. Women are largely excluded from the national myths that legitimate the Australian state. Australian egalitarianism is essentially of a masculine variety. Yet compared with the aura of long established patriarchal regimes, Australian 'fraternity' also has a certain adolescent quality which makes it vulnerable and malleable. The class structure probably is more open than its old-world equivalents, and high positions in the bureaucracy have been more accessible to the working class. Though this has mostly favoured men, the greater permeability of state structures has allowed for women's participation and, in recent years, made possible the rise of the 'femocrats'.

Pateman's account of the shift from patriarchal to fraternal discourses about sovereignty meshes with Foucault's 'bottom-up' analysis of power. The general drift of discourse analysis is away from 'grand theories' of power, particularly 'top-down' ones that see power as a unity residing in the state. Instead they stress the omnipresence of power, as being produced in every social relationship. Foucault warns that we should not

assume that 'the sovereignty of the state, the form of the law or the overall unity of a domination are given at the outset; rather, these are only
the terminal forms power takes'.[6] Foucault treats power as exercised
rather than possessed by individuals or groups, and existing in the
complex network of relations that permeate every aspect of life. 'The
state' is an overall effect of all these relations and cannot be assumed to
act coherently as the agent of particular groups. Power does not reside in
institutions or structures and rather than there being a 'unity of state
power', there is a 'complex strategical situation in a particular society'.[7]
He suggests that 'maybe, after all, the state is no more than a composite
reality and a mythical abstraction whose importance is a lot more limited
than many of us think'.[8]

To reduce the State to a list of functions is to give it both too much
and too little importance. This 'reductionist vision of the role of the state
in relation to everything else makes it absolutely essential as a target to
be attacked and a privileged position to be taken over'. And yet to place
it 'above' or outside society is to miss its main significance and to insist
on a homogeneity in the operations of power which simply is not there.
Elsewhere he says, 'I don't want to say that the state isn't important,
what I want to say is that relations of power, and hence the analysis that
must be made of them, necessarily extend beyond the limits of the state.
In two senses: first of all because the state, for all the omnipotence of its
apparatuses, is far from being able to occupy the whole field of actual
power relations, and further because the state can only operate on the
basis of other, already existing power relations. The state is super-
structural in relation to a whole series of power networks that invest the
body, sexuality, the family, kinship, knowledge, technology and so
forth'.[9] He shifts the emphasis away from the intentionality of the state;
rather than posing questions about how 'it' intervenes in the wider
society, he is concerned with its techniques and apparatuses of
regulation. These are intelligible not because they can be 'explained' but
rather 'because they are imbued, through and through, with calculation'.[10] This is not to revert to a pluralist analysis. While power is
diffused throughout society, it operates as a network, not as a collection
of isolated points, and each specific and localized struggle potentially
has serial effects on the entire network.

Foucault himself has been more concerned with strategies of power
that go beyond the state and its apparatuses, with techniques of surveil-
lance and control and discourses on reason and sexuality. The emphasis
on 'normalizing' discourses appears to play down the role of the state,
reduce it to one arena and by no means the most important. It is
important to stress the specificity of the state; the political realm is not
merely a reflection of the economic, it is the site of competing discourses

and practices. Foucault points here to the concern with 'governmentality' and at the new diplomatico-military and police techniques that
constitute it. Though he does not say so, these domains are clearly
masculine. 'Governmentality' was originally conceived on the model of
(a father's) management of a family, and family remains an important
instrument of government. The discourses that construct the state
assume a masculine subject rather than self-consciously defending or
creating 'men's interests'. In fraternal discourse, like the specifically
patriarchal ones that preceded it, women are treated as the objects of
recipients of policy decisions rather than full participants in them. What
feminists are confronted with is not a state that represents 'men's
interests' as against women's, but government conducted as if men's
interests are the only ones that exist. Claims to be representing 'women's
interests', however disunified these may be, may actually be tossed
around amongst groups of men and used as a strategy for achieving their
own goals. The interests of men as 'fathers' does not always coincide
with their interests as 'brothers' or mates', and each in turn will shift and
change each time they are articulated.

Feminist activists in Australia have not been greatly concerned to
theorize the state. They were initially content to treat it as an elite made
up of men[11] and to get on with the business of engaging with whatever
aspect of it they were involved in. This at least produced a healthy
cynicism about what it was they were dealing with. But underlying this
was an ambivalence about whether the state was inherently masculine or
whether, through the extension of full citizenship to women, it could be
turned into the neutral arbiter of liberal theory. Given the Australian
(and New Zealand) traditions of pragmatism and social reform ('Socialism Sans Doctrine' as Metin called it in the late nineteenth century), it is
not surprising that some feminists should have faith in the state's willingness to iron out gender inequalities once pointed out. Those of a more
academic bent attempted to theorize the structural features of the state
but it is not clear that our efforts have been of much strategic use. They
have tended to be rather abstract and, in emphasizing its overall unity
and coherence, leave little space for fluidity or change. There is a strong
functionalist heritage here, whether socialist, feminist or liberal, in
the institutional views of both state and family. It has been assumed
that their functions in preserving capitalism, patriarchy or just plain
'society' can be recited. They have not had much predictive potential
and all too often have trailed along and theorized situations after they
were all over. Often they have become out of touch with experience. In
the circumstances the spontaneous reactions of frontline activists have
frequently been more useful.

In Marxist theory 'the state' is an expression of class domination,

whose 'function' is to stabilize capitalist relations, to maintain unity and
cohesion in the face of class contradictions and antagonisms. It is recognized that the state is not a blunt instrument of the ruling class and that
the divisions between and within classes are actually inscribed in its
structures, resulting in frequent conflict between different state apparatuses. Nevertheless, in the long term at least, the state is thought to act
coherently, and political power to be a unity. In stressing that 'the
personal is political', feminists emphasized the continuities between
men's power in the state and in other domains. Nevertheless when
feminists have focused on the patriarchal nature of state structures, they
have tended to see the state as a reflection of what exists elsewhere
rather than an important site for the construction of gendered power
relations. It becomes difficult to account for historical change or regional
and individual variation. The passing of the Family Law Act, for
example, which created marital breakdown, as evidenced by one year's
separation, as the only grounds for divorce, does not seem to indicate
much support for the traditional family. Yet feminists cling to this idea,
in this case arguing that the purpose of the Act was to 'modernize' the
family. And there is a tendency to appear to be setting up as normative
the very things that are being criticized.

The last few years have already seen a shift in how feminists talk
about the family. It is no longer regarded as 'patriarchy's primary institution' but one of a series of sites of gender construction and gender
struggles. Stanley and Wise warned of the tendency towards abstraction
that was evidenced by a growing gap between 'the' family which was
oppressive and 'my' family which had mitigating features.[12] There has
been exploration of the variety of family forms, the contradictory nature
of their component elements, the complexities of their power relations
and their failure consistently to carry out its prescribed 'roles'. The
family, like the state, is seen less as an institution or a 'thing' and more
as a site of a variety of interventions and strategies of power. Though
feminists have been enraged by much of Jacques Donzelot's analysis[13]
they too have begun to look at the legal, welfare, medical, psychological
and other discourses which construct the 'social' and within it 'the
family' and the strategies available to men and women in relation to
these discourses.[14] We are now beginning to see how such an analysis
can be applied to the state and the domain of the 'political'.

The relationship between family and state has been of particular
concern to feminists. There has been analysis of the way they back each
other up, of interchangeability of function. In this context the 'welfare'
area, and the shifting of welfare responsibilities between family and state
has long been noted. Discourses around welfare and its provision are
central to the construction of gender relations. Feminist engagements

with the state have mostly been concerned with social and family policy, with criticizing the assumptions underlying such policies and attempting to make the state deliver better services to women.

Marxist-feminist analysis of the welfare state,[15] like Marxist analysis, has tried to avoid a simple functionalist approach by introducing notions of contradiction. The welfare state is thus theorized not only to be acting simply in the interests of capital in the reproduction of labour power. It also grants reforms with the same hand with which it takes them away. The welfare state is seen as deriving from both working class victories and ruling class victories in the same uneasy and often unexplained amalgam. Where the working class, women and disadvantaged win, we are usually reminded of the contradictory nature of capitalism which besets the state. That is, its need to maintain the appearance of neutrality in order to legitimate its power at the same time as facilitating the process of capital accumulation. More recently feminist theory on the welfare state has recognized the need to shift our analysis to the particular institutions of the welfare state and their specific histories, rather than assuming any unity of the state or integration of its parts.[16]

Feminist analysis extends the argument to place the family at centre stage. Here the welfare state is argued to produce and reproduce a patriarchal nuclear family form, where women are constructed as dependent, as mothers and carers, while men are the breadwinners. In relation to tax and social security, Hilary Land and others thus argue that social security reflects specific family ideology which derives from the Beveridge report and has little changed: 'The attitude of the housewife to gainful employment outside the home is not and should not be the same as the single woman: she has other duties'.[17] Indeed the current rhetoric of the right in Britain and the social policies pursued seem to provide further ammunition to the argument. In Australia it has similarly been argued that post-war reconstruction in the hands of a Labor government consolidated a particular family form and a working relation between family and state that has remained in place.

Others have explored the ramifications of this dominant ideology to suggest that the state thus has no interest in women as non-family members, as women outside their domestic and mothering role. One of us attempted to show how housing policy is a striking case in point.[18] It is also commonly argued that women are discouraged from full time participation in the labour market because of the disincentives built into the social security system. Shaver has noted that when welfare and taxation policies are taken together as a series of transfers, the state takes from women as individuals and redistributes to them as wives and mothers.[19]

Feminists who have distanced themselves somewhat from Marxist feminist discourses have stressed the patriarchal state, or emphasized the politics of masculine dominance. In Varda Burstyn's account the state is the 'great collective father figure', a new representative of 'men-as-a-group' who substitute for the absent fathers.[20] Policies controlling women's sexuality as well as labour are crucial. So too is men's conscious exclusion of women from positions of authority and defence of their power. Other feminists have shifted the terms of the debate yet further by emphasizing inequality of power as the central dimension. For Mackinnon then, the state institutionalizes male power in its forms of law, social policy and politics and formulates all its policies according to the interests and experiences of men.[21] Pateman takes a different tack arguing that 'within the patriarchal welfare state, to demand proper social recognition and support for women's responsibilities is to condemn women to less than full citizenship, where citizenship is constituted by men's capacity to work'.[22]

Discussions of the welfare state which invoke notions of contradiction, of masculine power, of legitimation, of mediation of class relations or class conflict, of reproduction of labour, of the creation and mediation of distinctive family relations, of accumulation of capital, fall into some rather serious traps. Each of these discourses suggest that the state has coherence and clear intentionality. Introducing the notion of contradiction does not solve the problem. Explaining equal employment opportunity legislation for women on the one hand, and the withdrawal of expenditure on child care on the other, in terms of contradiction implies certain assumptions. Contradiction can have meaning in only two ways. Either in terms of some kind of Marxist dialectic, that is, that we are in the process of transformation onto the next stage. Or, more importantly, the state can only be said to be contradictory if it is imputed to constitute a set of coherent intentions. That is, the discourse of contradiction implies a unity of state form which then surprises us when it appears to act in unexpected ways. We argue that the state is erratic and disconnected rather than contradictory. The extent of fragmentation cannot so easily be denied in a federal system where there may be considerable disjunctures between federal, state and local levels of government.

While the structures are important, the state is not an object or an actor so much as the site of a number of discursive formations. If we take this view we do not have to puzzle about why the state acts so contradictorily or, as in Judith Allen's examples of prostitution and abortion, why it fails to act at all.[23] We do not have to conclude in advance that it will act uniformly to maintain capitalist or patriarchal relations, or that this is its 'purpose'. The outcomes of particular policies will depend not purely on the limits placed by 'structures' but in the range of discursive struggles which define and constitute the state, and specific interest groups, from one moment to the next.

Current legislation on social security in Australia illustrates our point. The federal government has enacted legislation which makes single parents ineligible for supporting parents' benefit once the youngest child reaches sixteen. Instead they are required to sign on the unemployment register and claim dole. The rhetoric is that women should be encouraged back into the labour market through retraining programmes and not consigned to dependence on the state as mothers indefinitely. How can such a shift be explained? Marxist feminist analysis might suggest that the state is cutting back its public expenditure in the interests of supporting capital accumulation. And certainly the Hawke government is demonstrating an increasing tendency to kowtow to business interests and to stringently control welfare expenditure. But the argument that the state is defining women as mothers can hardly apply. In the broader structural framework then, why this specific measure when there are a range of options? We could see such a shift as a gain for feminism. Haven't we precisely been arguing that social security provisions reinforce women's dependence and militate against women's entry into the labour market?

The picture is not so simple. During the process of the policy formulation feminists have been up in arms against the new provisions. Their arguments are varied: that there are no jobs for women to go to; that training prorammes are unavailable or inaccessible to women; that women will be financially worse off on the dole, since they lose many existing pension entitlements; that it's a cost saving exercise; that it represents a refusal to recognize women's services as mothers and to support their future needs. An apparent feminist gain is revealed once more as the state fobbing us off. For other feminists the shift is perceived as being in the right direction. There is no one feminist position from which to confront the state.

How can we explain the policy? It does not appear to be the state supporting traditional familial relations even if, more broadly, it is acting in capital's interests by saving money. Neither is it a direct response to feminist pressure. A closer inspection of events suggests several possible explanations. In part, it illustrates the conflicts and compromises between different state apparatuses. The Department of Finance wanted cuts in the welfare budget and were keen to lower further the age beyond which dependence is no longer acknowledged. The Department of Social Security wanted to deflect this initiative with their own proposed less radical cut-off point. Single parents are notoriously the easiest group of pensioners to knock off, partly because of the dominant discourse of dole bludgers, partly because of their lack of voice and organization. In contrast, the government has no desire to see a cohort of blind pensioners rapping on the doors of parliament with their white sticks. The policy was formulated and the bureaucrats, reputed to be supportive of feminism, were left defending the move as part of the budget package. During a period when there has been the highest level of 'feminist' policy advice on social security matters, single parents have been the hardest hit. It is impossible to know if the presence of the femocrats has in part legitimized the changes or if, in their absence, the policies would have been worse. In a sense, the feminist arguments have been incorporated and thrown back in a distorted or qualified form.

Any number of illustrations of the state as an erratic beast could be cited. Feminists have long complained that the state has been lenient to separated fathers on the question of maintenance. In 1988 a system has been devised to collect maintenance from men through the tax system. There has been a variety of feminist responses from criticisms of the move as cost saving to an assertion that it forces women to declare paternity against their will. The absence of a coherent feminist position mirrors the lack of coherence, interest or clarity within the state. Some policies may reflect a patriarchal, some a capitalist, state. Each and every instance of policy-making reflects a different configuration of power relations and networks, of players, interests, financial relations, ideologies, politics and pressures which exist within and outside of the state apparatuses. No wonder that some policies are gains for women while others are not. If we include a perspective of heterogeneity of women and feminist response, no one policy will be a gain for all women. To say the welfare state supports the traditional patriarchal family is no longer useful, if it ever was. As Alison Smith suggests in her discussion of women's refuges, the legal agencies cannot be perceived as simply shoring up some 'archetypal conception of family relations but instead should be seen as contributing to their changing forms'.[24] Local, regional and national as well as historical and cultural specificities have to be acknowledged.

The modern industrial state is another arena. Kim Windsor's chapter addresses the exclusion of women from industry policy debates and initiatives. 'Australia Reconstructed' reflects the concerns and proposed strategies of the key trade union and government players. The mission to Europe to investigate the economic, employment and industrial strategies of Britain, West Germany, Sweden, Norway, and Austria endorsed the already prevailing view that some version of the Swedish corporate model was the way to go. To see the report as another illustration of the fraternal contract is to argue not just that the members of the mission were all (bar one) men, nor simply that women are barely mentioned in the report, nor that the focus is on industries where male workers are concentrated; nor even that the debate on new forms of work (flexible specialization etc) should have incorporated a discussion of the consequences for women. These are nevertheless significant criticisms. More fundamentally, the links between the modern industrial state and the welfare state are simply not made. Yet, it is somewhere in this interface that women's possibilities, opportunities and dependences are constructed. Sweden is admired for its low levels of unemployment, industrial democracy, female labour force participation and so on. What is neglected, however, is an analysis of how high levels of social housing allow worker mobility, or enable women to have greater independence, or how child care provision in that country enables women to have greater labour force participation. In Australia, the dominance of private home ownership and a relatively small welfare sector must have some meaning. Industry policy debates thus operate in a distinctively different arena. Is there a new form of patriarchal state to which this document is urging us to aspire?

In its attempt to curb the rising tide of job loss in manufacturing and competition from the South East Asian region as a cheap labour source, and to encourage investment in declining industrial areas, we see new strategies employed. Notions of masculinity, nation and industrial growth are invoked in tandem as new images of brotherhood are created. Thus James Lang Wootton, the industrial real estate agency, advertises the Alexandria Centre as a top relocation for Captains of Industry and Investment Generals. While Hooker's pamphlets on the Botany Bay Industrial Estate trumpet slogans like 'Bound for Botany Bay with Conviction . . . the costs are not criminal' or show images of men's backs in raincoats with the words, 'Where's the best place to expose yourself between the airport and the city?'

Finally, if the ideology of fraternity is to be taken seriously, we must look as well at the warfare state and men's use of military apparatuses and rituals in constructing and consolidating political and cultural power. As Fernbach and others have pointed out, it is strange that theories of the state tend to focus on government and administration and treat the military as an optional extra, there to obey civilian orders. Historically it may be more accurate to view the military as the first element in state formation, 'with the addition of warfare onto hunting as a masculine specialization'.[25] For Fernbach, the state represents the institutionalization of male violence. Important conceptual connections can be made here between masculinity, war, nationalism and citizenship. As Genevieve Lloyd[26] and other feminist philosophers have argued, the manliness of war is constituted by the woman somewhere at home, by the defence and transcendence of the private familial concerns of life, 'the feminine'. Through the experience of war, man as soldier emerges in the glory of selfhood and citizenship. Modern nationalisms have largely been forged through war and the commemoration of war. If war constitutes the nation, the state claims to be the political embodiment of the nation. Of course the right and the duty to bear arms have long been seen as the mark of the citizen, and woman's alternative duty to bear sons and warriors does not quite match up. The two conscription referenda during the First World War point this up for they cast a long shadow on women's newly won citizenship. What right had women to vote to send men to distant battlefields when they themselves could not go?

It cannot be assumed that war is always a means to an end and not an end in itself. While Australia is not a highly militarized country it constructs its national identity out of war experiences, particularly the obsession with Gallipoli and the ongoing creation of the Anzac legend. The very word 'Anzac' became so sacred that it was forbidden by law in 1921 to use it for commercial purposes.[27] The legend of the digger was further reinforced by Australia's participation in the Vietnam war. As in the US, women's involvement in the anti-war movement in the 1960s was important to the emergence and character of the women's liberation movement.

Opposition to militarism and war has thus been an important strand in Australian feminism. Feminists have, since the Vietnam days, analysed and confronted the links between masculinity and war. Perhaps the best-known in recent years have been the Anzac Day marches and the women's peace camps. Anzac Day is in a real sense Australia's national day, a kind of combination of Remembrance Day with 4 July. Australian patriarchy is symbolically assembled in the dawn services and solemn marches that mark the earlier part of the day, before the diggers retreat into boozing and punch-ups. While the Left has long challenged the meaning of Anzac Day and its glorification of war, it has never been so effective as the feminist marches, since the late 1970s, 'in memory of women all countries raped in all wars'. By dressing in black, and acting out the rituals of dignified, silent mourning, their critiques of masculinity have proved difficult to deal with. The Returned Services League (RSL), the guardian of the legend, accused the women of making 'a deliberate assault on the Anzac Tradition itself' and claimed they were 'a foe ... just as real as that on the battlefields of Flanders'.[28]

Feminists understood here the importance of the symbolic, in struggling to transform the meaning of the day, to expose the repressions and silences around masculinity and war, and to reject a national identity based on these things. Though the focus on 'rape in war' appeared to some to be narrow, it created widespread community debate about rape and patriarchy, war and militarism, sexual politics and everyday life in a way that few campaigns have succeeded in doing. And it forced the courts to use the language of patriarchy, collectives and non-violence.

Australia too has had its women's peace camps, which have played a role in exposing the complicity of the Australian State with US imperialism – mateship on an international scale. On November 11 1983 (anniversary of the Whitlam sacking as well as Remembrance Day), 700 women gathered outside Alice Springs and proceeded to the perimeter gates of the US military installation of Pine Gap. They had come from all over Australia to demand the closure of the base. They camped there in the desert, thousands of miles from anywhere for two weeks, to bring national and international attention to Australia's military and nuclear involvement. This was to be followed in 1984 by the presence of 300 women at a peace camp at Cockburn Sound, a naval base south of Fremantle in Western Australia. Though the base is Australian it is seen as 'de facto' American since it harbours US nuclear-armed warships. The intention was to link militarism with other levels of the oppression of women, for example through rape, prostitution and their use by sailors as recreational objects. Such actions draw pointed attention to the fraternal nature of the Australian state while simultaneously linking the state with other dimensions of gendered power struggle.

To conclude, it seems to us that feminists are necessarily involved in struggles in and through the state in all its aspects. But it no longer makes sense to treat the state as a unity, even a contradictory one, to see our political priorities in terms of 'bringing it down', or to evaluate our strategies in terms of whether we have been successful in finding 'its' weakest links and hence come one step closer to revolution. The focus should be on developing 'a strategic analysis appropriate to political struggle, to struggles in the field of political power'.[29] This will involve looking at the specificity of mechanisms of power rather than relying on abstract theory. By concentrating on the apparently surface phenomena rather than the underlying structures, feminists have more chance of establishing links and connections between the numerous and varied points of resistance.

Notes

1. Alison Smith, 'Women's Refuges: The Only Resort? Feminism, Domestic Violence and the State' in D. Barry and P. Botsman (eds) *Public/Private*, Local Consumption Series 6, Sydney.

2. Carole Pateman, *The Sexual Contract*, Polity Press, London, 1988.

3. See Barbara Sullivan's chapter in this collection.

4. Lorna Weir, 'Women and the State: A Conference for Feminist Activists', *Feminist Review* 26, Summer 1987, p. 98.

5. Francis Castles, *Australian Public Policy and Economic Vulnerability. A Compar-*

ative and Historical Perspective, Allen and Unwin, Sydney, 1988; and *The Working Class and Welfare: Reflections on the Development of the Welfare State in Australia and New Zealand 1890–1980*, Allen and Unwin, Sydney, 1985.

6. Michel Foucault, *The History of Sexuality*, vol 1, Vintage Books, New York, 1980, p. 92.

7. Ibid., p. 93.

8. Michel Foucault, 'On Governmentality', *Ideology and Consciousness 6*, Autumn 1979, p. 20.

9. Michel Foucault, 'Truth and Power' in C. Gordon (ed.), *Power/Knowledge: Selected Interviews and Other Writings 1972–1977 Michel Foucault*, Harvester Press, Brighton, 1980, p. 118.

10. Michel Foucault, *History of Sexuality*, Vol. 1, pp. 94–5.

11. See Anne Summers, *Damned Whores and God's Police*, Penguin, Melbourne, 1975.

12. Liz Stanley and Sue Wise, *Breaking Out*, Routledge & Kegan Paul, London, 1983.

13. Jacques Donzelot, *The Policing of Families*, Pantheon, New York, 1979.

14. Michele Barrett and Mary McIntosh, *The Anti-social Family*, Verso, London, 1982.

15. See for example Elizabeth Wilson, *Women and the Welfare State*.

16 Sheila Shaver, 'Gender, Class and the Welfare State: The Case of Income Security', *Feminist Review* 32, 1989.

17. W. Beveridge, *Social Insurance and Allied Services*, 1942, p. 51 para 114.

18. Sophie Watson, *Housing and Homelessness: a Feminist Perspective*.

19. Sheila Shaver, 'Sex and Money in the Welfare State', in C. Baldock and B. Cass (eds), *Women, Social Welfare and the State in Australia*, Allen and Unwin, Sydney, 1983.

20. Varda Burstyn, 'Masculine Dominance and the State', in R. Miliband and J. Sadler (eds), *Socialist Register*, Merlin Press, London, 1983.

21. Catherine MacKinnon, 'Feminism, Marxism, Method and the State: An Agenda for Theory', *Signs*, vol. 7, no. 3, pp. 525–44.

22. Carole Pateman, 'The Patriarchal Welfare State', in A. Gutman (ed.), *Democracy and the Welfare State*, Princeton University Press, 1988.

23. Judith Allen, 'Octavius Beale Re-considered: Infanticide, Babyfarming and Abortion in New South Wales 1880–1939', in Sydney Labour History Group (ed.) *What Rough Beast? The State and Social Order in Australian History*, Allen and Unwin, Sydney, 1982; 'The Making of a Prostitute Proletariat in Twentieth Century New South Wales', in Daniels, K (ed.), *So Much Hard Work: Women and Prostitution in Australian History*, Fontana, Melbourne, 1984.

24. Alison Smith, *Op. cit.*

25. David Fernbach, *The Spiral Path*, Gay Men's Press, London, 1981, p. 31.

26. Genevieve Lloyd, *The Man of Reason*, Methuen, London, 1984, pp. 63–75.

27. Sabine Erika, 'Rape: Our Window of Vulnerability. The Sydney Women Against Rape Collective' in *Anzac Day – Thinking About the Future: A Forum for Women*, Sydney, August 25, 1984.

28. Rosemary Pringle, 'Rape: the Other Side of Anzac Day', *Refractory Girl*, 26 June 1983, p. 31.

29. Foucault in Gordon, p. 145.